A Neighborhood in Ottoman Istanbul

SUNY series in the
Social and Economic History of the Middle East

Donald Quataert, editor

A Neighborhood in Ottoman Istanbul

Fruit Vendors and Civil Servants
in the Kasap İlyas *Mahalle*

Cem Behar

State University of New York Press

Published by
State University of New York Press, Albany

© 2003 State University of New York

All rights reserved

Printed in the United States of America

No part of this book may be used or reproduced in any manner whatsoever without written permission. No part of this book may be stored in a retrieval system or transmitted in any form or by any means including electronic, electrostatic, magnetic tape, mechanical, photocopying, recording, or otherwise without the prior permission in writing of the publisher.

For information, contact the State University of New York Press, Albany, NY
www.sunypress.edu

Production by Michael Haggett
Marketing by Michael Campochiaro

Library of Congress Cataloging-in-Publication Data

Behar, Cem, 1946–
    A neighborhood in Ottoman Istanbul : fruit vendors and civil servants in the Kasap Ilyas Mahalle / Cem Behar.
    p. cm. — (SUNY series in the social and economic history of the Middle East)
    Includes bibliographical references and index.
    ISBN 0-7914-5681-1 (hc alk. paper) — ISBN 0-7914-5682-X (pb alk. paper)
    1. Kasap İlyas Mahalle (Istanbul, Turkey) 2. Istanbul (Turkey)—Social life and customs—History. 3. Istanbul (Turkey)—Economic conditions—History. I. Title. II. Series.

DR738.5.K37 B44 2003
949.61'8—dc21
                                                                               2002030966

10 9 8 7 6 5 4 3 2 1

For Candan, my first reader

Contents

Preface ... ix

INTRODUCTION: THE CITY, THE *SEMT*, AND THE *MAHALLE* ... 1
    The *Mahalle* and the *Semt* ... 3
    The "Islamic City" ... 7
    The Kasap İlyas *Mahalle* ... 11
    Fluidity and Imprecision ... 13
    Sources and Issues ... 18

CHAPTER 1: THE CONTOURS OF A LOCAL IDENTITY ... 27
    Local Identity: The Formative Sixteenth Century ... 31
    Mahalle Topography: Boundaries and Landmarks ... 35
    Houses and Gardens ... 40
    Streets and Dead Ends ... 44
    The Population and Inhabitants of a Peripheral *Mahalle* ... 49
    Kasap İlyas' High Street: "Butchers' Road" ... 53
    Fire and Brimstone ... 58

CHAPTER 2: POWER AND LOCAL ADMINISTRATION IN
KASAP İLYAS: TANZIMAT AND AFTER ... 65
    The *Imam* and His Congregation ... 67
    The Benefits of Local Power: The Case of Aziz Mahmud Efendi ... 72
    A Case of Peaceful Transition: *Imam* and *Muhtar* in Kasap İlyas ... 78
    The Administered Body: Early Nineteenth-Century Perspectives ... 83

CHAPTER 3: MIGRATION AND URBAN INTEGRATION:
THE ARAPKİR CONNECTION ... 95
    The Formation of a Migrant Shelter in Kasap İlyas:
    Ispanakçı Viranesi and the *Arapkirlis* ... 97

Fruit Vendors and Civil Servants: Provincials and
   Arapkirlis in 1885 — 106
Legal Residence: Regionalism and Nepotism — 120

CHAPTER 4: "END OF EMPIRE": PORTRAIT OF A NEIGHBORHOOD
COMMUNITY IN THE LATE NINETEENTH CENTURY — 131
  Families and Households — 136
  Streets, Houses, Warehouses, and Shops: Residential and
    Commercial Areas in Kasap İlyas — 146
  The *Muhtar* and his *Mahalle*: Ruler, Representative,
    Middleman — 160

EPILOGUE — 173

Appendix — 183
Notes — 185
Bibliography — 209
Index — 217
Volumes in SUNY Series in the Social and Economic History
of the Middle East — 225

Preface

As frequently happens, this research came about by chance. It was in 1988, while working on marriage, family, and fertility in late Ottoman Istanbul, that I first came across the name of the Kasap İlyas neighborhood. This encounter materialized in the form of notebooks and loose folios. These documents had probably been waiting for some time on the stall of a secondhand book dealer in Istanbul. The book dealer, Turan Türkmenoğlu, managed to convince me that these disparate sheets full of an already pale scribble were somehow connected with my research on family and fertility patterns. A quick glance at some of the notes on marriage contracts that one of the notebooks contained, made me think that this might be true after all.

Upon closer scrutiny, it became clear that these manuscripts constituted an exceptional set of archival documents pertaining to the life and administration of a single Istanbul *mahalle:* Kasap İlyas. Some of the documents were from the seventeenth and eighteenth centuries and they had been carefully preserved by the successive *imam*s and by local headmen (*muhtar*s) of Kasap İlyas. These individuals had added, in the late nineteenth century, a large number of notes of their own that had apparently been handed down from one *muhtar* to another. The novelty and originality of the data was striking. The equivalent of these sources exist, to the best of our knowledge, for no other urban neighborhood of Istanbul or, perhaps, of any other Ottoman city. A small portion of these sources and documents have been used as partial and local illustrations in our book on *Istanbul Households*.[1] However, it did not then occur to me that these documents, highly interesting but nevertheless patchy and disparate, could be used as a basis for an historical study of this single *mahalle*.

The two articles on the Kasap İlyas *mahalle* that I have published so far (one in 1997 and another in early 1999) have been the object of fruitful criticisms coming from two colleagues: Ferhunde Özbay and Ayhan Aktar. It is due to their encouragement and enthusiasm that I began to consider writing an historical study focusing not on one Ottoman or Middle Eastern city but on a single neighborhood community (a *mahalle*) within an Ottoman city. The idea that these *prima facie* highly partial and chronologically patchy local sources of information on the Kasap İlyas *mahalle* deserved to be transformed into a—hopefully—consistent book is due to their moral support.

These exceptional local sources had to be supplemented with information relating to Kasap İlyas obtained from the Ottoman Religious Courts' Archives and with quantitative data from the 1885 and 1907 Ottoman population censuses (*Tahrir-i nüfus*). Thanks are due to Nurettin Çivi and Aysel Istanbullu, directors of the Istanbul Registry Office *(Istanbul Vilâyeti Nüfus Müdürlüğü)*, for allowing me to transcribe in their entirety the original Ottoman census documents for the neighborhood. The help of Dr. Abdülâziz Bayındır, director of the Istanbul Religious Courts' Archives *(Istanbul Müftülüğü Şer'iye Sicilleri Arşivi)* is also gratefully acknowledged. My heartfelt thanks go to Aysel Danacı, Emre Erdoğan, Tülây Gençtürk, Meriç Mekik, and Araks Şahiner for their assistance in transcribing the Ottoman Sharia' Court records for the Kasap İlyas *mahalle*, as well as the 1885 and 1907 late Ottoman census documents, and for cross-tabulating some of the results.

I owe a deep debt of gratitude to the elderly inhabitants of Kasap İlyas whom I interviewed and who have provided me with a perspective on what life and human relationships in Kasap İlyas had been, a perspective that I could not have obtained otherwise. Hasan Şarkalkan, *muhtar* of the neighborhood since 1994, made all of the interviews possible, and what is more, made me feel like a *bona fide* member of the highly extended familial network that the Kasap İlyas *mahalle* must have been in former times.

It gives me great pleasure to be able to thank those scholars and institutions that have helped me during the preparation of this book. Thanks are due to a grant from the *Population Council*, a grant which (MEAwards Grant MEA 323) made possible, in 1994 and 1995, part of the research and data collection on which this book is based. The contribution of the *Eurasian Project on Population and Family History* (International Research Center for Japanese Studies-Kyoto) is also gratefully acknowledged.

Edhem Eldem's lengthy article on eighteenth- and nineteenth-century Istanbul[2] has been an excellent source of inspiration. Nedret İşli and İbrahim Yılmaz (*"Simürg"* İbrahim) have been of great help in locating some rare publications on Istanbul neighborhoods. In the writing process, Mine Eder unfailingly supplied sharp lexicological advice. Two friends and colleagues, Selim Deringil of the Department of History, Boğaziçi University, and Şevket Pamuk, of the Ataturk Institute of Boğaziçi University, gave generously of their time, read the entire manuscript, and provided many discerning comments and suggestions.

In the end, I alone am responsible for the errors and deficiencies that remain.

Introduction
The City, The *Semt* and the *Mahalle*

The image of Istanbul as *the* city, or as "a world in itself" was often used to depict the size, the bustle, and the diversity of the Ottoman capital.¹ As the center of economic and political power of an empire stretching over three continents, Istanbul drew people from all Ottoman lands and even from beyond. Its population was no doubt one of the most disparate in the world, and the city itself was very large. The walled city itself, a triangular peninsula surrounded by water on two sides, was, at least until the industrial revolution, larger in area than most European cities.² Its three boroughs (Eyüp, Galata, and Üsküdar) were set outside the walls and, for two of them, across the water. The official Ottoman denomination of greater Istanbul, *Dersaadet ve bilâd-ı selâse* (the Abode of Felicity and the three boroughs), does reflect the feeling of size and distance, as experienced by its inhabitants in their daily lives. Many Istanbulites were leading a localized life, especially before the nineteenth century, and were only partially familiar with the city at large, especially those parts of it that were "across the water." Well into the nineteenth century, traveling from one part of the city to another was still something of an adventure, and daily "commuting" was unthinkable. Local identities and solidarities at the neighborhood and district level developed within Istanbul long before an overall urban conscience could impose its stamp on the inhabitants.

The population of Ottoman Istanbul, though it certainly had a number of ups and downs, always seemed to be tremendous.³ Among Ottoman cities, only Cairo could ever have stood the comparison. Though the hard data are lacking, Istanbul—and not London or Paris—might well have been the most populated capital-city of Europe between the sixteenth and the late eighteenth centuries. At the time of the Ottoman conquest, the population of the Byzantine capital had fallen to just tens of thousands of people. The policy of Mehmed II (the Conqueror) was one of bringing settlers to Istanbul, a policy of forced migration *(sürgün)* in an attempt to revive the city in the decades immediately following the conquest. About a century later, under the reign of Süleyman "the Magnificent" (1520–1566), the Istanbul population

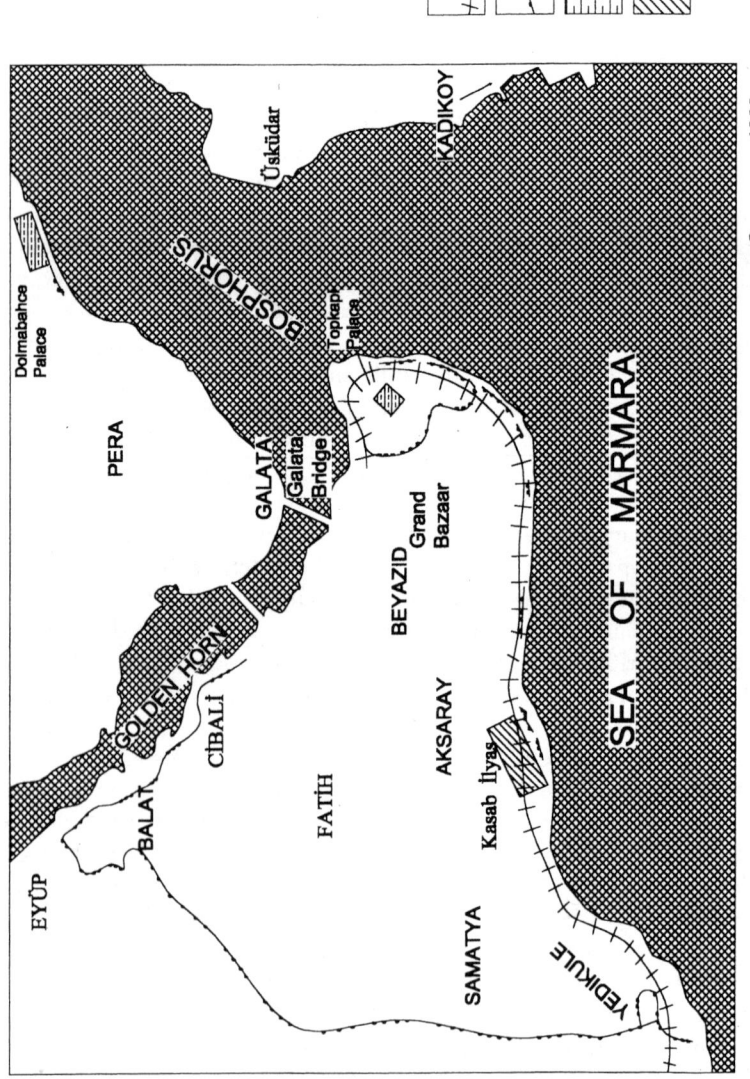

FIGURE 1 Istanbul (Map of the Walled City)

probably reached the quarter-million mark. It was then almost twice as large as that of Paris or London.

Throughout the centuries, the Porte was always worried about the uncontrollable crowding of Istanbul and tried to limit migration to the city and to push away all undesirable elements, if necessary *manu militari*. These efforts, however, were mostly to no avail. Except for some wild guesses made by a few European travelers, there are practically no data for the seventeenth- and eighteenth-century population of Istanbul. The earliest estimates for the first half of the nineteenth century point to slightly less than half a million inhabitants. Growth was slow but regular throughout the nineteenth century. The first citywide reliable count is that of 1885. The one-million mark will be crossed—for the first time, and only temporarily—just before the First World War, due to the sudden inflow of refugees fleeing the Balkan wars.

Not surprisingly, the historiographical heritage of Istanbul has tended to view this enormous conurbation not as an integrated whole, but rather as a patchwork, a colorful *collage*. There is a wealth of studies on the trade and commerce of Istanbul, its politics and government, its art and architecture, its religious/ethnic communities, and so forth. There have been very few efforts to examine Istanbul as a unified whole. The very problematic nature and—as often as not—the simple absence of historical documentation on the social life of the city and of its inhabitants, is a forbidding obstacle facing local and social historians of the Ottoman capital. Specific in-depth local studies as well as studies emphasizing the modes of articulation of the diverse sections of the city to each other are sorely lacking. Istanbul's topographical mosaic of well-defined individual cells did consist, on one side, of city quarters or residential neighborhoods (*mahalle*s), delineated on ethnic/religious grounds and, on the other side, of ethnically more mixed commercial/economic areas. There is, however, a very basic difficulty in finding references to individual *mahalle*s in pre- nineteenth-century Ottoman archival sources. The only Ottoman historical sources for Istanbul that are classified on a topographical basis and in which various *mahalle*s can be spotted are the Archives of the Religious Courts (*Şer'iye Sicilleri/Kadı sicilleri*); and even in these archives, homogenous, long, and uninterrupted time series are difficult to come by.

THE *MAHALLE* AND THE *SEMT*

Ever since the early sixteenth century, the urban fabric of the residential areas of intramural Istanbul has consisted of a juxtaposition of *mahalle*s. Some of them retained their name and topographical location for centuries. These *mahalle*s were usually not very populous, nor did they cover a wide area. On the eve of the First World War, for instance, the Istanbul *mahalle*s had an average population of around fifteen hundred people.[4]

Ten or fifteen streets at most, grouped around a thoroughfare or perhaps around a small square, and one or two small mosques (or a church or a synagogue, depending on the ethnic makeup of the neighborhood) defined most of the residential Istanbul *mahalle*s. The neighborhood also usually contained a public fountain or two and a few shops catering to basic necessities or services. There might also be some some public utility buildings (a public bath, or perhaps, a dervish convent or a primary school). Less basic goods and services were available either in the more central commercial areas, like the covered big bazaar (*çarşû-yı kebir*), or in the many weekly markets serving larger slices of the urban population. Many of these Ottoman *mahalle*s of Istanbul bore the name of the benefactor of the local mosque, the public bath or fountain, that of a mythical figure, that of a Byzantine monument, or even, in a few cases, the name of the geographic origin of its first Muslim inhabitants.

Although the borders and areas of each of the Istanbul *mahalle*s were never very strictly drawn, and they certainly did fluctuate in time, these urban neighborhood units were at all times perceived as an important protective and cohesive unit immediately surrounding the family and the household. They fostered a durable sense of *local identity* and *cohesion*. At least ever since the middle of the sixteenth century, and in the absence of accepted family surnames, many of the artisans and the ordinary folk of Istanbul were known or nicknamed as "from such and such a district (*semt*) or *mahalle*." Various types of rivalries or cooperative actions between adjacent neighborhoods and districts are well-known and have survived well into the twentieth century.

The *mahalle*s were well entrenched as basic communities at the local level and played key roles in shaping local identities and solidarities. This solidarity entailed a particular *modus vivendi*, plus some sort of collective defense, as well as various mechanisms of mutual control and surveillance, many of them designed for regulating and monitoring public morality. In many *mahalle*s collective social life was real, durable, and strong. In many of them, for instance, self-appointed bands of youths would act as militias to defend the mahalle's "honor" from outside "agressions." In others, there were, in the nineteenth century, self-organized amateur "fire-brigades" who took charge of the extinction of real and of the prevention of potential fires. These young mens' brotherhood type of groups (*tulumbacı*) also took upon themselves the task of defending the honor and reputation of the locals. Twentieth-century Kasap İlyas bears many reminiscences of these groups. The districts (*semt*s) and *mahalle*s of pre-twentieth-century Istanbul had their—real or imagined—honor and reputation to uphold.

The traditional *mahalle*s of Istanbul were generally very mixed in terms of wealth, social class, and status. Residential patterns usually ran along lines of ethnicity and religion. However, ethnically and/or religiously mixed *mahalle*s were not infrequent either. Recent studies have tended to show that even in the early periods of Ottoman rule, ethnic and religious identities did not necessarily exhaust the definition of a *mahalle*. The notion of the absolute homogeneity of the Islamic or Middle Eastern town quarter regarding its social composition and the idea that these neighborhoods were exclusively defined by religious, ethnic, class, or occupational affiliation have also seriously been challenged by recent studies on Ottoman cities, especially in the empire's Arab provinces.[5] In intramural Istanbul, large mansions of *pasha*s and *bey*s neighboring the shanty lodgings of beggars (*se'ele*) or of streetporters (*hamal*s and *küfeci*s) were quite a common occurrence. These different groups were not usually clustered in separate parts of the neighborhood either. Indeed, there were some *mahalle*s where, on the whole, the inhabitants fared better than those of other neighborhoods. However, really "exclusive" areas, or particularly well-off neighborhoods, or particularly destitute ones were quite exceptional.

Within intramural Istanbul, the distinction between the *semt*[6] (district) and the *mahalle* was of primary importance in the perception of urban space and in situating local identities. The *semt* is a nondescript area, a district, usually much larger than an average *mahalle*, indicative of a rather large section of the city. Most of the *semt*s took their name from a precise point, such as a city gate, a large market, or a building that was functional for the city as a whole (Edirnekapı, Fatih, Sultanahmet, Karagümrük, Unkapanı, Şehremini, Fener, etc.) and were therefore used as basic geographic markers. Sometimes, the toponymy of the *semt*s might indicate the city or region of the empire from which an initial population had migrated (Aksaray, Karaman, Çarşamba, etc.). Many people referred to their personal addresses by indicating both the *semt* and perhaps the name of a local landmark (a well-known mosque, a city gate, a wharf, a monument, etc.). These *semt*s and landmarks were no doubt better known by the inhabitants of Istanbul at large than the names of the numerous small traditional *mahalle*s. The *mahalle*s, notwithstanding some remarkable exceptions, were of vital importance only to their own denizens and their names might not be known to inhabitants of distant *semt*s.

A cadastral land survey of the city and a regular name for each street of intramural Istanbul (with a number for each house or gate) were to come only in the 1860s. Before the last quarter of the nineteenth century, even official documents—deeds of sale of real estate, for instance—in which a precise definition mattered, routinely used only very approximate addresses in which the *semt* and/or a well-known local landmark were mentioned. For instance, in the religious court rulings in which a resident of the Kasap İlyas *mahalle* was involved, that person was always identified as "such and such, from the Kasap İlyas *mahalle* near [the] Davudpaşa [wharf/gate]." The Davudpaşa *semt* and/or the Davudpaşa wharf clearly localized the small Kasap İlyas *mahalle*. For all practical purposes, this was deemed to be a sufficient "address." Once in the neighborhood, people were pretty sure of finding their way to a precise destination or of reaching the desired person simply by asking around.

The *mahalle* was an economic and social entity which, as far as the daily lives of its inhabitants is concerned, delineated their primary cultural milieu (family life, religious community, neighborhood, etc.). This is especially true of the period preceding the early nineteenth century, since local public coffeehouses began spreading in Istanbul only then.[7] Before that period, these public coffeehouses were concentrated in a few central or commercial areas of the city. The *mescit* and, perhaps, the *hamam* were the only public meeting places at the *mahalle* level. Therefore, the local *mescit*, which was of definitional importance to the neighborhood, was also the main available public space.

Local consciousness at *mahalle* level necessarily meant close and frequent contacts. As to the *semt*, its extent implied that routine face-to-face meetings were much less important. In Istanbul the *semt* was almost always related to the functionality of the area within the overall urban organization (trade, commerce, religion, politics, education, etc.). The sense of belonging to a *mahalle* was part of daily life, but that of being part of a *semt* certainly involved a somewhat higher degree of abstraction, a sort of open topographical self-positioning and status-seeking with respect to the rest of the city. A residential s*emt* could be more or less prestigious than another and there could be a—real or imagined—hierarchy of *semt*s, but not of *mahalle*s.

Unlike the *mahalle*, the *semts* never were legal administrative units. The *mahalle*, however, was always both a *basic urban administrative unit* and a *social and economic entity*. However, these two meanings never completely overlapped. The centrally determined administrative network of Ottoman Istanbul and the web of local identities did not necessarily coincide. This was so in the inceptive fifteenth and sixteenth centuries as well as in the "modernizing" nineteenth. The perception of the urban population regarding their environment and their self-definition in relation to their immediate surrounding was always more important than the religious/administrative matrix imposed upon the cityscape for purposes of control or tax collection.

In the residential quarters of the Ottoman city, the *imam* of the local mosque was considered, up until the Tanzimat reforms of the middle of the nineteenth century, as a local headman of sorts. As a mediator of the authority of the *kadı*, he had both administrative and religious powers and duties. His most important duty was to apportion and to collect the lump-sum taxes imposed by the Ottoman state. He also acted as a guarantor for every local inhabitant. Any newcomer who wanted to set up house in the *mahalle* had to have the *imam*'s approval, provide a guarantor, and also produce proof of his solvency. After the 1830s laymen (*muhtar*s) were appointed/co-opted as local headmen. The process of transfer of authority was generally smooth and a good example of this transfer can be followed in Kasap İlyas.

THE "ISLAMIC CITY"

Social and urban historians of Istanbul have often stressed the idea that these *mahalle*s, however diverse they may have been, defined on the whole a *static* configuration, typical of most precapitalist urban populations.[8] The *mahalle* is implicitly taken to be not only a basic level of social integration but also a community characterized by a high amount of autarky and an almost built-in inability to move. This static picture of the human topography of Istanbul *intra muros* is usually taken to mean, first, that the numbers, areas, and composition of the residential *mahalle*s were well-defined and relatively stable, and, second, that the restricted mobility of the population implied some rigidity in the ethnic/religious makeup of each of the neighborhoods.

The absoluteness of the ethnic, religious, and functional divisions embedded in the topographical makeup of the city, its cellular structure, and the absence of interpenetration between the ethnic and religious constituents were also used for claiming the existence of a specific and typical Islamic urban model, an archetypal *Islamic City*. The functional articulation of various parts of the city, the use of public space, and its overall architectural and urbanistic consequences (the functional triangle consisting of the mosque, the market, and the public bath) were also taken to have an unequivocal and unique connection to this model. Often even the sheer physical shape of the Islamic city was taken to be an unequivocal expression of its social structure, just an external sign of a system of law, social ethics, and social institutions. The presence of ruling elites that distantiate themselves from the population at large, the general lack of urban political autonomy and of oppositional political initiatives coming from the cities in Islamic lands—as opposed to "Western"/European cities—that were attributed to this structure were taken to be an *a posteriori* demonstration of the thesis.[9] Some proponents of the thesis went as far as denying the existence of any sort of permanent formal institutions within the Islamic city and of any sort of corporate personality within which there might grow up an exclusive solidarity that could take precedence over the community of "believers at large," the *umma*.[10]

The thesis on the existence of an essentially "Islamic city" was, for a long time, surrounded by the prestige and aura of its first proponent, none less than Max Weber himself. Weber had, in fact, adduced no historical evidence worthy of that name to support his thesis. His idea, however, was taken up by, and integrated into, other worldviews such as "Orientalism" or the "world-economy/world-system" paradigm. These two were obviously in dire need of defining (albeit sketchily, and notwithstanding the teleological vision involved), some overarching urban similarities that would account for the decline or "peripheralization" of Ottoman, "Islamic," and Middle Eastern cities in the nineteenth century. A classical Islamic scholar, Gustav von Grunebaum, came to the rescue in the 1950s, filled up Weber's historical lacunae with religious and philological scholarship and, for all practical purposes, codified the concept of the Islamic city for the coming decades, and it became part of a more general typology of urban forms.[11] The same codification had also been applied in the 1930s and 1940s to North African Muslim towns by the French Islamists William and Georges Marçais.[12]

The Eurocentric Weberian framework on urban development in Islamic lands received a more nuanced interpretation in the hands of such scholars as Ira Lapidus and Albert Hourani.[13] While sharing with Weber and von Grunebaum the basic view of a disaggregated and vertically segmented typical Islamic urban structure that lacked the elements of a true civil society, these historians had a more nuanced view of the politics and governance of these cities. They admitted the historical existence of a group of denizens who could, under certain circumstances and by common consent, come to represent an (almost European) civic community spirit, a strictly local *'asabiyya*. For a number of reasons, most of them concerning the available historical sources, scholars have so far considered the (North African as well as Middle Eastern) Arab case as the normative type of "Islamic city," although Anatolian and other Ottoman towns, and even Istanbul, have also been envisaged within the same paradigm.

More recent studies, however, while seeking neither to question nor to support the long-standing paradigm of the Islamic city have, first and foremost, tried to diversify their historical perspective by using a larger variety of local sources. Recent historical work tends to focus on the diversity of situations and on the singularity of urban societies in Islamic lands and in the eastern Mediterranean. Efforts are made to situate and represent a greater diversity of ethnic, religious, local, and professional identities. Scholars now rightfully insist not only on the *singularity* of each Ottoman city, but also on that of each of their constituent parts. As Lapidus candidly wrote in an article published in 1973: "When we speak of Muslim cities, we do not speak of a special type of city society, but we refer to the predominant religious and cultural identifications of their inhabitants and the institutions built around these identifications."[14]

In the residential quarters of Istanbul, settlement patterns did traditionally follow religious and ethnic lines. Socioeconomic determinants of housing patterns were, for centuries, of only secondary importance. The class- or income-based differentiation of the urban fabric did not take hold of Istanbul before well into the twentieth century. But from this observation to the idea that these residential patterns were, before the twentieth century, either frozen or at least largely predictable, there is a huge step that the proponents of this thesis would not hesitate to take. The reality is, as we shall see in the case of Kasap İlyas, that even in times of relative demographic stability, even before the "long" nineteenth century, both the population of Istanbul and of the traditional residential neighborhoods were in considerable flux. The demarcation lines between *mahalle*s were never so strict and the horizontal mobility of the residents was much higher than is usually admitted. At the local level, mobility and change seem to have been the rule, not the exception.

It is also usually understood, in the context of the same paradigm, that the guilds in Islamic cities did not essentially function as organizations defending the interests of craftsmen. Given the general weakness of urban organizations in Islamic lands, the guilds would be functioning basically as a means of supervising and taxing craftsmen, who would otherwise have totally escaped governmental control.[15] This centrally controlled rigid guild structure would then obviously have impeded the appearance of a class of "free" laborers, the social basis for industrialization and for capital accumulation. The administrative rigidity of the guilds' organization, another pillar of the "Islamic City" paradigm, will be clearly seen, in the case of Kasap İlyas, to be more an illusion than a reality. The fluidity and permeability of guild and nonguild activities will be illustrated by the fruit and vegetable peddlers who had been living for centuries in Kasap İlyas.

The *hara*s or *mahalla*s of some Arab or Middle Eastern cities, such as those of Cairo or Aleppo, were often barred by gates that had to be shut at night, a fact taken as a handy physical demonstration of the segmentation of Islamic urban structures. As to the borders of the various city quarters of Istanbul, or those of any other Turkish Anatolian city for that matter, let alone being physically barred, they were never even strictly drawn or well defined.[16] Over the centuries, there were orders issued by the *kadı* of Istanbul, especially in times of political trouble, demanding that the population construct gates to protect their *mahalle*s from outside aggressions. But these rulings were never fully implemented, or only haphazardly. As exemplified by the Kasap İlyas *mahalle* and by its adjacent neighbors, the areas of the traditional Istanbul neighborhoods have always been somewhat imprecise and fluid. The *mahalle* was essentially a basic urban community defined by a dense web of relationships, before being a "ward," a local administrative unit.

As to the continuum in local consciousness in Ottoman Istanbul, it may well be due not to any pre-set internal homogeneity, but to the very peculiar functional and topographical constraints which, from the very beginning, besieged almost all quarters of the Ottoman capital-city. The fact that the continuity in the topographic and administrative makeup of the capital-city of the Ottoman Empire implied a rigidity neither in the number nor in the human and social composition or the economic and social function of each of its cells is perhaps a further challenge to the essentialist notion of a clearly defined, archetypal, and immutable "Islamic city."

The resilience and the physical and social flexibility of our particular city quarter needs explanation, when viewed over a number of centuries. That the small Kasap İlyas neighborhood had the capacity and contained a multisecular mechanism designed to absorb rural migrants and integrate newcomers is striking enough. The fact that, in the last four centuries, it has more or less successfully survived a number of devastating fires, earthquakes, political instability, changes in the economic fortunes of Istanbul, and nineteenth-century throes of modernization must be a sign of its power of adaptation. Ottoman/Turkish cities were not amorphous conglomerates of homogenous, rigid, and isolated town quarters or guilds. The apparent lack of formal urban institutions before the nineteenth century signifies neither that townsmen had no means of articulating their specific interests, nor that particular public cultures, of the sort that the legacy of the "Islamic city" typology has contributed to obscure, did not exist.

True, no Muslim Istanbul neighborhood could exist or survive without a minimal level of autarkic organization centered around a mosque (and with a public fountain, a few shops, perhaps a school or a public bath, etc.). From that trivial fact to the notion of a city made up of homogenous and uniform cellular units, there is, however, a huge step which, if taken, will wear away much of the historical variety that characterized Ottoman cities and neighborhoods. We would suggest that any attempt at devising a normative "Ottoman neighborhood" or producing a programmatic "Istanbul *mahalle*" is bound to lose much factual wealth and historical variety. In organizing research into local history around such clichés as "integration," "local autarky," "staticness," or "topographical fragmentation" we would elude many issues. Much information would be put away by the a priori submission to such bulky concepts.

This book does not pretend to provide a paradigm to rival the idea of the Islamic city, and to replace one norm or one archetype by another. If anything, we would argue, in the context of Islamic/Ottoman/Middle Eastern cities, against any essentialist reductionism and in favor of the irreducible historical singularity not only of each city, but of each of its bits and pieces. The contribution of such a microstudy to the debate would be to show, perhaps, that not only the cities of Arab, Islamic, and Ottoman lands themselves, but also their topographical or functional or social constituent parts (i.e., the neighborhoods, *hara*s, or *mahalle*s) too, cannot be made to fit into a set of fundamentally unique and ghettoizing characteristics.

The Kasap İlyas *Mahalle*

Kasap İlyas ("Butcher İlyas") *mahalle* is a smallish neighborhood in south-central intramural Istanbul, bordering on the sea of Marmara and immediately to the west of the large Langa vegetable gardens. Set on one of the southern hillsides of Istanbul, on land gently sloping toward the sea, the neighborhood also includes part of the city ramparts bordering on the sea of Marmara, with a gate (Davud Paşa Kapısı) opening to an empty plot of land on the seaside. From this plot of land jutted out a small wooden wharf known as the Davud Paşa Wharf (Davud Paşa İskelesi). Both the gate and the wharf served as geographic markers to localize the neighborhood (see map).

Situated near the area known as Xerolophus or Hagios Emilianos in Byzantine Constantinople, the identity of this Ottoman *mahalle* is documented from the end of the fifteenth century on. With a couple of adjacent neighborhoods, it formed a *semt* of Istanbul known as Davud Paşa. The fifteenth-century mosque bearing the name of its founder, the grand vizier Davud Paşa (d. 1498) is located further up the hill, in another *mahalle*. Together with the wharf, the gate on the ramparts, and a building of public utility located within the *mahalle* (the public bath, Davud Paşa Hamamı), this mosque gave its name to the whole area. The Davud Paşa *semt* is surrounded by other well-known districts: Cerrahpaşa, Samatya, Langa, and Etyemez. As to the Kasap İlyas *mahalle*, it still exists as a small administrative unit, presently within the bounds of the Fatih District of the Istanbul Metropolitan Municipality.

Local legend tells us that Kasap İlyas was the chief butcher/meat provider to the Ottoman army that conquered Constantinople in 1453 and that in recognition of his services, the sultan bestowed upon him a large plot of land. On this plot of land he first built a small mosque bearing his name and endowed it. Around this local mosque, goes the legend, a whole neighborhood bearing his name then took shape. The elderly inhabitants of Kasap İlyas still recount the many foundation myths concerning Kasap İlyas and his arrival to the neighborhood, as well as his many exploits, religious and otherwise. Kasap İlyas has grown into a sort of mythical figure and he has been surrounded by an aura of sanctity by the locals for quite a long time. His deed of trust (*vakfiye*) was set down in 1494[17] and his small shrine standing in the small graveyard beside his mosque bears the date of 1495 as the date of his passing away. The present-day Kasap İlyas mosque was almost totally rebuilt after the 1894 earthquake. Of the original structure, nothing much remains.

The available *waqf* (philanthropic/pious foundation) registers for the neighborhood bear evidence to the existence of a durable sense of local identity. So do many elements of local folklore and ethnographic material.

Significant intracommunity links can be documented for a period extending back to the late fifteenth century. For instance, in the first half of the sixteenth century, the average number of pious foundations per *mahalle* in Istanbul was around 11. Kasap İlyas, however, had one of the highest number of foundations (26, to be precise) among all the 219 listed neighborhoods in traditional intramural Istanbul.[18] Less than fifty years after the Ottoman conquest, this is a sure indicator of a relatively high degree of social cohesion.

The first population census of our neighborhood was done in 1885. The neighborhood contained then about a hundred fifty houses, most of them wooden, one- or two-story traditional structures, set in a total of thirteen streets and blind alleys. Kasap İlyas also had a mosque, two dervish convents, three public fountains, a school for girls, a police station, and about thirty shops as well as a number of warehouses for the storage of bulk goods (coal, wood, timber, sand, gravel, etc.). It also contained a large double *hamam* for men and women, surrounded by a number of shops. The presence of a large public bath in such a small neighborhood is something quite exceptional for Istanbul, for most of the public baths were located in or around the central commercial areas of the city. This large fifteenth-century *hamam* certainly attracted customers from other *mahalle*s as well.

The irregular and dense maze of streets and houses in the *mahalle* acquired a topographical stability only toward the middle of the nineteenth century, after a number of devastating fires which, together with large areas of the city, also ravaged our neighborhood. According to a rough calculation based on a map of Istanbul dating from around 1875, the Kasap İlyas *mahalle* covered an area of approximately six hectares.[19] Quite a large portion of the *mahalle* was occupied by gardens and vegetable gardens (*bostan*s), sometimes called the "Davudpaşa gardens." These were extensions of the neighboring Langa Gardens (see map). Kasap İlyas, though relatively large in area, has never been very densely populated. Well into the twentieth century parts of it still had a clearly semirural character.

From about the sixteenth century on, Kasap İlyas was a predominantly Muslim city quarter with always, as far as we know, only a minority of Greek orthodox inhabitants. Armenians and Greeks were a sizable majority in the neighboring Langa and Samatya *semt*s. The last Ottoman census of 1907 tells us that Kasap İlyas contained about eleven hundred people.[20] Its sixteenth- and seventeenth-century population must have been about half that figure, or even smaller.

Kasap İlyas is not topographically central to the walled city, nor is it situated anywhere near the political heart (the Palace) or near the traditional business or shopping areas of the walled city. The central commercial areas were situated either along the southern shores of the Golden Horn or in and around the large covered bazaar. As was the case with all *mahalle*s located near the city walls and city gates, Kasap İlyas was, throughout the centuries, considered to be *peripheral* (in all senses of the term) and it was inhabited by relatively poor people. Notwithstanding the presence of a number of mansions (*konak*s) belonging to the high-ranking military and bureaucrats, Kasap İlyas was always a much less prestigious residential area than some of its immediate neighbors.

Kasap İlyas housed, in the late nineteenth century, a large number of street peddlers, itinerant vendors of fruits and vegetables, some beggars, a group of—mostly female—manumitted black slaves, and a considerable number of families of quite modest means. Many of these were immigrants from the eastern Anatolian town of Arapkir. Nevertheless, all of the elderly inhabitants we interviewed, while recognizing that Kasap İlyas or the Davudpaşa District had never been very wealthy or particularly prestigious, still took great pride in its allegedly "aristocratic" (read: "old Istanbul") character.

Kasap İlyas' economic and social articulation to the rest of the capital-city of the Ottoman Empire took shape through two of its main topographical assets: the wharf and the vegetable gardens. From the sixteenth century on, the neighborhood appears in official documents as "the Kasap İlyas *mahalle* near the Davudpaşa wharf," thus signaling the fact that the wharf preexisted the *mahalle* and/or that it had a topographical and commercial importance that superseded that of the neighborhood as such. The Davudpaşa wharf was indeed an important geographic marker on the Marmara shores of the walled city and, as we shall see, a was nonnegligible disembarkation point for a number of goods. As for the large Langa orchards, and their extensions right to the middle of the neighborhood, they played an important role in local fruit and vegetable production and distribution and provided employment to many of the less-favored inhabitants of the *mahalle*.

FLUIDITY AND IMPRECISION

At no period in the history of Istanbul can the number of *mahalle*s within the walled city be taken as a datum. Their number in the early and formative decades of the Ottoman city after the 1453 conquest is not clear.[21] The estimates for the late fifteenth and early sixteenth centuries range between 60 and 130 *mahalle*s. New *mahalle*s were still being formed more than half a century after the Ottoman conquest. Whether the increase in the number of *mahalle*s that occurred in the first half of the sixteenth century is due to population growth by immigration, that is, in many cases, by forced settlements (*sürgün*s) of provincial groups, or simply to local population spillover is highly uncertain. The total number of Istanbul *mahalle*s was put at no less than 219 in a listing of pious foundations done in 1546.[22]

About two centuries later, however, a trustworthy and often cited source of the late eighteenth century puts the total number of neighborhood communities in intramural Istanbul at only 181.[23] In the post-Tanzimat era there was a tremendous change in the number of these basic urban entities. A listing of Istanbul *mahalle*s drawn in 1876 for electoral purposes contains 251 items. The 1907 population census contains population data from 147 intramural *mahalle*s. Another administrative list dated from 1913 contains no less than 346 names of neighborhoods. Only ten years later their number has fallen to 282, according to another official listing published in 1922.[24] The 1927–1928 Republican municipal reorganization finally reduced the number of Istanbul *mahalle*s situated within the walled city to 114. It also redefined and stabilized their borders. In many cases, these newly defined and redrawn, "rational" and republican *mahalle* borders were not in conformity with previous usage, nor were they necessarily in agreement with traditional perceptions of local urban space. The number and area of these intramural Istanbul *mahalle*s is, however, still the same today.

The number, the borders, the areas, and the modes of transformation of the quarters of Istanbul, as well as the social, demographic, and economic reasons behind their fluctuation, is still a moot question. Population growth—whether because of immigration or simply as a result of an excess of births over deaths—might have resulted either in a multiplication of neighborhoods or in an overcrowding of existing ones. Demographic growth certainly caused an increase in the number of *mahalle*s in the fifteenth and sixteenth centuries, but not necessarily in the nineteenth, when overcrowding was the result in many cases.

Besides, many local or large-scale fires frequently devastated Ottoman Istanbul, in whose residential areas houses were, especially after the sixteenth century, built more and more frequently of wood. As a result of the large-scale fires, many neighborhoods were frequently burned down.[25] In the reconstruction process, however, some neighborhoods were reconstructed and survived almost intact (e.g., Kasap İlyas) but some less fortunate *mahalle*s did not. They disappeared and/or were absorbed by one or more surrounding *mahalle*s.

A well-documented example is that of the *Servi Mescidi mahalle*, situated in central Istanbul. In 1826 a local fire completely destroyed the neighborhood. The *mahalle* contained at the time of the fire a total of forty-four houses, its namesake *mescit* and a *han*.[26] After the fire, new houses and shops were rebuilt on the vacant lots, but these were somehow attributed to the two neighboring and larger *mahalle*s of *Mahmud Paşa* and *Cezerî Kasım Paşa*. The unfortunate *Servi Mescidi* neighborhood then disappeared from the official records. It does not appear in the 1876 listing. The efforts at revival and restoration by the trustees of the local pious foundation (*vakıf*) and by the *imam* of the local mosque—who had lost his sources of revenue in the fire—

were of no avail. As late as 1902, the trustees of the foundation related to the small mosque filed an application to the Council of State (*Şûra-yı Devlet*) to make their point. The Council of State issued a ruling stating that the *Servi Mescidi* pious foundation was still valid, that the charred remains of the mosque were still standing, and that, therefore, the destroyed neighborhood had not lost its legal right to exist. But the court ruling could never be implemented, and the local mosque, and the Servi Mescidi *mahalle* were never rebuilt.[27] In the municipal reform of the 1920s its area was included within *Mahmud Paşa*.

What is it that made such a difference possible between the "stable" Kasap İlyas, which survived all the fires, and the unfortunate *Servi Mescidi* neighborhood that succumbed to the first large-scale fire and could not be restored? The answer is not clear. Whatever it may be, the lesson is that the physical, mental, and social boundaries of the Istanbul neighborhood communities were basically imprecise. The topographically amorphous nature of many of these urban cells could make them extraordinarily resilient as well as prone to sudden and accidental change. There is even a relative instability in the very *names* of many *mahalle*s, when considered over a long period of time.

The case of a "new" *mahalle*, just next to Kasap İlyas is a good example of an attempted but aborted neighborhood. Its existence is documented as far back as the second quarter of the sixteenth century, and it seems to have then occupied an area around the Davud Paşa gate. It was at that time called a "new *mahalle*, adjacent to Kasap İlyas," probably because it did not yet have a mosque of its own from which to derive a name. In the 1630s, however, Bekir Paşa, one of the *defterdar*s[28] to Sultan Murad IV, built a two-story wooden mosque on the seaside just outside the ramparts, endowed it, and appointed an *imam* and a *muezzin* to officiate in it. With a number of people already living in the area, and a newly established and endowed mosque, the new neighborhood was thus set to acquire its independence from Kasap İlyas.

It appears, however, that a bona fide "Bekir Paşa *mahalle*" could never be launched. This "new" neighborhood does not appear in a late seventeenth-century Istanbul *avârız* list of neighborhoods[29] composed just a few decades after the building of the Bekir Paşa mosque. About a century and a half after the foundation of the mosque, an exhaustive and authoritative listing of Istanbul mosques does contain the Bekir Paşa *mescit*, but does not omit to mention that this small mosque "has no *mahalle* attached to it."[30] Similarly, a "Bekir Paşa neighborhood" appears in none of the post-Tanzimat nineteenth-century official *mahalle* listings. Yet another source calls the small mosque not by the name of its founder but as "the *mescit* next to the Davudpaşa wharf."[31] In the second half of the nineteenth century the mosque must have fallen totally in disuse, for during the Ottoman 1885 census it was already abandoned and in ruins. In the last Ottoman census of 1907, it had completely disappeared.

The Bekir Paşa *mescit*, as a building, had stood the test of time for about two and a half centuries. However, at no point in time had it succeeded in giving its name to a neighborhood independent from the Kasap İlyas *mahalle* from which it was supposed to have emerged. Was the congregation of the small seaside mosque too small or too poor and/or was the initial endowment and incomes of the *waqf* insufficient for the upkeep of an *imam*? Why didn't the "new" neighborhood expand beyond its initial area? Why didn't it annex new groups of streets and people?

There was no Muslim neighborhood in Istanbul that did not have at least one proper *mescit*. But there were plenty of mosques that had no attached *mahalle* of their own.[32] At least three other such small mosques without a *mahalle* of their own were situated not too far from our Kasap İlyas neighborhood. One was the *Şah ü Geda* mosque, situated to the west of our neighborhood and part of the Kürkçübaşı *mahalle*. The second was the *Şah Sultan* mosque in the neighboring Etyemez District. The third was the *Çavuşzade* mosque situated at the northern border of Kasap İlyas. All of these mosques were sixteenth-century constructions and the Çavuşzade mosque is even said to have been built by the master architect Sinan. None of these small mosques ever had their own *mahalle*. We shall probably never fully understand the social and economic dynamics that lay behind Bekir Paşa's unsuccessful attempt at pioneering the establishment of a new neighborhood "independent" of Kasap İlyas.

The city quarter, as a location, was always both *socially and physically flexible*. This was perhaps even more so in topographically very large and—at least until the second half of the nineteenth century—relatively sparsely populated Istanbul, than in other Ottoman cities of a more normal extent. Suraiya Faroqhi, for instance, points to a relative stability in the numbers but to a very frequent change in the *names* of the *mahalle*s in the central Anatolian towns of Ankara and Kayseri in the sixteenth and seventeenth centuries.[33] In Istanbul, both borders and areas could vary even over a relatively short period of time. "Mergers and acquisitions" of *mahalle*s were probably as frequent as new formations and split-ups.

An example is again provided by our—still relatively stable—Kasap İlyas *mahalle*. As detailed in the 1885 census documents, the inhabitants of the Kasap İlyas *mahalle* lived within a total of 14 streets and *culs-de sac*s. Only twenty-two years later, the official rosters of the last Ottoman census of 1907 show us that the population of the same *mahalle* had spilled over an adjacent street and that the neighborhood—as defined jointly by census officials assisted by the local headman (*muhtar*) during the census operations—now included 15 streets instead of 14.[34] The Kasap İlyas *mahalle* had, in the meantime, spilled eastward and encroached on a street that had formerly "belonged" to the Bayezid-i Cedid *mahalle*. This neighborhood, whose existence is documented from the sixteenth century on, appears, however, in none of the nineteenth-century official *mahalle* listings and must, in the meantime, have merged with another neighborhood, probably with the one called "Sancaktar Hayreddin" situated just to the west of Kasap İlyas. A *mahalle* at one point in time is a still photograph of a complex process of building and destroying, and of organizing and reorganizing.

The flexibility of the notion of the *mahalle* is also shown by the many cases of *"a neighborhood within a neighborhood."* These are instances where part of a *mahalle* is called by a different name. The aborted "Bekir Paşa *mahalle*" is a case in point, albeit unsuccessful in the long run. But some of these smaller entities might have found their way into some historical sources and have appeared as a distinct city quarter in some listings, and not in others.[35] At some point in time, an Istanbul *mahalle* could have, embedded in it, a subgroup of streets or even of a few building blocks that bore a special name.

For instance, Çavuşzade Street has always been part of the Kasap İlyas *mahalle*. Nevertheless, it was considered by many of its twentieth-century inhabitants as forming a separate entity having distinct characteristics. The nineteenth- and twentieth-century inhabitants of *Ispanakçı Viranesi*, another small area within Kasap İlyas, also formed a subgroup. People living in these two *submahalle* entities were distinguished due to their—real or imagined— social, ethnic, professional, or religious backgrounds. *Ispanakçı Viranesi* housed new rural migrants to Kasap İlyas, especially in the nineteenth century, and Çavuşzade Street was inhabited mostly by Istanbulites. But there never officially existed a separate Ispanakçı Viranesi *mahalle*, nor was there ever one named Çavuşzade. These two names never found their way into official *mahalle* listings. It remains that a subset of a given *mahalle* could sometimes, or just for a certain period of time, be considered a totally separate neighborhood. This adds a further element of imprecision to the already fluid local perception. In a sense, a *mahalle* was always a process in the making and only a fleeting picture is provided by the few available cross-sectional snapshots.

Gradual changes in the makeup of Istanbul *mahalle*s were also induced by the simple horizontal mobility of the inhabitants. The ethnic/religious composition of neighborhoods could not have been totally static either. This mobility is impossible to document for periods preceding the second half of the nineteenth century. The few reliable figures that exist for the Kasap İlyas *mahalle* in the Hamidian period, however, strongly suggest that even in earlier periods urban mobility must have been far from negligible.

The *turnover rate* of the population in our small neighborhood was very high in the second half of the nineteenth century. Between 1885 and 1895 the yearly entry and exit rates to and from the *mahalle* totaled around 3 percent. That is, for a population of around 1,000 to 1,100 inhabitants, the *muhtar*'s notebooks reveal that there there were about 30 people moving in or out of the neighborhood every single year. This is a very high rate of circulation. We should add to this figure of 3 percent the yearly births and deaths that occurred among the population of the *mahalle*. This would mean that the demographic and social composition of the neighborhood could be completely transformed within a generation or so. Indeed, over the last quarter of the nineteenth century the population of Kasap İlyas changed almost to a degree of unrecognizability. Practically none of the families and households present in the *mahalle* during the 1885 census are to be found twenty-two years later, in the last Ottoman census of 1907.

Sources and Issues

What is known of the demographic structures and the social relationships within the capital-city of the Ottoman Empire, especially in the eighteenth and nineteenth centuries, mostly concerns either the Palace itself and its web of political relationships or the more "Westernized" suburbs of Galata and Pera, whose inhabitants were mostly the Levantine or the non-Muslim. In any case, the available information concerns mostly middle- or upper-middle-class strata. The stock of published sources and materials (novels, memoirs, biographies, travelogues, etc.) also concern, for obvious reasons, more or less the same groups. Besides, they are, for the most part, concentrated in the post-Tanzimat period.

As exemplified by the history of Kasap İlyas however, grassroots Istanbul, much less "visible" both to contemporaries and to historians, was certainly quite different. The majority of the Istanbulites, especially those living in the intramural city, shared more modest households and neighborhoods, and it is they and their movements that ultimately put their stamp on Ottoman Istanbul. However, not much of significance has been written either on the daily lives of ordinary citizens, on the structure and the web of relationships of average neighborhoods or, for that matter, on the human fabric of Ottoman cities at large.

As far as the Anatolian towns are concerned, the picture is not all that different. In the heyday of their discovery and frenetic exploitation as a new source, it was hoped that the early Ottoman tax *cum* land cadastral surveys of the fifteenth and sixteenth centuries, the *tapu-tahrir* registers (the *Defter*s), could be used to reconstruct quarter by quarter their demographic and economic structure. These documents, however, have proven to be too schematic, too isolated, and too incomplete to provide anything more than a simple indication of relative population densities and, in some cases, of global population trends[36] in these cities. Besides, consistent long-run series are almost impossible to obtain for the fifteenth and sixteenth centuries.

As to the Ottoman/Turkish tradition of local history, this literature deals quite extensively with the archaeological remains and the architecture, the historical monuments, the urban layout, and so forth, of various cities. Notwithstanding a few notable exceptions, much of this literature, especially that concerning Anatolian cities, is little more than undigested raw historical source material with almost no attempts at detailed comment or synthesis. Besides, this literature is, mainly for lack of historical documentation, largely silent on what is the basic element of any community object of study: the people and their daily lives in the Ottoman period.

There is a small number of brilliant exceptions to this sad state of affairs. Faroqhi on seventeenth-century Ankara and Kayseri, André Raymond on various Arab cities under Ottoman rule, Haim Gerber on seventeenth-century Bursa, Abraham Marcus on eighteenth-century Aleppo, Daniel Goffman on Izmir, and Özer Ergenç on sixteenth-century Ankara deserve special mention. All of these studies use the archives of the local religious court records as one of their main source of documentation.

Local Archives

We know, however, of no equivalent historical study focusing on a *single mahalle* within an Ottoman or Middle Eastern city. Indeed, one of the reasons why, among all of the neighborhoods in traditional Istanbul, the Kasap İlyas *mahalle* has been picked up for such an in-depth, demographic, and historical study is, first and foremost the availability of a really exceptional set of archival sources pertaining to its population. The equivalent of these historical sources exist, to the best of our knowledge, for no other urban neighborhood of Istanbul, or for that of any other Ottoman city, for that matter.

These quite exceptional archival sources consist of three thick notebooks accompanied by a number of loose folios, all handwritten by the successive *imam*s of the Kasap İlyas mosque and by the *muhtar*s of the Kasap İlyas *mahalle* in the second half of the nineteenth century. These notebooks and folios contain, among other items of information:

1. a nominative list of 654 marriage contracts registered by the *imam*s of the Kasap İlyas mosque in the second half of the nineteenth century;
2. a complete list and description of *waqf* property in the neighborhood starting from the 1660s and ending about the middle of the nineteenth century, as well as the uses to which these *waqf* buildings and land have been put and the revenues that accrued;

3. a nominative list of population movements in and out of the neighborhood in the last quarter of the nineteenth century, as well as a (very incomplete) list of births and deaths in the *mahalle*;
4. a very precise descriptive count of all real estate property, public and private, in the neighborhood conducted in 1885 with names of owners and of tenant(s), if any.

The care with which the successive *imam*s and *muhtar*s of the the nineteenth-century Kasap İlyas *mahalle* took note of the demographic events that occurred in their neighborhood is truly surprising. Prior to the late nineteenth-century regulations on registration, there was no Ottoman/Muslim tradition of registering or centralizing vital events. A particularly zealous scribe (the local headman, *muhtar* Osman Efendi, of whom more will be said later) was instrumental in preserving these local documents. We have used these exceptional local records to complement the official census documents, to obtain an insider's perspective about the social and economic makeup of the neighborhood, and to trace the process of rural migration and integration into the *mahalle*. The marriage records contain little demographic information, for neither the ages, nor the dates and places of birth of the spouses were noted. These records are, however, a good indicator of the progressive secularization of vital registration. As to the local *waqf* records kept by the *imam*, the local trustee, they furnish important glimpses on intra*mahalle* relationships in the seventeenth and eighteenth centuries. The movements in and out of the neighborhood have provided a means of analyzing a multisecular migration model from the Anatolian town of Arapkir.

Quantitative Data (Late Ottoman Censuses)

Two other important Ottoman archival sources have been delved into, for the purposes of this book: The archives of the religious court (*Şer'iye Sicili Arşivi*) for the Davud Paşa District, spanning the period from 1782 to 1924, and the 1885 and 1907 late Ottoman Population Census (*Tahrir-i Nüfus*) documents. The censuses and registration schemes developed in the Ottoman Empire in the second half of the nineteenth century provide a rich source of data for historical studies. The two late Ottoman *de jure* censuses (*tahrir-i nüfu*s) of 1885 and 1907 and the population registers that were built upon them comprise a rich array of information on many aspects of Ottoman population and society.[37]

Until recently, these data had been utilized only in a superficial way.[38] Census-taking was an age-old Ottoman habit and a census of each newly conquered territory was indeed taken in the fifteenth and sixteenth centuries.

But these early counts were done for the purpose of assessing agricultural output and potential tax returns. Besides, they were discontinued after the first decades of the seventeenth century.

The two censuses of 1885 and 1907 were in fact the first empire-wide censuses designed specifically for purposes other than either taxation, agricultural revenue assessment, or military conscription. They were the first "modern" censuses in which precise demographic and social information was collected for each individual. All census registrations were nominative and they permit, therefore, the reconstruction of family and household structures. The 1885 census was also the first to record information about females. Individuals were recorded as members of residential groups of various types, the most common of which was the house or household (*hane*). The houses and other premises were all registered together by neighborhood and street address, and these are very helpful in drawing the social topography of the neighborhood.

Registration in the Ottoman capital during these two censuses is known to have been quite thorough, both for males and females. Strict measures were implemented to make sure that the census officials carried out their tasks. Each registered individual was then issued with a sort of population certificate (*nüfus tezkeresi*), which was a combination of a birth certificate and an identification card. This certificate was later to become an essential document for transacting all official and legal business, buying and selling property, seeking government employment, obtaining travel documents, and so forth. There is reason to suppose that census regulations were most strictly applied in the capital-city. In the Kasap İlyas *mahalle*, for instance, both the local headman and the *imam* of the mosque assisted the census officials in the registration process and signed the local census register upon completion of the operations as a testimony of the exhaustivity of the count. The data from these censuses are the most reliable source for the study of population, households, and families in late Ottoman society.

The basic rosters for the 1885 and 1907 censuses in the Kasap İlyas *mahalle* are kept intact in the Population Registry (*Nüfus Müdürlüğü*) of the Fatih District of metropolitan Istanbul. These two late Ottoman censuses were designed to also function as permanent population registers, probably under the influence of Quételet's Belgian population registers, and the census totals were to be regularly updated with the day-to-day registration of all subsequent vital events. All births, deaths, and in- and out- migrants to and from each neighborhood and city were to be recorded on the basic census rosters and these were to be kept *in situ*. The total failure of the postcensus registration schemes, however, stand in sharp contrast with the thoroughness and the reliability of the initial census registration itself. These rosters, which contain personal and confidential information, are still protected by a privacy law. They have not yet been turned over to the Ottoman Archives of the Prime Ministry and are not yet, properly speaking, public archival documents. They can be consulted by special permission only.

We have done an exhaustive and systematic transcription of both the 1885 and the 1907 census documents for the Kasap İlyas *mahalle*. In the 1885 census, the non-Muslim population of the neighborhood was registered in a separate roster, which is unfortunately lost. As to the 1907 census, there is only one basic roster that contains both the Muslim and the non-Muslim inhabitants of the neighborhood. In 1885, the Kasap İlyas *mahalle* had 925 registered Muslim inhabitants and, in 1907, a total of 1,160 inhabitants, 1,039 of which were Muslim.

Other Written Sources

Quantitative data and sources for the pre-nineteenth-century Istanbul population are difficult to come by. The available estimates, most of them by European travelers and Orientalists, are approximations with a usually low degree of reliability. Besides, Istanbul was never taxed in the same manner as the provinces, never had a *Tapu Tahrir Defteri*, and was never, even immediately after the Ottoman conquest, subjected to a census. There are, for the sixteenth, seventeenth, and eighteenth centuries, only a few sparse *cizye defteri* (head-tax registers for the non-Muslim population) and some partial household counts for the occasional *avârız* taxation. As to the urban local level, population figures are non-existent. The first citywide reliable count is that of 1885.

The Archives of the Religious Courts (*Şer'iye Sicilleri Arşivi*) for Istanbul are classified on a topographical basis, given that many of the courts of justice were also responsible for law and order in specific chunks of the city. The archives for the Davud Paşa District, of which the Kasap İlyas *mahalle* is a part, span the period between 1782 and 1924. The Davudpaşa Court of Justice, always headed by an aide (*na'ib*) of the *kadı* of Istanbul, was one of the oldest courts of the city. Its foundation is probably contemporaneous with the namesake mosque and dates therefore from the last decade of the fifteenth century. The court operated at first *within* the Davudpaşa mosque itself but was moved, in the eighteenth century, to a two-story wooden building just adjacent to it. The devastating fire that ravaged a large part of Istanbul in 1782 destroyed both the Davudpaşa Court Building and its three centuries of accumulated archives.

As to the post-1782 religious court records for Kasap İlyas, they contain mostly deeds of sale of property, settlements of debts and of commercial disputes, cases of inheritance with litigation, and cases of divorce. The cases of divorce include declarations of outright repudiation as well as cases with mutual consent and financial settlement. There are also a number of rulings that amount to an outright rejection of the plaintiff's case. A 10 percent sample spanning the 1782–1924 period has been drawn from among these court records. A total of 173 detailed court records have thus been transcribed, classified, and analyzed. A first screening was done by previously selecting the court cases where either the plaintiff, the defendant, and/or the object of discord were living or were situated in the Kasap İlyas *mahalle*.

Interviews and Personal Narratives

A small number of in-depth interviews have also been conducted with elderly inhabitants of Kasap İlyas. Nine of them were with Kasap İlyas-born men who were still in touch with their *mahalle* of origin, and one was with the wife of a former *muhtar*. The interviews were conducted either in their homes or in a coffeehouse in the *mahalle* where elderly people regularly met on Sundays. We attempted to obtain informants from as wide a range of social strata as possible but the paucity of the numbers involved invalidates any claims of "representativity."

Not surprisingly, we have had difficulty in obtaining precise chronological information about occurrences in the neighborhood. The temporal construction of each of the biographical narratives hinged on the remembrance of a past and lost "imagined community." Nevertheless, these interviews have provided very useful general information on daily life in the neighborhood and on its inhabitants in the first half of the twentieth century. We have thereby also obtained important clues on intracommunity relationships, on the self-image of the neighborhood community as a whole as well as, more generally, on twentieth-century local identities in Istanbul. Local myths and legends seem to have played an important role in the definition of the inhabitants of the *mahalle*.

The interviews also provided us with insights into the values and aspirations of men and women living in the integrated atmosphere of a traditional Istanbul neighborhood before the Second World War. During the interviews, most of the older Kasap İlyas inhabitants have spontaneously referred to the "foundation myths" of their *mahalle* with a mixture of pride and nostalgia, and have all expressed deep regret at the disappearance of the local *'asabiyya* in Istanbul. Many of the interviewees, for instance, took great pride in the "authentic old Istanbul" nature of their *mahalle* of origin, which they viewed as a proof of aristocracy. They all missed and deeply regretted the former internal solidarity networks.

The Istanbulites, in their public life, often saw their *mahalle* as a direct extension of their untouchable individual private space, of their inner personal domain. Their doorstep, their (often dead-end) street, and their *mahalle* were indeed transitional stages between their private and public spheres of activity. Therefore for many people, to talk about a *mahalle* implied conducting, in a sense, a first-person narrative discourse.

On the other hand, Ottoman historians have sufficiently stressed the fact that there was no widespread tradition of first-person narrative writing, no "personal" literature, or autobiographical materials worthy of that name in Ottoman times, at least not before well into the second half of the nineteenth century. There are exceptions, of course, but the exaggerated value attached to them is of a kind that tends to confirm the rule. The dearth of Ottoman/Turkish historical sources centered on the singularity of individual lives has been sufficiently underlined. The personal voice, the distantiation of the observer to the observed, the autobiographical touch, and the opinionated observation of daily events is something that is virtually impossible to find before the winds of "Westernization" could seriously affect daily social life in Ottoman cities.

As to the very few available personal narratives, they do not furnish sufficient material for the construction of personalized histories. Nor are they numerous enough, or do they constitute a fruitful perspective leading to a view of society "from the bottom up."[39] This state of affairs, for the time being, erects almost insuperable barriers to the detailed study of Ottoman popular life and culture in past centuries. The building of a meaningful, consistent, and continuous Ottoman/Turkish *histoire des mentalités* is, by the same token, a formidable enterprise. As things now stand, therefore, an Ottoman/Turkish equivalent of a Montaillou or of a "Merchant of Prato" seems quite impossible to reconstruct.

Take, for instance, our exceptionally conscientious late nineteenth-century Kasap İlyas *muhtar*s and *imam*s. These two officials have very carefully noted down hundreds of local events, filled up pages and pages with notes of local occurrences, and kept a personal archive full of various official matters of sometimes minor local importance. Some of the events that happened in the neighborhood didn't even require the official seal and did not even need to be officially registered.

Nevertheless, these two people, through pages and pages of local records, never give as much as a single clue either about themselves, their families, or their daily lives. Besides, they have never put down in writing a single personal opinion or viewpoint. The tone that prevails in their handwritten documents concerning the *mahalle* is a totally flat and impersonal one. The events that took place in Kasap İlyas were uniformly related in a crisp, dry style, often evocative of shorthand notation. Nowhere does the mental attitude of the *muhtar* and the *imam* toward these events, their work in general, their immediate social environment, or themselves transpire in any way. The tone is that of a zealous scribe who does his job well, often does more than what is required of him, and puts down in writing a maximum of information. But the scribe never distantiates himself from the duty of officially recording events. That these events in the Kasap İlyas *mahalle* were taking place in a very close environment and that almost all of them involved people who were well-known both to the *muhtar* and to the *imam* have made no difference. The selectivity among the types of recorded events is not revealing either. All social and demographic events, whether a birth, a death, the arrival to the *mahalle* and the registration of a newcomer, or even a simple signature apposed on a sales contract, get exactly the same flat and impersonal treatment.

Besides, these zealous and careful scribes always chose to remain *incognito*. Not once do they directly sign their books or documents, or mention their own names and identities, which we have had to discover by following the changes in handwriting, by cross-checking with other sources, and by capitalizing on minor textual hints. Official or unofficial *local chronicles* are a type of historical source that is not to be found in Ottoman Istanbul. Whether all of this constitutes sufficient reason for explaining the absence, especially before the second half of the nineteenth century, of any documentation on life in the Istanbul *mahalle*, is a matter to reflect upon. Microscale social and economic studies have not yet managed to appear as a promising research area for Ottoman and Middle Eastern historians.

We do not go so far as asserting that the Kasap İlyas *mahalle* was, in any sense of the word, *representative* of the whole of traditional Istanbul—or even of its more modest portion; nor can we say that it was a "typical" Ottoman/Turkish urban community neighborhood. Whether such a thing as a "typical" Ottoman city, which would also impose unique characteristics upon their various quarters and their inhabitants, ever existed is doubtful. To situate and describe a precise Ottoman local urban identity and to document its demographic and social evolution is, in itself, a sufficient challenge.

Otherwise, it might well be that Kasap İlyas has followed a strictly individual and inimitable path, that it has had an evolution that is totally *sui generis*. The highly unusual set of historical documents that have survived for this *mahalle* would, if anything, tend to set our neighborhood apart from the others. The care with which the successive *imam*s and *muhtar*s of nineteenth-century Kasap İlyas took note of the demographic events that occurred in the *mahalle* is truly surprising. This is even more of a contrast when set against the background of a total absence of any Ottoman/Muslim habit of registering, reporting, or centralizing vital events. The impressive collection of local *waqf* documents that the local *imam*s carefully preserved is just as unusual. These quite exceptional local headmen might well have been the products of an exceptional *mahalle*. The lesson, if any, to be drawn from Kasap İlyas would be to emphasize the extreme diversity and dissimilarity of urban neighborhoods, as well as their fluidity.

Ironwork above the tomb of the founder of the *Mahalle*, Kasap İlyas (author's photograph).

1

The Contours of a Local Identity

It was a chilly November day of the year 1494 (*Safer* 900 a.h.). İlyas slowly climbed the steep hill toward the large mosque of the Grand Vizier Davudpaşa. Its lofty dome and tall minaret overlooked the whole district, the large semt to which it had come to give its name. Obviously, the Davudpaşa mosque was much larger and loftier than the small mescit İlyas himself had built down the hill. But how could he, a simple butcher, have ever competed with the fortune of a grand vizier? There was no point in being dissatisfied with the comparison. Turning back, İlyas looked down the hill toward the Marmara Sea and marveled at all that had been accomplished.

İlyas had seen glorious days indeed. He sometimes felt that the whole city of Istanbul was his. True, he was only a simple butcher. But he had been given, in his time, the incomparable honor of feeding and serving the army that conquered this magnificent city. He had been appointed chief butcher of the sultan's army, and had served his master as best as he could. He did not only feed the Blessed Army; he was also part of it. This meant that he too had waged a Holy War in his own right. That was more than four decades ago. For weeks and months in the spring of the year 1453 (857 a.h.) İlyas and his aides had borne the heavy responsibility of slaughtering sheep and providing the besieging army with a sufficient amount of meat. Once Constantinople was taken, who could deny his vital contribution to the victory?

And yes, after the conquest, when the time came for sharing the spoils, he was not forgotten. The glorious Sultan Mehmed the

Conqueror allotted his chief butcher, İlyas, a large piece of land within the walled city. The other chief butcher of the conquering army, Demirhan, had also received his share. He had, however, died soon after the conquest. Demirhan's lot was perhaps better situated, as it overlooked the bustling Golden Horn from the top of a steeper hill near the Byzantine church of Christ Pantocrator and was nearer to the commercial center of the city. But it was much smaller in area and already rather densely populated by Christians. As to his own share, near the city walls and overlooking the sea of Marmara, it was much larger and virtually empty. Luckily, İlyas had to face a territory that was practically a *tabula rasa*. Indeed, after the conquest the quasi-deserted city had to be almost totally repopulated. Settlers had to be brought in, new neighborhoods had to be formed, mosques had to be built, and Byzantium had to be given a new and Muslim stamp. So, in a sense, Kasap İlyas' Holy War was far from having ended with the capture of the city. His personal Holy War was in fact only beginning.

He remembered the very day he had set foot on "his" bit of Istanbul. That was also the first time he had entered the conquered city itself. Approaching his territory on a boat, he had found landing on a small old wharf made of a few creaking planks. The infidels called it the Agios Emilianos wharf. Part of the Muslim army had already used it as a landing place during the two-month long siege of Constantinople. This wharf was the nearest sea access to his portion of the city. İlyas had then looked at the area in and around the city walls bordering on the sea of Marmara and he had chosen the best place to build his mosque: not too close to the sea and the city walls, but not too high up the hill either, a plot of land bordering on the small side road that led from the Forum Bovis of the infidels to the city walls near the Seven Towers. Then he had boats bring to the seaside blocks of stone, limestone, and sand to make mortar, wood for construction, and so forth. Workers were hired and building began.

Very soon, however, the building of the mosque had to come to a temporary halt. İlyas remembered why. He was sitting on a block of stone watching the workers unloading the boats and carrying the various building materials from the wharf to the construction site of the mosque. The actions of one of these workers struck him. The man took a heavy stone or a sack full of limestone from the boat moored at the wharf, brought it to the building site and, without leaving it there, carried the same sack or stone back to the boat again. The action was repeated quite a few times. İlyas was puzzled.

When asked for the reason for his strange behavior, the man answered that "he felt he had to do his share of daily work, and that he had no choice but to work for a living; however, as he was impure, he felt he should not contribute to the building of a holy place of worship while in a state of ritual impurity." İlyas was struck by the man's honesty and piety. On the spot, he gave the order to stop all work on the building site of the mosque. Then, he gave priority to building a large hamam first, so that the workers could wash and regularly perform their ritual ablutions. A location just across from the mosque was selected for the purpose. The mosque itself was finally completed only after the public bath was built and in operation. With the mosque and the shops built just next to it, the providential public bath would become an essential part of the new *mahalle*.

Many of those who worked on Kasap İlyas' construction site were also among his former aides in his work as a butcher. They were all used to slaughtering sheep and cattle and all of them enjoyed a good bite of mutton or beef. Save one. This odd man was strangely averse to eating meat and would never even have a taste of it. No wonder he was nicknamed "Etyemez" (meat-averse!). It was very strange, therefore, that this man could take part in a long-term enterprise whose very existence rested on the provision and consumption of animal meat. Naturally, İlyas ended up by banishing this misfit. The man was told to go and settle as far away as possible from the mosque and from the center of İlyas's new *mahalle*. The vegetarian went and settled on a small bit of land at the extreme western tip of the large area put by the Sultan under İlyas's responsibility. The vegetarian's place of banishment was later to become a separate neighborhood known as Etyemez. Nevertheless, this neighborhood always remained morally part and parcel of Kasap İlyas's dependencies.

But all of this was a long, long time ago. İlyas the butcher was now old and felt tired as he climbed up the hill on a narrow dirt road. He knew that the end was not very far, but he was ready to go, and at peace with himself. He had already accomplished the pilgrimage to Mecca, the Haj. Besides, he had just made his will and had given away all of his possessions to endow a holy foundation. The foundation, his perpetual vakıf, was to take care of his mosque, the mosque he had built himself, the visible product of his dedication, of his piety and hard work. This mosque that bore his name, the Kasap İlyas mosque, was standing just below him, toward the foot of the hill on land gently sloping toward the sea. He had indeed richly endowed it. Apart from the yearly revenues accruing from the thirty thousand aspers in cash that had bequeathed to his foundation, there would also be the rental incomes from no less than sixteen shops and six rooms, all adjoining the mosque. These moneys would certainly be more than sufficient for the upkeep. An imam as well as a müezzin would be appointed on a permanent basis and the imam would be the trustee of his foundation. The wages of the Coran reciters, those of the Friday preachers and of the cleaners and caretakers of his mosque, as well as the expenses for the necessary upkeep and repair work would be paid out of his foundation's revenues.

Besides, with the public bath and the shops all near the city gate leading to the seaside and to the wharf, he was sure that a small center of attraction had already taken shape. Through his efforts, a durable neighborhood community, a real mahalle had been formed. However rich or prestigious the adjacent *mahalle*s might become, he was sure that his mahalle would always have both chronological and spiritual precedence over its surroundings. In time, the *Kasap İlyas* mahalle would, no doubt, put its stamp on the whole district. It seemed then that Kasap İlyas had waged his personal Holy War with a great deal of success.

As for himself, he had made sure that, when the time came, his body would be laid to rest in the small plot of land just behind the mosque. That would be a perfect location for watching his neighborhood, the Kasap İlyas *mahalle*, grow and prosper—and forever remain a basic building block of Muslim Istanbul.

It is not totally impossible for these events to have really taken place. This narrative is, as a matter-of-fact, just a combination of various local myths and legends of Kasap İlyas with the few elements of truth that can be gathered from sixteenth-century sources.

As to the first serious historical source of detailed information on the *mahalle*, it dates from 1546, no less than half a century after the putative decease of its mythical founder and almost a century after the conquest of Istanbul.[1] In the detailed list of *vakıf*s established in 1546 and published by Barkan and Ayverdi, the Kasap İlyas *mahalle* is listed as one of fourteen neighborhoods that were then part of the Davud Paşa area.[2] In this collation of Istanbul pious foundations, the details of no less than 2,490 deeds of trust are enumerated and these are distributed over a total of 219 *mahalle*s of Istanbul *intra muros*. This shows an average of 11 *vakıf*s per Istanbul neighborhood, though for most of the *mahalle*s the number of deeds of trust did not exceed four or five. Among the neighborhoods adjacent to Kasap İlyas, for instance, only three *vakıf*s were registered for the Sancaktar Hayreddin *mahalle*, two for Abacızâde, eight for Kürkçübaşı, nine for Hubyar, and eighteen for Davud Paşa. With a total of twenty six local pious foundations Kasap İlyas was indeed the record holder in and around the Davud Paşa area, and was also among the ten *mahalle*s of Istanbul having the highest number of local *vakıf*s.

Local Identity: The Formative Sixteenth Century

Less than a century after the conquest, Kasap İlyas had already acquired the location that it still occupies within the *semt* and *mahalle* topography of Istanbul. Set on the slopes of the last of the "seven hills" of the historical Istanbul peninsula, on land gently sloping toward the sea south of the Davud Paşa Mosque, Kasap İlyas was then, as it is today, embedded in the larger Davud Paşa *semt*.

The high number of endowments for local common benefit established in Kasap İlyas is a sure indicator of a strong sense of local identity and of a relatively high degree of social cohesion. The decisions that many of the inhabitants of the *mahalle* took, in the first half of the sixteenth century, concerning the transmission of their property, shows that they really believed in the perennity of their neighborhood. Those who established a foundation for local common benefit in their neighborhood chose to dispose of their goods in a manner that would establish an eternal link between them and their neighborhood community. A local identity, a sense of local belonging, was evidently already there, for such potent material effects would not have been produced without a strong collective belief in local common goals and benefits. The first deed of trust (*vakfiye*) established in the neighborhood is, as a matter-of-fact also the earliest within the whole Davud Paşa district and is dated May 1501 (Şevval 906 a.h.). That first local *vakıf* provides for the repair and maintenance of a local public convenience, a well for public use *(bi'r-i mâ-yı müşterek)* situated in the neighborhood.[3]

Was the comparatively large number of local endowments due to the fact that Kasap İlyas was particularly populous or particularly well-off in the sixteenth century? On the matter of populousness, just the contrary is true. As we shall see, though large in area, the *mahalle* was always, in the sixteenth as well as in later centuries, rather sparsely populated. As to riches, the available sources do not allow for that sort of a comparison at a *mahalle* level in the sixteenth century, but, as we shall see, eighteenth- and nineteenth-century data would, if anything, point in just the opposite direction.

Starting from the very end of the fifteenth century, the inhabitants of that small bit of Istanbul seem to have strongly believed that they could meaningfully bequeath their possessions (in cash or as real estate property) for a strictly *local* cause and purpose. Besides believing in the perennity of the mosque and of the *mahalle* itself, the inhabitants who endowed a foundation for local common benefit must have put a good deal of confidence in the personality of the local religious leaders (i.e., the *imam* and the *müezzin* of the Kasap İlyas mosque) who would automatically have to function as trustees and would have to manage the trust fund or the real estate property in accordance with the desires of the founder.

Besides, Kasap İlyas, through the prestige of its local religious leaders, seems to have acquired a particular urban aura. Indeed, the trusteeship of a number of houses situated in Arap Taceddin and in the adjacent "new" *mahalle* had also been given to the *imam* of the Kasap İlyas mosque. However, not even a single item of property situated in our neighborhood had been given in trust to a local religious foundation situated elsewhere in the city in the first half of the sixteenth century.

Points of Reference

In the last quarter of the fifteenth century three buildings played a definitional role in the formation of our neighborhood and of its local identity: (1) the Davud Paşa complex (*külliye*) which gave its name to the whole area and was situated up the hill above Kasap İlyas. Built in 1485 by the grand vizier Koca Davud Paşa (d. 1498), it was composed of a large mosque, a shrine (*türbe*), a small theological school (*medrese*), and a soup kitchen for the poor (*imaret*); (2) the Kasap İlyas mosque, built probably not long before 1494, which is the date of its deed of trust; and (3) the large Davud Paşa double bath (*çifte hamam*[4]) situated right in the middle of our *mahalle* and built probably at the same time as the Davud Paşa complex itself. As it was nearer to the city walls bordering on the sea of Marmara than to the Davud Paşa complex, the Davud Paşa public bath was often designated as Deniz Hamamı, or Denizciler Hamami (The Seamen's *Hamam*).

Together with the Davud Paşa gate on the city walls bordering the sea of Marmara and the small wharf that jutted out from the piece of land just outside the gate, these three buildings were the main formative landmarks of both the Davud Paşa *semt* and the Kasap İlyas *mahalle* in the last quarter of the fifteenth century. These three buildings put their imprint on the area, became the basic topographical points of reference for a local identity, and contributed to the formation of a durable local consciousness. Indeed, neither the name of the Davud Paşa District nor that of Kasap İlyas appear in a previous listing of Istanbul pious foundations dated from 1472.[5] The last quarter of the fifteenth century was crucial in that respect.

Were there any traces of any Byzantine building, monument, road, church, and so forth or of any other pre-Ottoman center of attraction that could have served as a point of reference to the newly formed *mahalle*? Judging from the speed with which local identities were formed in the neighborhood after the Ottoman conquest, the answer seems to be negative. The Byzantine monument nearest to the Kasap İlyas *mahalle* would be the *Arcadius column,* at the center of a small *forum* that was situated about a quarter of a mile to the north and was within the bounds of the Cerrahpaşa District, where the basis of the column can still be seen. To the west of Davudpaşa, the neighboring *semt* of Samatya derives its name from the Greek *Psammathia.* To the east of Kasap İlyas are the large vegetable gardens of Langa, whose Turkish name is a direct descendent of the Byzantine *Vlanga.* No onomastic or topographical traces have been transmitted to Ottoman Istanbul, however, either of *Xerolophus,* the Byzantine denomination of the hills of the Davudpaşa District, or of *Hagios Emilianos,* the name of a church and of a gate in the city ramparts, both in the same district.[6] The district was in no way an important Byzantine economic or political center. It did not become a primary urban center under Ottoman rule either. The construction of durable local identities in Ottoman Davudpaşa and in Kasap İlyas seem to have owed little to what the district had contained in Byzantine times.

The area was very sparsely populated in the late Byzantine period. Sources show that the whole Marmara coast from the point of the Seraglio to the Castle of the Seven Towers was hardly inhabited.[7] Buildings were rare in the first decades of the Turkish conquest as well. Many maps and engravings of the period show vast empty areas all along the coast. The Buondelmonti map of the end of the fifteenth century as well as the Vavassore map dating from the 1520s show, despite the usual inaccuracies of scale and perspective, that the seacoast of the walled city of Istanbul was lined with gardens, vineyards, orchards, and windmills and contained large areas of empty land. In all of the fifteenth- and sixteenth-century historic maps and charts, very few houses, churches, and mosques appear along the Marmara coast of intramural Istanbul.[8]

Deserted though it was in the decades preceding the Turkish conquest, the Davudpaşa area was not given priority when Istanbul had to be repopulated after the Ottoman takeover. Some of the neighboring districts did receive an influx of immigrant population, but not Kasap İlyas and Davudpaşa. As part of the policy of repopulating Istanbul, for instance, many Armenian communities were brought from around the Anatolian towns of Tokat and Sivas in the years immediately following the conquest, and they were settled in the neighboring districts of Samatya, Langa, and Sulumanastır.[9] For all we know, our district and *mahalle* were not directly concerned by any of these forced population movements. The neighborhood identities that took shape in the *mahalle* and in the district were not connected to any "imported" network of preexisting relationships (a common geographic origin, ethnic or religious groupings, etc.) which would have simply been superimposed upon a new topographical *locus*. The available evidence seems to indicate that local identities and local solidarities in Kasap İlyas were formed on the spot, the two mosques, the *hamam* (a place for meeting as much as one for taking baths) and the wharf having served as basic mental and geographic landmarks.

The account-books of the large and central *Süleymaniye* mosque, built between 1550 and 1557, barely a decade after the 1546 list of pious foundations, contain another bit of evidence indicative of this early formation of the Davudpaşa and Kasap İlyas local identities.[10] In the absence of family surnames, almost all of the workers employed on the construction site of the large sultanic mosque were clearly identified by their place of origin. For those coming from outside the capital, the name of their town of origin was added to their name and for the Istanbulites, that of their district within the city. Next to those coming from the adjoining districts of Langa or Samatya, many workers (stonemasons, carpenters, etc.) on the construction site, from 1550 on, were clearly identified as "such and such from Davudpaşa."

Endowments, Donations, and Foundation Aims

The specifications of the sixteenth-century Kasap İlyas *vakıf*s list the broad range of endowments that were set up by the local inhabitants.[11] First of all, various amounts of cash, ranging from one thousand to thirty thousand aspers (*akçe*) were donated. In most of the deeds of trust it was clearly specified that the yearly return of these moneys would be 10 percent. Then there is real estate (a total of sixteen houses and five shops, all situated within the *mahalle*) which had been endowed. This is quite considerable, given that Kasap İlyas could not, in all probability have contained at the time much more than fifty or sixty houses. Besides cash and real estate, some utensils for daily use (a cauldron, a large tray, a copper bucket, a basin, a pickaxe, a spade, etc.) were also bequeathed to the Kasap İlyas mosque, as well as, more appropriately, some manuscript copies of the Coran.

Three of the twenty-six *vakıf*s provided funds for the upkeep of a dervish lodge (*tekke*) situated elsewhere. The Süleyman Halife *tekke* belonging to the Halvetî Sufi order was situated in the neighborhood of Sofular, about a kilometer to the east, and three Kasap İlyas deeds of trust dating from 1515 and 1521 provided funding for this lodge. This leads us to presume that there existed no such *tekke*s in or near Kasap İlyas in the first half of the sixteenth century.[12]

The deeds of trust directly and openly state that their object is one of local common benefit. The upkeep and repair of the Kasap İlyas mosque is the most often-cited aim and endowed moneys and their future revenues are clearly earmarked for that specific purpose. The provision of oil for the oil-lamps of the mosque and the purchase of candles for lighting the mosque on special days is also important. The care and cleaning of the two communal water-wells of the *mahalle* have also been provided for, as well as the expenses of a small local primary school (*muallimhane*) which was endowed as early as 1514. In another important chunk of the deeds of trust both the management of, and the revenues that would accrue from, the bequeathed property (houses and shops) are directly left to those who are to officiate as *imam* and/or as *müezzin* of the Kasap İlyas mosque. These indirect donations to the *imam* are often conditional upon his regular recitation of Coranic prayers for the rest of the soul of the deceased donor. The existence of officiating local religious leaders must be seen as an object of common benefit from the point of view of the local community.

From a strictly technical and legalist point of view, though, about half of the sixteenth-century Kasap İlyas pious foundations belonged to the type called hereditary (*evlâtlık* or *zürrî*) *vakıf*s. Technically, this means that the initial donor could decide that the donated cash or property forming the initial endowment would at first be entrusted either to one or more of his direct descendants or to another person of his choice. The endowed property would then be managed by these selected "heirs" and would revert to the trusteeship of the *imam* of the local mosque only after the death of those persons or the complete extinction of their line of descendants. As suggested by Barkan and Ayverdi in their introduction to their modern edition of the 1546 list of Istanbul *vakıf*s, this mode of constitution of the *vakıf*s could also have been used as a way of bypassing the very strict Islamic rules (*ferâiz* or *muhallefât*) concerning the partition of inheritances.[13]

In the middle of the sixteenth century, the *imam* of the Kasap İlyas mosque who was also the local leader of Kasap İlyas, was managing the revenues of twenty-six different local pious foundations. From among these, the use of, and/or the revenues accruing from, six houses and three shops had been given to him by the various donors. As we shall see, the *imam*s of the Ottoman Kasap İlyas *mahalle* have always enjoyed fairly comfortable income levels, and the basis for their regular income flow seems to have been already established in the early sixteenth century.

MAHALLE TOPOGRAPHY: BOUNDARIES AND LANDMARKS

To determine the precise boundaries of the sixteenth-century Kasap İlyas *mahalle* is an attempt both vain and impossible. The *mahalle*s—or, rather, those that survived until the twentieth century—were officially assigned precise and artificial boundaries only in 1927.[14] For centuries the Kasap İlyas mosque, the Davudpaşa complex, the *hamam*, the wharf, and the city ramparts bordering on the sea of Marmara were sufficient definitional landmarks. There is nevertheless reason to suppose that the area and borders of the Kasap İlyas *mahalle* did not change to a very considerable extent during the last few centuries. To the west and to the east of it, the two neighboring *mahalle*s (Sancaktar Hayrettin *alias* Bayezid-i Cedid, and Kürkçübaşı) have always been the same. The southernly limits of Kasap İlyas were, then as now, naturally set by the city walls and by the sea of Marmara. To the north, there were two neighboring *mahalle*s (Hubyar and Abacızade) in the sixteenth century but these had later disappeared and had been absorbed into other northernly neighborhoods.

To sum up, Kasap İlyas extended, then as now, over a rectangular area, with the long sides of the rectangle being oriented approximately in the east-west direction. Compared with the other intramural Istanbul *mahalle*s, Kasap İlyas has never been a *small* neighborhood. In the nineteenth century, Istanbul neighborhoods usually covered an area ranging from one to five hectares.[15] Kasap İlyas, toward the end of the nineteenth century, had a total area of no less than six hectares. Only a little more than half that area was effectively inhabited, though, and the Davud Paşa vegetable gardens took up the rest.

The streets of Istanbul received official names only in the 1860s. The people of Istanbul gave names to the more important streets before the nineteenth century, but nothing points to the existence of street names as early as the sixteenth century. There were no house or gate numbers either and the modern construct of an "address" could not apply.

The truth is that none of the real estate property in Kasap İlyas set up as a pious foundation in the sixteenth century can now be located with any degree of precision within the *mahalle*. For in the deeds of trust, these properties were always described with reference to the nearest well-known landmark and to the names of the owners of the neighboring houses or property. The landmarks most often used in the sixteenth-century Kasap İlyas *mahalle* were, besides its namesake mosque and the *hamam*, the city ramparts, the Davud Paşa gate on the same ramparts, and the wharf.

The Wharf

Among these ontological markers of Kasap İlyas, the Davud Paşa wharf is of special importance. This wharf, which probably preexisted the *mahalle*, was far from being essential to the general port activities of a large city like Istanbul. The most important wharfs were always, in Byzantine as in Ottoman times, located along the coast of the Golden Horn, which was a magnificent natural harbor. To these were brought most of the goods imported to the city and the main wharfs used for passenger transportation were also situated along the coast of this harbor. The Davudpaşa wharf was nevertheless one of the very few jetties situated on the Marmara Sea coast of the walled city. Along a one-mile stretch of coastline from Langa to Samatya, among the vegetable gardens and the fishermen's huts, there were but two small jetties: that of Yenikapı, mostly used for bringing fruits and vegetables from the Asian coast in the nineteenth century, and our Davudpaşa wharf.[16] The Davudpaşa wharf served as a basic point of reference for a much wider area than our neighborhood.

This wharf epitomizes the functional articulation of Kasap İlyas to the rest of the city. To this small wooden wharf, barges brought such construction materials as wood for burning, timber, coal, straw, sand, and gravel. These were then stored in a number of nearby warehouses within the Kasap İlyas *mahalle*, all situated between the Davudpaşa wharf and the main thoroughfare of Kasap İlyas that passed between the mosque and the *hamam*. Records suggest that the presence of warehouses in the area was as ancient as the wharf, or as the neighborhood itself. As early as 1511 a deed of trust mentions the existence of a "seller of wood/timber near the Davudpaşa wharf."[17] Traces of these shops and warehouses are to be found throughout the centuries.

These warehouses obviously did not address themselves to the sole inhabitants of Kasap İlyas, or even to the larger Davudpaşa area of which Kasap İlyas was a part. Most of these goods were commodities of first necessity, whether for fuel (wood and coal), for transportation (straw), or for construction and repair work (sand and gravel). As a matter-of-fact, the general layout of the city of Istanbul commanded that an important part of the import, transportation, and domestic distribution of these bulk goods be done by sea, to avoid the hilly and dense maze of narrow streets in the city center. They had to be stored in warehouses situated not too far away from their port of disembarkment. From there, retail trade and distribution could proceed. The Davudpaşa wharf and the warehouses in our *mahalle* serviced a large portion of the city, in fact almost the whole of the Marmara seacoast west of Langa. Our neighborhood therefore had an urban commercial function whose importance exceeded the narrow limits of a small and residential *mahalle*. Wood and timber was brought to the capital-city of the Ottoman Empire from various Black Sea ports and their first points of entry were situated along the southern shore of the Golden Horn (in *Cibali* and *Odun iskelesi*, to be more precise).[18] The Davudpaşa wharf and the warehouses in the Kasap İlyas *mahalle* served as one of the main transiting points for urban retailing and distribution.

The centuries-long presence of the wharf and of the attached warehouses did put a durable imprint on Kasap İlyas. The owners of the warehouses used local labor and facilities, and many of the street-porters living within the *mahalle* were partly or fully employed in the transportation and distribution of timber, sand, and so forth. The whole area acquired, as we shall see, a certain disrepute due to the presence of the porters and of various warehouse workers, a largely "nonfamilial" and mostly migrant group within an otherwise almost completely residential area. The small wooden Davudpaşa wharf was also sometimes also used for public transportation. Seventeenth- and eighteenth-century listings of boats and barges operating in Istanbul show that a few, though not many, of them were permanently attached to the Davudpaşa wharf. These boats and barges must have carried passengers to and from the city center, that is, to and from other wharfs situated on the Golden Horn. This public transportation activity probably continued until the 1860s, when the *mahalle* was connected to central Istanbul by a tramway line. Although Istanbul is a typical port-city surrounded by water on three sides and where various types of boats were, for centuries, the most important means of public transportation, there are few serious studies on the history of marine transportation within the city.[19]

The Davudpaşa wharf also had its political heyday in the early sixteenth century, for it was, in a way, involved in the political fight between Selim and Korkut, both sons of Sultan Bayezid the Second (reigned between 1481 and 1512) and potential heirs to the Ottoman throne. When the throne seemed to be up for grabs Korkut, who was then governor of Manisa, secretly moved to Bandyrma, took a boat that crossed the Sea of Marmara, and landed in Istanbul on April 9, 1512. His intention was to rally the various Janissary corps stationed in Istanbul and to convince them to join him in order to overtrow his father. The attempt was not crowned with success and it was Selim, later nicknamed "The Grim," who finally mounted the Ottoman throne. What pertains to the Kasap İlyas *mahalle* in this adventure is that, to mount his political coup, Prince Korkut had chosen the Davudpaşa wharf when he disembarked upon his arrival at Istanbul.[20] That is hardly surprising for, in all military and political logic, he needed a wharf that was both well-known to navigators and was not too centrally situated. It can be surmised that, had Prince Korkut's political gamble succeeded, the fortunes of the small and secondary Davudpaşa wharf and of the *mahalle*s in its environs might well have received an economic and political boost.

Even in the early sixteenth century, however, the significance of this minor wharf was not limited to the sole Kasap İlyas *mahalle*, within the bounds of which it happened to operate. The Davudpaşa wharf, minor though it was, was used as a basic topographical landmark for a much wider area. In fact, the whole of the Marmara coast all the way from the Langa vegetable gardens to the Greek and Armenian quarters of Samatya were using this wharf as a topographical marker. For instance, in two deeds of trust dated April 1530 and October 1542,[21] the small mosque of Bayezid-i Cedid, situated about half a mile to the west of the Kasap İlyas mosque, and nearer in fact to the district of Samatya than to Davudpaşa, is described as "the mosque of Sultan Bayezid near the Davudpaşa wharf." Moreover, in the seventeenth and eighteenth centuries, not only this or that particular building or plot of land, but whole *mahalle*s were described with reference to the Davudpaşa wharf. In many of the local deeds of trust drawn in the late seventeenth century, the neighborhood where the donated property is situated is described as ". . . the Kasap İlyas *mahalle* near the Davudpaşa wharf."[22] So is the neighboring *mahalle* always referred to as ". . . the Bayezid-i cedid *mahalle* near the Davudpaşa wharf."

Later, the inhabitants of Kasap İlyas even came to be designated, in some nineteenth-century sources, as those from the Davudpaşa wharf (*Davudpaşa Iskelelı*). This designation was meant to differentiate those who lived in the parts of the Davudpaşa District nearer to the seaside and to the wharf—that is, in the Kasap İlyas *mahalle*—from those who resided up the hill, near the grand vizier's mosque and the religious court contiguous to it. These people were therefore called those from the Davudpaşa Court (*Davudpaşa Mahkemeli*).[23] When local fire brigades were constituted within Istanbul in the middle of the nineteenth century, the volunteers from the Kasap İlyas *mahalle* were, almost naturally, incorporated into the Davudpaşa Wharf fire brigade, and those from the upper parts of the district into the Davudpaşa Court brigade.

The Ramparts

The city ramparts bordering on the Sea of Marmara, the natural southern border of our rectangular neighborhood, constituted yet another important definitional landmark for the Kasap İlyas *mahalle*. A gate on the walls (*Davudpaşa kapısı*) opened on a small plot of land from which jutted out our wharf. These walls had lost all defensive function after the capture of Constantinople and had not undergone any substantial repair work.[24] Materials were often extracted from them to build houses. Among the sixteen houses donated to a pious foundation in Kasap İlyas in the first half of the sixteenth century, no less than nine were set very close to these city walls. As the description in the deeds of trust shows *(cidar-ı kal'a ile mahdud)*, either the houses themselves or their gardens were abutting on the waterside ramparts. Many shops and warehouses were also contiguous to the city walls in the sixteenth century. We know that three of these shops were endowments of pious foundations, in 1511, 1521, and 1529. The last two were shops/warehouses for timber and wood. Then as now, there were vegetable gardens as well under the city walls, and one of them, too, had been bequeathed to a foundation in 1515.[25]

All this leads us to believe that the center of gravity of the sixteenth century population of Kasap İlyas had been nearer to the sea. There probably was a relatively greater concentration of houses, shops, and people in the part of the neighborhood between the Kasap İlyas mosque, situated more or less in the center of the *mahalle*, and the southernly ramparts. Compared to this part of the neighborhood, the slopes of the hill toward the Davudpaşa mosque must have been more sparsely settled.

Houses and Gardens

The sixteenth-century deeds of trust contain a number of important clues on houses, land use, and general patterns of settlement in the Kasap İlyas *mahalle*. The houses and other real estate property donated to a local *vakıf* are often described in some detail.[26]

Houses as Dwellings

The usual *nomenklatura* of houses and dwellings in Ottoman Istanbul comprises four different status markers. These markers are, in ascending order of prestige: *süfli* (shabby, run-down), *tahtanî* (level with the ground), *fevkânî* (elevated), and *mükellef* (luxurious). These adjectives are the expression of a hierarchy in both size, quality, and social status of the house. The last qualifier was usually reserved for palatial houses and for the larger dwellings of the high-ranking military and bureaucrats.[27] The *tahtanî* houses were on average, single-story houses, and the *fevkânî* usually had two stories.

Out of the sixteen houses set up as a foundation in Kasap İlyas in the first half of the sixteenth century and whose descriptions are given in the deeds of trust, no less than thirteen are qualified as *hane-i tahtanî*. That is, they all had only a ground floor.[28] Two others were qualified as *süfli*, that is, they also had one single floor but they were smaller and/or shoddier than the others. Only one of the houses in Kasap İlyas was qualified as a *fevkanî* house and therefore had more than one floor, most probably two. In the sixteenth century, just as in later centuries, and notwithstanding the presence of a few large mansions, the houses in the Kasap İlyas *mahalle* were mostly of an average size and of a quite modest appearance.

From the little that remains of the old *mahalle*s of Istanbul today, one gets the distinct impression that the wooden two-story type of residence was definitely the most common one. But this contemporary impression concerns mostly the surviving nineteenth-century wooden buildings. Back in the sixteenth century, the most common type of Istanbul dwellings seem to have had only one floor. Many sixteenth- and seventeenth-century European travelers also report that one-story buildings were pervasive in most of Istanbul.[29]

Moreover, it is probable, as Barkan and Ayverdi also point out,[30] that most of these one-story *süfli* or *tahtani* houses in the Kasap İlyas *mahalle* only contained a single "room," the main living quarters. The word *hane*, or "house," most probably designated the whole construction, while the individual dwelling-units included therein were designated by the word *bab*, which means "door," "gate," or "entrance." When and if the two did not coincide, it was openly specified in the deed of trust, for instance, a house with two gates (*iki bâb hane*) was being donated to a *vakıf*. A patent example of the distinction between house and residential unit is given by a deed of trust established in the Kasap İlyas *mahalle* and dated December 1526. According to this deed, "a house with two gates" was being set up as a pious foundation, but the donor had clearly specified that the incomes accruing from the large room (*beyt-i kebir*) were to be put to a different use than the moneys that were to accrue from the renting of the small room (*beyt-i sagir*).[31]

The assumption that most of these houses must have contained a single living space is also supported by the abundance of outhouses and annexes attached to each of them. The roofed single space was functioning both as a living room and as a bedroom, because most of the other domestic chores and functions were banished to these outhouses and extensions. The houses in the Kasap İlyas *mahalle* all possessed one or more of these extensions. The kitchen (*matbah*) and the kiln or oven (*furun*), for instance, were invariably separated from the house itself, and so, for obvious reasons, were the toilets (*kenif*). Some houses had a well, others an open veranda (*zulle*), and still others a cellar or a granary (*serdab* or *anbar*). The extensions attached to the same *hane* were obviously being used in common by all of the households living within the same dwelling-unit. Indeed, a water-well that is donated to a Kasap İlyas *vakıf* is mentioned in the deed of trust as being an extension of a house and is described as a common water-well (*bi'r-i ma-yı müşterek*).

The Kasap İlyas houses, as were most dwellings in sixteenth-century Istanbul, were wooden constructions that had a basic timber structure, and brick, mud or stone filling in between. The outside walls might have been covered with boards or planks. More probably, they were simply plastered.[32] Sixteenth- and seventeenth-century European travelers to Istanbul are unanimous in observing that all of the large public buildings (mosques, public baths, *han*s, *medrese*s, etc.) were solidly built of stone, whereas most private housing was basically built of wood. Wood was a cheaper and more readily available building material than stone, and this was important for the more modest neighborhoods of Istanbul.

The sixteenth-century Istanbulites had been eyewitnesses to the terrible havoc of the 1509 earthquake. This violent earthquake (later nicknamed "the minor doomsday") had destroyed more than a hundred mosques in intramural Istanbul, as well as the larger part of the ramparts of the city. No stone minaret was left standing.[33] After this devastating earthquake, wooden constructions acquired in Istanbul the reputation of being both more resistant to shocks and the cause of less casualties in case of destruction. However, time and time again the public authorities in Istanbul tried to discourage and even to forbid the widespread use of timber as a basic building material. Time and time again official edicts were issued by the *kadı* of Istanbul to regulate the height of wooden houses, to limit the width of their eaves, to set standards concerning their roofing, to set the minimum distance between these types of houses, and so forth,[34] all in order to keep the risk of fires under control.

These efforts were to no avail, though, and the regulations could not be obeyed or upheld, for a very simple reason. First, the population at large could afford but the cheapest of building materials and, second, the number of available craftsmen such as stonemasons, carpenters, and brickmakers was limited. And a large number of these craftsmen were often commandeered for the building of a sultanic mosque, the repair of a fortress, and so forth, and wars often created shortages of masons and builders. Fires, large and small, continued to ravage the city. The havoc wrought in the Kasap İlyas *mahalle* by the two large fires that cut through Istanbul in 1660 and again in 1782 is proof that, as far as housing is concerned, wood continued to be the main building material throughout the centuries, at least in our neighborhood.

Only ten years after the fire that ravaged half of Istanbul in 1782, G. A. Olivier, a representative of the French government who traveled through the Ottoman Empire is surprised by the difference in the quality of the public and private buildings in Istanbul. His testimony confirms that nothing had really changed between the sixteenth and eighteenth centuries as far as building techniques were concerned. Olivier writes:

> The houses have a skeleton made of oak and this skeleton sits on foundations which are not very deep. The beams are either nailed or fitted with tenons. The empty spaces within the wooden structure are then filled with a sort of mortar made of a mixture of mud, hay and bits of hemp. The walls are covered on the outside with rather irregular painted planks. The roof is covered with long and half-cylindrical tiles similar to those we use in the south of France. In the houses the floors are always wooden. Only public and official buildings such as hans, hamams, bedestens etc. are ever built of solid blocks of stone."[35]

We shall return to the subject and to the destructions caused by fires.

As to the sixteenth-century wooden houses of Kasap İlyas, they were certainly not in a contiguous row, nor were they attached to each other. Almost all of the houses, even those qualified as *süfli*, seem to have had a garden, or at least a flower bed (*sofa*), or a plot of land of some sort. Out of the sixteen houses set up as a foundation in Kasap İlyas in the first half of the sixteenth century and whose descriptions are given in the deeds of trust, five had a small garden (*cüneyne*) and four of them a small vegetable garden (*bahçe*). Two of these houses were flanked by stables (*ahır*) and one of them had even a vineyard (*kerm*). For another house, the deed of trust specifies that it was surrounded by just an empty plot of land (*arz-ı hâliye*).

The Bostans

There were also many larger vegetable gardens (*bostan*s) in sixteenth-century Kasap İlyas. One of these vegetable gardens, situated right in front of the Davudpaşa gate, was given as an endowment to a local pious foundation by one Kethüda Sinan in February 1515.[36] The planting of trees, and the sowing and reaping of fruits, vegetables, and flowers was an important activity in sixteenth-century Kasap İlyas. With the extensions of the large and neighboring Langa vegetable gardens penetrating right into our *mahalle*, and given that many of the gardens attached to the Kasap İlyas houses were also probably used as orchards and vegetable gardens, the area had an agricultural character, an almost semirural atmosphere. In many cases, the resident household units living enclosed in a more or less self-sufficient dwelling coincided with an agricultural unit of production. Many of the houses that had been donated to a local foundation in the early sixteenth-century Kasap İlyas *mahalle* had a water-well that went with it. These wells were used for watering the vegetable gardens and orchards rather than for drinking. Some of the wells also had, perhaps, a water wheel drawn by a horse, also used for ploughing, and put in adjoining stables, donated with the house.

As communications were slow and relatively scarce, most of the fresh fruit and vegetables consumed within the city of Istanbul came, until well into the twentieth century, from the many local vegetable gardens and orchards. These *bostan*s were located either within the quite sparsely populated walled city itself, or in its immediate surroundings. One of the largest vegetable gardens within the walled city was indeed that of Langa, immediately to the east of Kasap İlyas. These large Langa gardens extended right into our neighborhood. Most of the fruit and vegetable sellers in Istanbul were of the itinerant type and they carried and marketed the fresh fruit and vegetables to the areas of Istanbul where there were no nearby *bostan*s.

Just as the wharf, the presence of these vegetable gardens—which gave our "peripheral" neighborhood a quasirural appearance—also put their stamp on the social and occupational structure of our neighborhood. This was so in the nineteenth century as well as in the sixteenth. Many fruit and vegetable street vendors lived in the vicinity of the large Langa and Davudpaşa vegetable gardens, which were a permanent source of provisioning for their retail trade. As we shall see, this group of street vendors came to be the backbone of the non-wage-earning population of Kasap İlyas in the late nineteenth century.

Besides the mosque, the *hamam*, and a few shops clustered around the mosque, what other public amenities did our neighborhood contain in the sixteenth century? Was there a bakery, for instance? We do not know for certain. Some of the houses donated in the sixteenth century had an oven or kiln (*furun*). If the baking could have been done at home, what about the wheat and the flour? There were some windmills in Istanbul in the sixteenth century and some of these were situated on the nearby windy hills overlooking the sea of Marmara. We also know that in the late eighteenth century there was a privately owned mill within our neighborhood and that this mill was donated to a foundation.[37] This is not sufficient evidence, however, to deduce that the locals used to systematically take their wheat to the mill and then to bake their bread at home.

As for other public amenities, we know that there was at least one public fountain for drinking water in the neighborhood in the first half of the sixteenth century. Drinking water had been brought to the neighborhood through the so-called Kırkçeşme (forty-fountain) water conduit system that was part of Soliman the Magnificent's foundation that provided waterways for Istanbul. That fountain was situated right in the middle of the *mahalle*, where the mosque, public bath, and shops were situated.[38] There was also another public fountain midway up the hill on the road that climbed from the Kasap İlyas *mahalle* toward the Davudpaşa mosque. It was probabaly connected to the same large system of water conduits. This second public fountain somehow disappeared in later centuries but nevertheless left a durable imprint on the *mahalle*, for the name of this fountain (*Yokuşçeşme*, i.e., "sloping fountain" or "fountain on the slope") was given to the same street. The street still bears the same name.

Streets and Dead Ends

Out of the sixteen houses set up as a foundation in Kasap İlyas in the first half of the sixteenth century and whose detailed descriptions are given in the deeds of trust, nine were surrounded by a wall on all sides. These houses, with their gardens, and all sorts of outhouses and extensions included therein, were enclosed, walled (*muhavvata*). This is a critical detail that allows to visualize more clearly the patterns of land use, the streets, and the general outlook of the *mahalle* in the sixteenth century.

There was no reason why these one-story houses whose gardens were surrounded by walls should be facing each other. Besides, only those that had a second floor (and these were quite rare, especially in Kasap İlyas) could be overlooking the street or the neighboring gardens. The presence of walled-in areas, of various gardens also meant that the houses were somewhat at a distance from each other. The gates or facades of these houses did not have to face each other or to run parallel to the street. They did not have to follow any preestablished symmetry, building plan, or pattern either. The plots of land on which these houses were built in the sixteenth and seventeenth centuries were apparently of different sizes and of sometimes quite irregular shapes. The deeds of trust usually situate each house and plot of land by referring to the owners of the neighboring houses or plots. And some of the endowed properties in the Kasap İlyas *mahalle* had two neighbors, some three or four, and some even five. Some of the gardens and plots of land are described as being triangular. There was no clear cluster of houses, except perhaps just around the mosque itself and around the Davudpaşa *hamam* just across it. Houses were sparsely distributed over the neighborhood, and so were the inhabitants. A single house, donated in 1524, was described as being contiguous to another building, and that building was the Kasap İlyas mosque itself.

It appears that what is perceived nowadays as the "traditional Istanbul housing pattern" does not date from as far back as the sixteenth century, at least not in or around our *mahalle*. The almost canonical image of the two- or three-story wooden houses with tiled large eaves, overhangs, and latticed bay windows, all regularly lined up on narrow and badly cobbled winding streets is an image that dates from the late eighteenth century at the earliest. It was certainly not until the eighteenth and nineteenth centuries that wooden houses of two or three stories spread beyond the wealthier areas around the seat of government and the markets. The sixteenth- and seventeenth-century streets and housing patterns were very different, especially in a relatively peripheral neighborhood like Kasap İlyas.

Ottoman towns were not anarchic or sprawling but they were sketchily planned. When a new center was endowed and founded in Ottoman Istanbul in the inceptive fifteenth and sixteenth centuries, the result could be only a new neighborhood made of wandering lanes governed by rigid laws of property. For there was no town planning that could have preexisted the settlements in the conquered city and no time for preestablishing an ideal grid of streets and settlements. When the Kasap İlyas *mahalle* came into being, for instance, the various buildings were certainly not erected according to the fixing of a street map or of any sort of development scheme. Just the opposite happened. For land was plentiful, both in Istanbul and in the whole Davudpaşa District. So, the Kasap İlyas mosque, the shops, and the *hamam* were probably built first. With them, or after them, came the houses with their gardens and multiplicity of extensions and outhouses, and all of these, as we saw, were enclosed within a wall or a fence. The space that remained became the streets of the *mahalle*. All of the strictly private spaces were built up, and the public passageways of the neighborhood were then defined by default, so to speak.

It is highly doubtful that the modern concept and image of a "street" could in any way fit the situation in sixteenth-century Istanbul. This is especially true for those "peripheral" parts of the walled city which, like the Kasap İlyas *mahalle*, had salient rural characteristics. A low population density as well as an agricultural and horticultural outlook were, as a matter-of-fact, the lot of many other sixteenth-century neighborhoods of Ottoman Istanbul. Many neighborhoods in the area all along the land walls from the sea of Marmara to the Golden Horn and many of those—like Kasap İlyas—that were located along the walls bordering the sea, as well as those situated within the alluvial plain of the Bayrampaşa stream (the "Lycus valley" in Byzantine times) shared the same fate.

Public Thoroughfares *(Tarîk-i 'amm)*

These Istanbul "streets" that accompanied the formation of various *mahalle*s and that gradually took shape in the fifteenth and sixteenth centuries had to espouse the city's quite uneven ground and unusually hilly topography. There were, of course, a few main arteries whose location did not change from early Byzantine times.[39] Their configuration was essentially dictated by the crestline of the intramural Istanbul hills and by their relation to the surrounding sea and to the main gates of the city ramparts. The road that was (and is still) considered Kasap İlyas' "high street" was precisely one of those older roads. This Ottoman artery was superimposed upon the Byzantine road that went from the Forum Bovis, situated right in the middle of the city, to one of the main gates on the land walls. But apart from those very few main arteries that remained intact for centuries, it is unlikely that many of the secondary "streets" of old Istanbul could have retained for long the configuration that they had in the sixteenth century.

What did these "streets" of Kasap İlyas in the sixteenth and seventeenth centuries look like? First of all, they were unpaved, and therefore dusty in the summer and muddy in the rainy winters of Istanbul. The regular paving of the Istanbul streets began to be considered a normal municipal activity only after the 1850s. Before that, if streets were to be paved the expense had to be paid by the locals,[40] and it is improbable that the modest dwellers of Kasap İlyas could have afforded that expense. Second, these "streets" did not necessarily have the same width; they could be quite narrow at some points and uselessly wide at others. The attempts at regulating the width of Istanbul streets were the work of a special municipal committee created only in the 1860s (*Islahat-ı Turuk Komisyonu*). The sixteenth-century streets had no sidewalks worthy of that name. Third, they had not been leveled and were full of all sorts of bumps and holes. Fourth, these "streets" did not have any official name. In sixteenth- and seventeenth-century documents all of these streets are named the public thoroughfare (*tarîk-i 'amm*), and the dead ends simply the private thoroughfare (*tarîk-i hass*). Besides, as we saw, these streets were surrounded by walls, thus limiting—and protecting—the visibility of the (mostly single-story) enclosed houses on both sides.

People used to circulate in the city either on foot or on horseback, so, for most of the minor streets in traditional Istanbul they just had to be wide enough to allow the passage of a horse-drawn carriage. In the seventeenth century the streets in the Davudpaşa area must have been particularly narrow, for they were, so runs the legend, at the origin of an interesting political crisis. When, in 1647, Sultan Ibrahim (nicknamed the "Mad") went strolling through Davudpaşa on horseback (and also in disguise), his way happened to be blocked by a horse-drawn carriage. Getting angry, he instantly ordered the Grand Vizier Salih Paşa to forbid all carriages from entering Istanbul. A short while later, the same thing happened again in the same area, but this time the Sultan was furious and had the Grand Vizier removed from office and then executed.[41]

These events might well be an outright fantasy, produced by a politically minded official Palace historiographer and chronicler, with the intention of demonstrating that Ibrahim was really out of his wits and thereby justifying his overthrow in 1648, and subsequent assassination the same year. As to Grand Vizier Salih Paşa's removal from office and execution, they were most probably due to more complex political reasons. Whatever the case may be, it remains that, first, a real or imaginary "traffic jam" that occurred in or near our neighborhood was used as a justification for a very important political execution and that, second, the story found its way into standard Turkish history books. The sixteenth- and seventeenth-century Davudpaşa and Kasap İlyas streets must have been, at some points, barely wide enough for a single horseman. The area must also have had at the time quite a bad reputation due to the narrowness of its streets and to the ensuing circulation problems.

The narrow streets of the Kasap İlyas *mahalle* were seldom straight; they had many bends and curves. They clearly lacked both greenery and perspective. They had to follow the hilly Istanbul terrain, as they followed an itinerary almost randomly determined by the borders of the various houses and by the enclosed gardens and vegetable gardens of the neighborhood.

Thus constituted, these streets were, strictly speaking, just passageways. Their spatial configuration did not allow for any other social function involving any durable intracommunity relationships. The Kasap İlyas *mahalle* did not contain any public square/piazza or any equivalent that might have the same spatial meaning and social/cultural functions. The "streets" of sixteenth-century Kasap İlyas could obviously in no way function as open public spaces where the locals could come together to trade, communicate, exercise an innocuous pastime, or even simply to chat. Even their functioning as a simple playground for children must have been limited by their physical characteristics. Besides, there was at the time in the *mahalle* neither a coffeehouse nor a *tekke*.[42] The only two places where the locals could have met and shared common experiences were the Kasap İlyas mosque and the Davudpaşa public bath.

Besides, the fact that most houses had only one story and so many walled enclosures meant that it was impossible to sit at one's window and talk to one's next-door neighbors or to those across the street, or just to watch the passersby. True, there was nothing of much interest that could happen in the streets of a peripheral *mahalle* like Kasap İlyas. In sum, this type of a house and street configuration in our *mahalle* entailed a local spatial perception radically different from that connected with the late nineteenth- and early twentieth-century houses and neighborhoods. It is this last perception that still survives in Turkish memories and that is sometimes teleologically extended backward to the earlier centuries. However, uses and perceptions of private and public spaces had greatly changed in Ottoman Istanbul in the meantime.[43]

Blind Alleys *(Tarîk-i hass)*

Many of the "streets" in sixteenth-century Kasap İlyas were in fact simply blind alleys. Out of a total of sixteen houses donated to a foundation in the first half of the sixteenth century five were on a dead end. The deeds of trust describe them as bordering on a blind alley (*tarîk-i hass ile mahdûd*, literally, "limited by a private street"). These streets were not considered a public thoroughfare, but were qualified as "private." These blind alleys were narrower and shorter than the other Kasap İlyas streets. The short dead ends were considered a kind of entrance hall to the few houses whose gate opened onto it, not as their property but as their private space, in a way. Not being a public passageway, these alleys also functioned as a protective element, guarding the private life of the households who lived within it. It was obviously seen as a sort of lock, a transitional stage between the public space of the streets and the privacy of the houses.

The inhabitants of the houses whose gates faced these blind alleys were sharing this semiprivate space; this fact entailed mutual obligations and responsibilities. As they were shared by more than one household, none of them could infringe with impunity on the tacit agreement that made the alley an area of common privacy, so to speak, or a meeting point of many private domains. For instance, such building activities as the construction of a new house, the extension of an existing one, the adding of a second floor, of an overhang, or of a bay window that might overlook either the alley or the neighboring gardens, the opening of another gate to the alley, and so forth, were all pending on the tacit agreement of all of the other inhabitants of that blind alley. This, in most cases tacit, building permission was called, in Ottoman legal parlance, a partners'/shareholders' permission (*izn-i şürekâ*). The absence of such a permission meant the possibility of a court case, or, more frequently, the request for an *ad hoc* official legal opinion (*fetva*) to be obtained from the Şeyhülislâm, and that would have force of law.

The problems that arose in these blind alleys did not necessarily exclusively concern the respect of mutual property rights. Any intervention on that communal space was *ipso facto* a direct intervention on somebody else's privacy. That is why building activities in these dead-end streets often gave rise to legal disputes; a new window overlooking the neighbor's garden, an extension slightly dimming somebody's sunlight, or any sort of noisy activity could be the occasion for a legal opinion emanating from the highest religious authorities. Quite a large number of these disputes between neighbors thus found their way into the *fetva*-collections of such reputed and authoritative seventeenth-century Şeyhülislams as Feyzullah Efendi and Çatalcalı Ali Efendi.[44] These collections of legal opinions were then used later as precedents for the settlement of similar conflicts.

A *modus vivendi* between all neighbors had to be eventually found, for the rules of communal life in the dead-end streets of residential Istanbul had to both respect all legal property rights of the inhabitants and to be mindful of their perception of their respective private domains. It remains that the interface between the public and the private domains in Ottoman cities, and its evolution and its relationship to Ottoman urban culture in general is a topic not yet sufficiently investigated.

THE POPULATION AND THE INHABITANTS OF A PERIPHERAL *MAHALLE*

The sixteenth-century Kasap İlyas *mahalle* consisted of mostly single-story wooden houses, all set at some distance from each other with their enclosed gardens, and of narrow and irregularly winding streets and dead ends. Apart from the central area with the mosque, the *hamam*, and a small "shopping center" around it, the neighborhood was generally quite sparsely populated, as it contained large vegetable gardens and some vacant lots. We know that, in the first half of the sixteenth century, one of the shops around the public bath[45] was a butcher. Another shop housed a maker and seller of *boza*.[46]

In the sixteenth and seventeenth centuries, the *semt*s and *mahalle*s around the Davudpaşa wharf could in no sense of the term have been *central* to the life of the city. They were not near the main political (the Palace) or commercial (the harbor and the Grand Bazaar) areas of Istanbul. Nor were they part of the more densely populated residential districts situated in the central, northern, and eastern parts of the peninsula. Ayverdi states that the center of gravity of the sixteenth- and sevententh-century Istanbul population was situated around the large and central Bayazit complex and that the density of settlement decreased as one moved westwards.[47] Many seventeenth-century local sources also show that, just as two centuries ago, the coastline of the Marmara sea west of Kumkapı was still hardly built at all. This coastline was lined with gardens, orchards, and empty land. The great seventeenth-century Ottoman traveler Evliya Çelebi, as well as the Armenian historian Eremya Kömürcüyan, his contemporary, describe the Davudpaşa area as one most suitable for walks and for general recreational activities.[48]

Though it is quite impossible to give a plausible estimate of its sixteenth- and seventeenth-century population, it is sufficiently clear that the Kasap İlyas *mahalle* never had a large number of inhabitants. A list of taxpayers and *mahalle*s of Istanbul dating from 1634 provides another illustration.[49] The tax to be collected that year was an *avârız*-tax. These *avârız*[50] taxes were occasionally levied from the inhabitants of the capital, either when the treasury was in dire need of funds or when a state of imminent war was the cause of extraordinary government expenditure. Whenever a tax of this sort was to be levied, a number of *avârız* households was attributed to each Istanbul *mahalle* and the total amount to be levied was apportioned among the neighborhoods according to the number of households attributed to each of them. The number of households was not arbitrary, for it depended on the population of the *mahalle* and was also supposed to reflect the overall "ability to pay" of the inhabitants. The tax attributed to each *mahalle* was then apportioned between the locals and collected by the *imam* of the local mosque. In 1634, a tax register *cum* listing of neighborhoods was established for Istanbul. According to this listing, the Kürkçübaşı *mahalle*, immediately to the east of Kasap İlyas, was attributed 10 households, and the Sancaktar Hayreddin *mahalle*, its immediate western neighbor, had a total of no less than nineteen. As to Kasap İlyas itself, it was lumped together with the Davudpaşa *mahalle* and these two had been assigned a total of fifteen households only. This clearly comes to mean that, in the first half of the seventeenth century, and compared to the surrounding areas and districts, Kasap İlyas was neither particularly populous nor noticeably well-off.

The population of Istanbul has always been overestimated or exaggerated, by European travelers, by well-meaning Orientalists, and also by many eminent Turkish historians. Fantastic figures have often been bandied about, such as a figure of over a million inhabitants for the middle of the sixteenth century.[51] The real number couldn't have been much above a quarter of a million, still a really extraordinary figure for that period. The population of Istanbul was to reach the one-million mark for the first time at the eve of the First World War only, but to fall again below that benchmark soon after the end of the hostilities.

The first complete and fairly reliable count of the population of the capital-city of the Ottoman Empire was conducted as part of the census of 1885. At that date, Istanbul had a total of 875,000 inhabitants, that is, about three times its sixteenth-century population. The city had grown throughout the nineteenth century and the density of settlement, especially within the walled city, had tremendously increased.[52] The population of Kasap İlyas stood at about eleven hundred people.[53] The same census, however, puts the average population of a traditional intramural Istanbul *mahalle* at about fifty percent above that figure. Though the transposition and extrapolation of figures taken from the city at large to the level of a small neighborhood is perilous, it seems quite certain that the sixteenth- and seventeenth-century population of the Kasap İlyas *mahalle* could not possibly have exceeded a few hundred inhabitants.

Who were then those sixteenth-century inhabitants of Kasap İlyas? The wharf, a crucial transiting point in the urban transportation and retailing of wood, timber, and other construction materials and the large vegetable gardens provided the main local opportunities for employment and were certainly the main local sources of income. The carrying, storage, and distribution of those bulk goods, as well as the rents and other revenues accruing from the cultivation, distribution, and sale of fresh fruits and vegetables were certainly providing the means of subsistence of a substantial proportion of the inhabitants of the neighborhood.

There was, as we saw, a small "shopping center" right in the middle of the *mahalle*. Its main feature, the large double *hamam* (a place for socialization as much as for ablutions), proved to be a durable center of attraction which, together with the Kasap İlyas mosque right across the street, certainly contributed to attract some customers for the local shops. A document dating from 1782, for instance, shows that the small conglomerate of shops was still there at that date. In the month of August of that year, a large fire had devastated the city and spread havoc in many of the Istanbul neighborhoods, built mostly of wood, like Kasap İlyas. A report on the widespread devastation caused by that fire contains the following statement ". . . a tentacle of fire went into the Seamen's Hamam and the Marketplace inside the Davudpaşa Gate and, from there, reached the dervish convent of Etyemez. . . ."[54] This small marketplace in the Kasap İlyas *mahalle* was well-known to the Istanbulites at large.

The sixteenth-century deeds of trust contain a number of useful clues on various social characteristics of the inhabitants of our neighborhood. The descriptions of the endowed properties include, for instance, the names of the owners of each of the neighboring properties.[55] Among a total of about 60 inhabitants of the Kasap İlyas *mahalle* mentioned in the deeds of trust of the first half of the sixteenth century, there is only *one* non-Muslim. The same remark applies to the whole of the Davudpaşa District. Among hundreds of property-owners whose names are cited in the 122 Davudpaşa deeds of trust, the names of only 6 non-Muslims are mentioned, 5 of which appear to be Greek Orthodox. At the time of Süleyman "the Magnificent," then, Kasap İlyas was a predominantly Muslim neighborhood, with but a tiny minority of non-Muslims, and so was the whole Davudpaşa District. Armenian chroniclers and historians of Istanbul confirm that this was still the case throughout the seventeenth and eighteenth centuries.[56] By opposition to its two neighboring districts of Langa, to the west, and Samatya, to the east, and whose Greek and Armenian churches are lavishly described by the Armenian chroniclers of Istanbul, Davudpaşa receives scant attention, and only by virtue of its gate on the ramparts and, not surprisingly, because of its wharf.

The account-books of the building site of the Süleymaniye mosque confirm our local sources. This monumental sultanic mosque, commissioned by its eponymous ruler to Sinan, chief architect of the empire, took seven years to be completed (1550–1557). The account-books of the construction have been transcribed and extensively published by Ömer Lütfü Barkan.[57] These detailed account-books include listings of all those who had worked on the construction site, with mention of their ethnic/religious background as well as specifics on their neighborhood of residence within the city, or of their town of origin for those who had come from outside the capital.

Among the hundreds of master builders and construction workers who, at sometime or other, had worked on the building—site of Süleyman "the Magnificent's" complex, there were *twenty* stonemasons (*sengtraş*) and carpenters (*dülgers*) who had come from Davudpaşa. All of them were Muslim. By opposition, the same account-books contain the names of 28 workers who were residents of the neighboring district of Langa. Only three of these were Muslims, though, the remaining twenty five being either Greek or Armenian. As to the westernly neighboring urban districts of Samatya and Sulumanastyr, they had provided a much larger contingent (about 70 workers) to the Süleymaniye construction site. Not a single one was a Muslim. Both the Davudpaşa District and the Kasap İlyas *mahalle* were, throughout the greatest part of the Ottoman centuries, areas populated mainly by Muslims, but were embedded between some of the predominantly non-Muslim areas of Istanbul, along the sea of Marmara.

Many construction workers were then living in Kasap İlyas in the sixteenth century. Indeed, none of the sixty dwellers of the *mahalle* mentioned in the deeds of trust have ever been honored with such titles and status-markers as *paşa*, *bey*, or even *ağa*, indicative, respectively, of high-level militaries or bureaucrats or more simply, with the last, of just an above average social status. Except for the *imam* officiating in the Kasap İlyas mosque itself, no one in the neighborhood was ever qualified as *efendi*, a title then attributed to persons belonging to the higher ranks of the religious hierarchy such as religious judges, and teachers in theological schools. That not a single house donated in the neighborhood was qualified as luxurious (*mükellef*) in the deeds of trust is also another indication on the general socioeconomic picture of the *mahalle*.

There were also, however, as there would always be, a few of the more well-to-do living in Kasap İlyas, inhabitants who were wealthy enough to own slaves. Two of the houses in the neighborhood (one of them with two floors) had indeed been bequeathed by their initial owners to their manumitted slaves, who were to act as the trustees of the pious foundation they had just established. But that type of social mix was a quite common occurrence in traditional Istanbul and does not constitute sufficient reason to suppose that Kasap İlyas was any wealthier for that.

As they were appointed trustees of the pious foundations, the identities of some of the *imam*s and *müezzin*s of the Kasap İlyas mosque in the first half of the sixteenth century are known to us. As early as 1506 the small mosque already had a permanent *imam*, who was probably living in one of the endowed houses nearby. His name was Murad, and he seems to have kept his post until at least 1510. In 1533 Ahmed bin Veli was the mosque's *müezzin* and between 1542 and 1546 the *müezzin* was one Ali, who was being supervised by Ayas Efendi, the *imam* of the Kasap İlyas mosque.

The sixteenth-century deeds of trust in Kasap İlyas also tell us about the donators' sex. Interestingly enough, seventeen out of a total of twenty-six local foundations had been endowed by women. Some of these women had even set up more than one foundation. Safiyye Hatun bint-i Hamza,[58] for instance, had bequeathed three houses situated in the *mahalle* between 1531 and 1538. As to Aişe Hatun bint-i Mehmet, in two different deeds of trust, both dated 1509, she had given a two-story house and an amount of cash of no less than thirty thousand aspers, a considerable sum of money. This relative overrepresentation of women among the donators to pious foundations in the Kasap İlyas *mahalle* will not disappear in later centuries.

Kasap İlyas' High Street: "Butchers' Road"

It is only toward the end of the eighteenth century that documents mention, for the first time, a street in Kasap İlyas having a specific name. This name is one with which the Istanbulites at large were quite familiar. The road concerned here is that which was, and still is, considered Kasap İlyas' "high street." It crosses the whole neighborhood from one end to the other in the east-west direction and, while within the Kasap İlyas *mahalle*, runs between the mosque and the public bath, right in the middle of the neighborhood's small marketplace. This Ottoman artery had been superimposed upon an old Byzantine road that went from the Forum Bovis to one of the main gates on the land walls (the small gate called "The First Military Gate" and situated just north of the Castle of the Seven Towers-Yedikule). This road had no particular name in Byzantine times. But the man in the street in Ottoman Istanbul called it, and for good reason, The Road of the Butcher/Butchers (Kassab/Kassablar Yolu). We shall shortly see why.[59]

When, in the 1870s, the first tramways were put into service, the Aksaray-Yedikule line that went from the location of the Byzantine Forum Bovis to the Castle of the Seven Towers passed through this road. As it was too narrow, houses on both sides of the road had to be demolished to allow for the simultaneous passage of two streetcars. The name "Butchers' Road" given to this road before the nineteenth century has absolutely nothing to do with the fact that this artery happens to run through a neighborhood that bears the name of a famous and heroic butcher (Kasap İlyas). As a matter-of-fact this road, which has a total length of about three kilometers, starts off just south of the *semt* of Aksaray, heads west, borders around the large Langa vegetable gardens, and passes through no less than eight different neighborhoods before reaching the city walls. This street came to be called "Butchers' Road"[60] simply because, throughout the sixteenth, seventeenth, and eighteenth centuries, some of the butchers of Istanbul had to carry their merchandise through that road very often, sometimes every day.

Ever since the Ottoman conquest of Istanbul, and perhaps even before that, all activities linked to the production of meat, leather, and related animal products had been concentrated within a large and empty area called "Kazlıçesme" just to the west of the Castle of the Seven Towers, immediately outside the city walls. By imperial decree, all of the slaughterhouses and tanneries, for sanitary reasons, had been relegated to that particular area. Small slaughterhouses did from time to time exist here and there within the city and some butchers slaughtered animals in their backyards. As a consequence, there were complaints from the populace about the filth and the stench, but also about unfair competition and noncompliance with guild regulations. Sometimes the Istanbul butchers themselves filed in complaints about the distance between the slaughterhouses and their shops and requested an official authorization to slaughter animals where they pleased. Time and time again imperial *fermans* were edicted, and the *kadı* of Istanbul issued warnings to that effect, forbidding the slaughtering of animals within Istanbul *intra muros* and reminding the butchers that the initial edicts of Mehmed II the Conqueror were still in full force.[61] The number and frequency of edicts of a similar nature and purpose suggest, however, that they were far from being fully complied with.

However that may be, the Kazlıçeşme area remained, throughout the Ottoman centuries, the main area for animal slaughtering and hide tanning, as well as for meat, leather, glue, and gutstring production in Istanbul.[62] And the meat produced in the Kazlıçeşme slaughterhouses had to be delivered daily to the various butchers within the city and therefore had to pass through the "Butchers' Road" that ran through the Kasap İlyas *mahalle*. This meat distribution operation was carried out almost every single day in the sixteenth, seventeenth, and eighteenth centuries. Obviously, no other name was more fitting for that kind of a road. As Sarkis Hovhannesian, the eighteenth-century Armenian historian of Istanbul notes: "... [outside the ramparts] The slaughter-houses are near the sea and from there the slaughtered animals are distributed to the butchers of the city every day. As for the Janissaries, they have their own butchers who prepare the meat and take it to their old and new barracks every day."[63]

There was one particular instance in which the daily transportation and delivery of meat—which always, lest we forget, passed through Kasap İlyas—was done collectively, so to speak, and took the form of a stately and frightful ritual. The event was the daily transportation and delivery of their rations of meat to the Janissary barracks called the "new barracks" and situated in Aksaray, precisely where the Byzantine Forum Bovis used to be. Large amounts of meat in the form of carved-out animal carcasses were carried in carts or on horseback and were accompanied by special attendants belonging to the Janissary corps. This blood-dripping convoy traveled every morning for about three kilometers, the whole length of the "Butchers' Road," all the way from the slaughterhouses beyond the city walls to the Janissary barracks. Very appropriately, the old Byzantine Forum had been, in the meantime, renamed Etmeydanı, or Meydan-ı Lahm, that is, literally, "Meat Square."

During the transportation of meat through the Butchers' Road early every morning, the long line of carts and horses was preceded by special attendants belonging to the Janissary corps called *seğirdim çavuşu*. These attendants, all clad with bloodstained leather overcoats, kept shouting all the time, signaling their coming and warning the populace not to block the road. For to have an open and free road was a privilege of the Janissary butchers, and anyone who dared to block the road, or even to inadvertently cross the convoy's path, could be sentenced to death. This sentence was indeed executed a few times during the seventeenth century. As to the effective distribution of the meat brought from the slaughterhouses, once arrived in Meat Square, it was accomplished with a real ceremony, full of religious symbolism

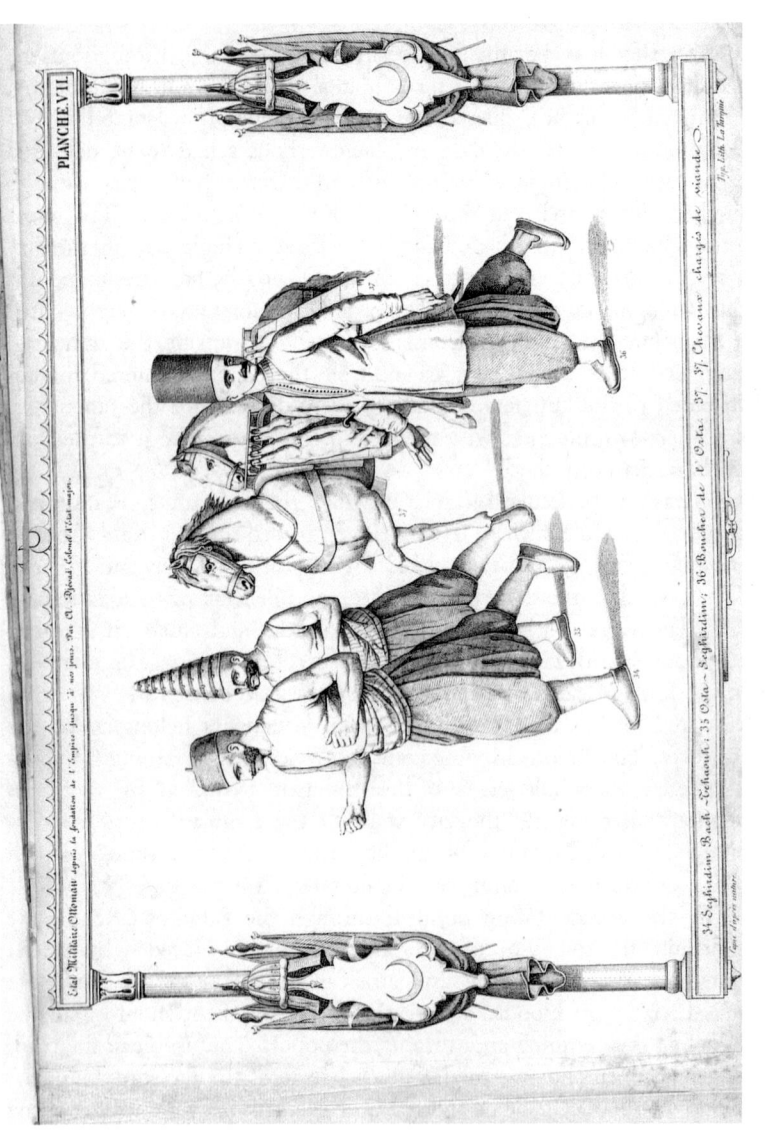

FIGURE 1.1 Procession of Butchers and Janissaries Conveying Meat to the Janissary Barracks
Source: A. Djevad *Etat Militaire Ottoman depuis la Fondation de l'Empire jusqu'à nos jours*, Paris, Ernest Leroux, 1882

and reminiscent of the ritual of the Bektaşi order of dervishes, to which many of the Janissaries are said to have been affiliated.[64]

The inhabitants of Kasap İlyas' "High Street," just as those of seven other *mahalle*s, were witness to this bloody daily procession for centuries. The overall reputation of the neighborhoods must have suffered. The artery that went from the center of the walled city eastward to the entrance of the Topkapı Palace is the direct descendant of the central Byzantine Mêsê. That is also the relatively wide avenue that the Ottoman viziers and the other grandees took—most often on horseback and in a procession with great pomp—on their way to the meetings of the Imperial Council, the Divan. That road naturally came to be called Divanyolu (Divan Road/the Road to the Divan). Though much less prestigious, Kassab Yolu, the "Butchers' Road," was just as memorable.

Such a relatively narrow road, with the daily passageway of convoys of freshly slaughtered and butchered mutton and beef carcasses could obviously not have been clean and proper. And when, in 1793, a well-meaning rich woman named Nazperver Kalfa built both a Coranic school for children and a public fountain on the "Butchers' Road," the point certainly did not go unnoticed.

Nazperver Kalfa—most probably a slave of Circassian origin—had been, in the 1760s, a nanny (*dadı*) to Selim, then heir to the Ottoman throne. When Selim (Selim III, who reigned from 1789 to 1807) finally ascended the throne, she was appointed as one of the treasurers of the Imperial Harem (Hazinedar) and was, from then on, known as Hazinedar Kalfa.[65] She then built a Coranic school for children and a large and magnificently decorated marble public fountain right on our "Butchers' Road." The small school *cum* fountain complex is situated at approximately the junction point of two *mahalle*s: Kasap İlyas and its immediate western neighbor Kürkçübaşı. A chronogram in verse is incised in marble just above the fountain and contains, as was customary, a panegyric of the benefactor of the school and of the fountain and gives 1792–1793 (1207 a.h.) as the date of completion of the construction. The verse ends on the following optimistic note: The former imperial *dadı* / Finally cleansed the butchers' road (*Sabıkan dadı-yı şeh-i vâlâ / Kıldı kassablar yolun tathir*).

Clean or not, "Butchers' Road" was an important and topographically unavoidable artery in intramural Istanbul. It was used by almost everybody, not only to enter the city but also to leave it. Sovereign Selim III himself, for instance, for whom Nazperver Kalfa had been first a nanny and then a protégé, seems to have used that road quite often. A few years after the building of the fountain, on October 13, 1795, on his way to watching some wrestling contest, Selim III had gone on horseback ". . . through the Samatya avenue and the Butchers' Road and out of the city through the Seven Towers, to the

Veliefendi Green. . . ."[66] On another occasion, a note in the diary of Selim's confident reads: ". . . [April 30, 1796] on horseback through . . . the Butchers' Road and out through the Seven Towers directly towards the gunpowder factory. . . ."[67]

A couple of other streets within the Kasap İlyas *mahalle* also bore a particular name toward the end of the eighteenth century. Çavuşzade Street, for instance, is already mentioned as such in a deed of trust dated from 1773. It apparently took its name from that of a family possessing a large house that was completely destroyed in the 1782 fire. In another deed of trust dated from July 1796 appears the name of Hamam Odaları (Hamam rooms) Street. These "rooms" that gave their name to that street might have been the living quarters of people associated with the public bath, or only a remainder of the shops given away as endowment together with the *hamam* back in the late fifteenth century. These two streets were just relatively small local thoroughfares, however, and none could compare in importance with the Butchers' Road.

Fire and Brimstone

Nazperver Kalfa's decision to build her school and public fountain in 1792 precisely on the "Butchers' Road" was no coincidence. A few years ago, the area had greatly suffered as a result of a catastrophic fire, one of the most destructive that ever hit Istanbul, and there were plenty of vacant plots of land along that road.

Ottoman—and wooden—Istanbul has been the theater of hundreds, if not of thousands of fires. Many of them were strictly local affairs that left no permanent scars on the city's texture and ended up by destroying just a few houses and shops, or sometimes a whole neighborhood. The city, however, did not suffer in its structure. But some others, such as the fire of 1660 or that of 1782, were a real cataclysm. Due to the strong northerly winds, the absence of any effective preventive action, and the nonexistence of fire brigades worthy of that name, everything that they met with turned to ashes. These fires could last for days on end (those of 1660 and 1782 lasted for three days each) and spared no public building, be they mosque, church, palace, or school. Many were killed in those large fires, tens of thousands were left homeless, and thousands were often forced to migrate elsewhere.[68]

The probability that any new fire would quickly spread to the neighboring houses and shops was perhaps less likely in such sparsely populated areas as Davudpaşa and Kasap İlyas, as compared to the more densely settled central districts. Indeed, all of the fires that devastated big chunks of the city started either in the commercial areas bordering on the southern shores of the Golden Horn, or right in the residential center (in Fatih, Aksaray, Saint

Sophia, etc.) and quickly spread to the neighboring districts. It is hardly surprising that the name of the Davudpaşa District and that of the Kasap İlyas *mahalle* do not frequently occur in the numerous accounts of the fires in Istanbul. The sparsely distributed population and distant houses, as well as the many gardens and orchards and the small number of shops might have been a protective factor. So were presumably the presence of the city walls and the proximity of the sea. These proved to be insufficient "protection," however, whenever the fires were violent. The fact remains, however, that no fire that started in the Davudpaşa District and then spread to other parts of the city has ever been recorded in Istanbul.

The Fire of 1660—Ihrâk-ı kebir (The Great Burning)

On Saturday July 24, 1660, a fire that started in a timber shop near Ayakapısı, on the southern shores of the Golden Horn, quickly spread throughout Istanbul and could not be put out for more than forty-eight hours, wreaking havoc in the city. When the cataclysmal fire finally stopped on the third day, hundreds of mosques, churches, markets, palaces, and thousands of houses and shops had been reduced to ashes. Thousands had perished. Tens of thousands had been left homeless and many disastered families had to be resettled after the fire in the towns of Çorlu, Silivri and Çatalca, all of them a few miles from Istanbul. Among the hardest-hit Istanbul districts were those along the Marmara: Kumkapı, Nişanca, Langa, Davudpaşa, and so forth.[69]

After the fire, popular rhymed pieces (*destan*s) were composed to lament and to commemorate the dreadful event. One of them, signed "Kâtipzade" is important in that it relates *how* the disaster had reached Kasap İlyas. Here is part of that rhymed piece:

> *Vardı andan Yenikapı semtin âteş kapladı / Gelmeden kaldırdılar esbabı Cellâtçeşmeli / Langa bostanı içine döktüler esbabların / Geldi yaktı nâr-ı ibret kaldı yerinde külü / Geldi andan Davudpaşa iskelesine geçip / Etyemezde dökündü üçüncü kolu hâsılı / Yandı bazı kalekapısı kanatları dahi / Kaldı mıhlarla demirleri eşikte dökülü.*

(From there the flames engulfed the district of Yenikapı / The Cellâtçeşme people took their belongings away / They put their belongings in the vegetable gardens of Langa / The exemplary fire came and left but ashes / From there it moved to the Davudpaşa wharf / The third branch finally reached Etyemez / Even some of the city gates were burned / Their nails and irons were strewn on the doorstep).[70]

More than the effective destruction it caused, it is the itinerary followed by the fire that is strikingly related in this piece of popular rhyme. It appears that the fire moved south from around Aksaray toward the sea and then progressed westward, probably along "Butchers' Road." The large Langa vegetable gardens were burned to ashes too, and with them the belongings that were carried there by their owners who thought that they would be secure. Unaffected by the *bostan*s, by the ramparts, and by the sparse population and houses, the fire's progress was not slowed down, and ran across our neighborhood from east to west, ending up at Etyemez, Kasap İlyas' western neighbor.

There is every reason to think that the Kasap İlyas *mahalle* suffered greatly, though one cannot document the destruction in any detail. One of the houses that was completely burned down left, however, a few traces in the records. According to a document dated May 11, 1663,[71] this house, belonging to a pious foundation whose trustee was Mustafa Efendi, then the *imam* of the Kasap İlyas mosque, is being rented out to Mehmet Çelebi and to his wife Amine Hatun. What is being rented, however, is not a house but in reality just an empty plot of land with, in the middle, the charred remains of a house. The document openly specifies that the house that belongs to the foundation was completely burned in the big fire (... *vakıf menzil harik-i âlide bilküliye muhterik olup*....) and that what was being now rented was only a plot of land with the remains of a house (... *arsa-yı merkume enkaz-ı mevcudesiyle*....). Obviously, Mehmet Çelebi and Amine Hatun were renting this plot of land from the pious foundation in order to build themselves a new house. Moreover, particular modes of expression used in the text suggest that it was written *ex post facto*. It's likely that the couple first got oral permission from the *imam* in order to begin building the house and then, once the building was in progress—or perhaps completed—had the *imam* put down the agreement in writing. Whatever the case may be, less than three years after the devastating fire, houses were being rebuilt and the *mahalle* was being repopulated, an example of resilience that also applies to many of the traditional neighborhood communities of Istanbul that went through such a cataclysmal event.

The Fire of 1782—Harîk-i Ekber (The Greatest Fire)

Fire started on Thursday night, the fourteenth of the moon of Ramadan 1196 a.h. (August 22, 1782), this time in a house but, just as in 1660, on the shores of the Golden Horn. It then split into many branches and lasted for three whole days and nights.

This time the catastrophe reached the Kasap İlyas *mahalle* by not just one but by two of its different branches. The first branch followed the "usual" itinerary, westward from Aksaray and through the "Butchers' Road," going right across the neighborhood to reach Etyemez, then the Greek and Armenian quarter of Samatya, and finally to Yedikule, having thus traveled and wrought destruction along the whole length of the "Butchers' Road." This branch was so violent that even some houses situated within the Castle of Seven Towers were completely burned down. The second branch of this monstrous fire came to the *mahalle* not from the east but from the north. It arrived from the northeasternly neighbor of Cerrahpaşa and stopped just at the northern tip of Kasap İlyas, though not before having destroyed a few houses situated within our neighborhood, among which two mansions (*konak*s) belonging to the Çavuşzade and Ispanakçızade families.

The first branch of the fire, however, was certainly by far the more destructive. As narrated by Derviş Mustafa in his observation of the fires of 1782, ". . . the fire split into many branches before morning and a tentacle of fire which followed the Butchers' Road went into the Seamen's Hamam and into the Marketplace inside the Davudpaşa Gate and, from there, reached the dervish convent of Etyemez. . . ."[72] The small marketplace with the shops that had been, in a way, the "community center" of our neighborhood ever since the very early sixteenth century, was completely destroyed. Even the mosque and the public bath, albeit both built of stone, were not left unscathed, since some of the wooden houses of the neighborhood were directly abutting on the walls of the bath or of the mosque. The wooden roof of the mosque must also have greatly suffered.

The records of the Davudpaşa Religious Court[73] show us that an unusually large number of houses and plots of land within the Kasap İlyas *mahalle* had changed hands within the few years that immediately followed the fire of 1782.[74] Between 1783 and 1788 no less than eighteen deeds of sale of real estate property within Kasap İlyas have been recorded in the Records of the Davudpaşa Religious Court. Some other sales of property within the *mahalle* might also have been recorded elsewhere.

For a relatively small neighborhood which, at the time, could not have had more than a hundred houses, that is a very high number indeed. The type of record concerning the Kasap İlyas *mahalle* occurring most frequently in the records of The Religious Davudpaşa Court in the decade that immediately followed the fire is the real estate property sales agreement. Of these eighteen sales of real estate, at least eight concerned houses that had been burned down in 1782. These eight legal acts of sale concerned basically the transfer of an empty plot of land. A closer look at the texts of these deeds of sale clearly shows, however, that some of these plots of land might include such items as the well-known remains of the house (*enkaz-ı mâlumeyi müştemil arsa*), and that some of them were qualified as the land of the burned-down private house (*muhterik mülk menzil arsası*). Another was qualified as a piece of burned-down house (*bir bab muhterik menzil arsası*). We are also sometimes told that the plot of land was burned down, so that now only the land is left (*muhterik olup arsası sırf kalmakla*).[75]

Besides the sale of these eighteen "houses" that were all private property (*mülk*), we also have records concerning two more "houses" that belonged to one of the local pious foundations and that had changed hands in the same postincendiary period.[76] The first of these houses is mentioned in a *vakıf* record dating from November 1789. Before the fire, this house had been rented by the trustee to one Mustafa Çavuş, who had died sometime between the date of the fire and 1789 without leaving any legal inheritor and without having rebuilt the house. The record tells us that the house ". . . was, by God's will, completely burned in the great fire and the land was left empty. . . . "[77] In 1789 the *imam* of the Kasap İlyas mosque rented this empty plot of land to one Ömer Ağa, who was also allowed to build a new house. Four years later, when the property was passed on to a new tenant in October 1793, the record tells us that it was not a plot of land anymore, but a "*vakıf* house."

The second house is first mentioned in another *vakıf* record dated January 1792, when a new tenant came forward to rent an empty bit of land belonging to the local foundation. Quite exceptionally, the measurements of this burned-down plot of land (*muhterik arsa*) are also given in the *vakıf* record. This plot of land had a total perimeter of 157 *zira*,[78] that is, just enough for an average-size house and a smallish garden. There was certainly feverish construction work on this plot of land, too, because when about a year and a half later, in May 1793, a new tenant came along, the rented property was not described as the charred remains of a burned-down house in the middle of an empty plot of land anymore. It was just a proper *hane* (house). Here, too, ten years after the catastrophe, there was a new house and new inhabitants.

The social and economic havoc as well as the destruction caused by fire have obviously been followed by a large increase in the rate of turnover of both the inhabitants and of the property-owners in the *mahalle*. Though house by house data are lacking, it seems not excessive to hypothesize that it is not only the houses and the grid of streets that changed after the fire, but also, to a certain extent, the social fabric of the *mahalle* itself. Those who had to leave the *mahalle* or who had no means of rebuilding their house after the fire simply sold their property if they were owners, or tried to transfer their legal right to—often lifelong—usufruct if they were only tenants of a local pious foundation.

Whatever the case may be, and provided the central pillars of the neighborhood community (the mosque, the *hamam*, or any other building of similar local importance, as the case may be) were not completely destroyed, the *mahalle* itself always could recoup its losses. As shown in the case of the two large catastrophies that befell Kasap İlyas, within ten years of the disaster many of the burned houses were rebuilt and the new owners or tenants were settled. We also have reason to suppose that the 1782 fire also largely contributed, once and for all, to the stabilization of the street plan of Kasap İlyas.

2

Power and Local Administration in Kasap İlyas
Tanzimat and After

In the Muslim *mahalle*s of pre-nineteenth-century Istanbul, the central figure of the neighborhood community was the religious leader of the local mosque, the *imam*. He was indeed an influential man and, at times, a local potentate of sorts. Certainly not because of the meager powers given him within the administrative setup of towns in the central Ottoman lands but rather, as we shall see in greater detail in the case of the Kasap İlyas *mahalle*, simply because he was often relatively well-off—if not outright wealthy. Besides, his legal position as trustee of a number of pious foundations put him in command of a nonnegligible amount of local economic resources.

For the larger or sultanic mosques, the appointment of *imam*s was a matter of seniority and, most probably of some haggling within the official religious hierarchy. As to the *imam*s of small neighborhood mosques in Istanbul, such as that of Kasap İlyas, there was, to the best of our knowledge, no standard method or procedure for selecting or appointing them. The process must have certainly involved a combination of widespread local concensus and open or tacit approval of higher religious authorities. The *imam* needed at least tacit local concensus as the source of his religious authority since, from a strictly theological point of view, he was nothing but a *primum inter pares* within his congregation. But he also needed approval of the political/religious authorities because many of his functions constituted a link between the populace and the government.

The flexibility of the process of appointment sometimes created real dynasties of *imam*s officiating in the same local mosque and sons often succeeded fathers as leaders of small Istanbulite local communities. Although the appointment procedure for *imam*s in republican Turkey has greatly changed—

the *imam*s are nowadays no more than ordinary government officials and their appointment procedure obeys the rules that apply to all civil servants—even in the present-day Kasap İlyas *mahalle*, a father and his son have been the officiating imams of the mosque since 1970.[1] Local dynasties of *imam*s may therefore have survived to a certain extent.

Before the middle of the nineteenth century, the *imam*s officiating in the small neighborhood mosques of the capital-city of the Ottoman Empire were not only religious figures, leading the prayers, reading sermons, and officiating in case of marriages and funeral ceremonies. They were also supposed to act as a link between the *kadı* of Istanbul, responsible for order and security in the capital, and in the population at large. The orders of the *kadı* were to be transmitted to the population by the *imam* after the Friday sermon, and so were the contents of imperial *ferman*s, when these touched upon matters of everyday life. Besides, these *imam*s were supposed to be in full control of their small neighborhood and of their congregation. They were considered guarantors for each one of the inhabitants of their *mahalle*. The *imam* was, in an informal manner, morally responsible for his congregation's behavior.

Adequate supervision and effective control of the local *imam*'s activities were often lacking, however, particularly in times of political and economic trouble. This gave rise, in early nineteenth-century Istanbul, to a number of complaints about the arbitrary decisions and abuses of power of many local *imam*s. These *imam*s, so went the complaints, never consulted anyone when taking a decision concerning the neighborhood and were "cruel" to the populace.[2] The Istanbul *imam*s were accused of bribery, of favoritism, of misusing *vakıf* property placed under their trusteeship, of being unfair in the apportioning of the *avârız* taxes within the *mahalle*, and of squandering the funds that had accumulated in the *avârız* foundations of their neighborhoods. Perhaps more importantly, they were blamed for not taking seriously their duty of contributing to the city's security and for letting the inhabitants of their *mahalle* get out of control. They were accused of being sloppy in controlling the travel documents of newcomers, rural migrants, and foreigners to the city who wanted to set up house in their *mahalle*, thus putting the security of Istanbul in jeopardy.[3]

These complaints and accusations seem to have prompted the reformist authorities of the Tanzimat period to introduce new and "secular" local administrative structures involving local headmen (*muhtar*s) instead of *imam*s. This "secularization" meant, for all practical purposes, that the new basic administrative relationship between the government and the population at large was to exclude members of the religious hierarchy. The *kadı*, the chief religious judge for Istanbul was totally deprived of his previous authority on municipal, economic, commercial, and security matters, and so were, therefore, the *imam*s. From the late 1830s and early 1840s on, *muhtar*s were appointed in both villages and urban neighborhoods and the administrative powers of the *imam*s were gradually transferred to these "secular" local headmen.[4] Probably in order to prevent further abuses of power, the new local headmen were flanked by a second muhtar (*muhtar-ı sânî*) and by an electoral committee (*ihtiyar heyeti*).

THE *IMAM* AND HIS CONGREGATION

As shown by local *vakıf* documents of the seventeenth, eighteenth, and nineteenth centuries,[5] the *imam* of the Kasap İlyas mosque continued to muster a nonnegligible amount of local resources. Ten *vakıf* documents, all carefully updated and kept by the successive *imam*s of Kasap İlyas have survived from the seventeenth and eighteenth centuries. These contain ten texts of the initial deeds of trust, plus, for each of them, various acts of rent or transfer of the endowed property, all signed by the foundation's trustee, that is, by the *imam* of the Kasap İlyas mosque himself. The first registered item dates from 1663, and the last from 1855. The bulk of the information contained therein, however, relates to the period roughly from the early 1770s to around 1850.

The large number of local pious foundations is, just as in the sixteenth century, a good indicator of the fact that local solidarity and a basic trust in the local mosque and in its *imam* did continue to play a definitional role in the constitution of the neighborhood community, the Kasap İlyas *mahalle*. Besides, in all of the deeds of trust, our neighborhood was still defined by reference to the same basic topographical landmark: the Davudpaşa wharf. The *mahalle* is defined as the Kasap İlyas *mahalle* near the Davudpaşa wharf (Davudpaşa Iskelesi *kurbünde* Kasap İlyas *mahallesi*).

Nine out of these ten seventeenth- and eighteenth-century Kasap İlyas *vakıf*s were meant to secure a regular revenue for the *imam* and the *müezzin* of the mosque to live on, and to provide for the upkeep of the mosque itself. As to the tenth, it was an *avârız vakfı*,[6] which must be taken as another strong sign of the existence of a durable sense of local identity and solidarity.

Indeed, these strictly local *avârız* foundations, usually set up by one of the better-off inhabitants of the neighborhood, were essentially meant to compensate for the insolvency of the poor local taxpayers in the case where an occasional and unexpected *avârız* tax was to be levied by the government. Given the mode of apportioning this tax, the insolvency of some of its inhabitants might also have meant the insolvency of the *mahalle* as a whole. In the absence of an *avârız* tax, however, the regular income accruing from the endowed property and money was, in principle, to be used by the *imam*—the trustee of the *avârız* foundation—to provide some help to the most destitute in the *mahalle* and to contribute to some enterprise of public utility, such as the clearing of a street, or the building or the upkeep of a public fountain or of a primary Coranic school.

That is certainly why these particular philanthropic foundations were also often called *avârız sandığı* (*avârız* cash-box). In 1772, the Kasap İlyas *mahalle* had an *avârız vakfı* of its own. To this foundation had been bequeathed, by one Ismail Ağa, a house, a shop for charcoal/timber, and a mill. Half a century later, in 1825, however, only the shop was left,[7] the rest having probably been destroyed in a fire.

The *Imam* with the Forty Keys

What is crucial from the point of view of intraneighborhood relationships is not that many of the seventeenth- and eighteenth-century deeds of trust stipulated that, as an appointed trustee, the *imam* was to receive a small fee for his services, or that he or the *müezzin* of the mosque, if any, were to pay no rent when occupying a house donated to the local *vakıf*. These houses were called *meşruta*, *imam meşrutası*, or *müezzin meşrutası*, for they were to be occupied free of charge on the strict condition that the occupant be the *imam* or the *müezzin* of the local mosque. Otherwise rent would have to be charged to the occupant by the trustee. That was only fair enough, as the *imam*s or *müezzin*s had no regular salaries.

What is much more important is that a number of houses and other real estate property situated within the neighborhood, as well as the revenues accruing from them, were directly under the *imam*'s control. Alongside his moral authority over the inhabitants of the *mahalle*, this certainly gave him considerable economic power especially when, as in Kasap İlyas, the neighborhood itself was neither too populous nor too big, but there existed nevertheless a relatively large number of local *vakıf*s.

For instance, it was the *imam* who decided if and when and to whom a house, a garden, or a plot of land belonging to a local *vakıf* were to be rented, and what the amount of the rent and its mode of payment were to be. Who would have to pay for the repair work of houses belonging to the *vakıf*? The owner, or the tenant? Would the tenant, for instance, be allowed to build a house on an empty piece of land belonging to the local *vakıf*? If yes, who would this new house then belong to? To the builder or to the owner of the land? Would this decision have an appreciable effect on the amount of the rent? These were matters over which the *imam*, being the trustee, had an absolute right of say.

Indeed, in many instances in the Kasap İlyas *mahalle*, the respective rights of use and of property had to be clearly specified in the *vakıf* documents. "Whatever is built belongs to the holy *vakıf*"[8] is a note we often came across in the documents. In that case, simple repair work done by the tenant to the house owned by the *vakıf* could be "deductible from his ordinary rent."[9] In other cases, however, the tenant of the *vakıf* plot of land was allowed to own the house that was built on it.[10] In that case, all repair work was paid by the tenant. In any event, that was a matter for the trustee of the pious foundation to decide.

More generally, any new use to which the *vakıf* property was to be put first had to be approved by the *imam*. Whether the endowed property could be subdivided into a number of parts to be let to different persons, whether that property could be used for a different purpose than its initial destiny, as set down by the founder, or whether the right of usufruct of the *vakıf* property could be, either by right of inheritance or by donation, transferred by the tenant to another person, were dependent on the *imam*'s approval. Whether the tenant would be allowed to use his right of usufruct of the *vakıf* property for a commercial operation (e.g., for a mortgage, or as a collateral to a loan), was also a matter to be approved by the trustee of the *vakıf* before any official step could be taken. Besides, before many of these transactions were concluded and put on record, a "donation" was made to the *vakıf*, payed in cash and recorded with the transaction itself. This "donation" constituted a nonnegligible portion of the *imam*'s income.

The *imam* of the Kasap İlyas mosque was obviously not left totally to his own devices. He had to abide by the Islamic law on pious foundations and he was supposed to use the property that was under his trusteeship in conformity with the wishes of the initial founder of the *vakıf*. Besides, the balance sheets of the *vakıf*s could, from time to time come under the examination of controllers (*nâzırs*) appointed by the higher religious authorities.[11]

It remains that, in a (population-wise) relatively small neighborhood like Kasap İlyas, where, nevertheless, local *vakıf*s were relatively numerous, the *imam* came to wield considerable local power and authority. Take the case of Hâfız Mehmet Efendi, who officiated as *imam* of the Kasap İlyas mosque between 1784 and 1799. At the beginning of his priesthood, he acted as trustee for seven different local *vakıf*s. In their endowments there were four houses, a "garden" (most probably a rather large "vegetable garden," a *bostan*), and a shop. Two new *vakıf*s were founded in the Kasap İlyas *mahalle* in the 1790s, and a house and another "garden" were added to the real estate property under his control. As to Hacı Aziz Mahmud Efendi, *imam* between 1822 and 1844, in the early 1820s he had the control of, and the incomes accruing from, three houses, two "gardens," and a shop in the *mahalle*.

The total number of houses in the Kasap İlyas *mahalle* could not have much exceeded 50 or 60, during the whole period going from the sixteenth to the early nineteenth centuries. Any residential Istanbul *mahalle* containing more than 100 houses would have been considered as a very large one. The number of houses in Kasap İlyas will reach 150 only toward the very end of the nineteenth century, after a prolonged period of steady population growth for the city as a whole. Given the size of our small neighborhood, then, a nonnegligible portion of the local wealth was under the *imam*'s control. This added a crucial element of economic power and influence to his moral authority over his congregation. We shall see to what use Aziz Mahmud Efendi, one of the prominent *imam*s of Kasap İlyas, chose to put it.

Some mosques of traditional Istanbul were nicknamed "the mosque with the forty keys," and the *imam* thereof "the *imam* with the forty keys." This was how the "bottom up" view of the local economic power wielded by the *imam* reflected itself in the popular parlance of the imperial city. The quantity of real estate property governed and managed by a single *imam* must have strongly impressed the man in the street. The expression "forty keys"—with its obvious numerical exaggeration—suggests a mixture of respect and apprehension, perhaps a fairly good description of how ordinary people really felt about the *imam* of their neighborhood mosque. The "forty" keys are of course those of the "forty" houses and shops that popular imagination construed the *imam* to "possess." To these "forty" houses and shops, so it must have been feared, the *imam* must always have had access with his key ring. Perhaps this potential access was perceived by the poor locals as auguring an unhappy occurrence such as an eviction from their lodgings, a distraint on their goods, or a rise in rents. There always was, in the least, the danger of intrusion into their privacy.

The Kasap İlyas mosque, although situated, as we know, in a rather peripheral, not particularly opulent, and not densely populated *mahalle*, was until recently one of those "mosques with forty keys." This almost magical power of numbers was even heightened by its present-day *imam* who, with a bit of regret and a good amount of nostalgia, mentioned the glorious past of his mosque and called its *imam*s "the *imam*s with seventy keys," and the Kasap İlyas mosque itself "the mosque with seventy keys."

The *Imam* and His Revenues

When the *imam* was trustee of a pious foundation endowed with real estate property, every operation on this property could become a source of income for the *vakıf*, and for him. Whenever the right of usufruct of this property changed hands, it was often the case for the acquirer to make a "donation" to the *vakıf*, a donation whose amount varied with the value of the property and its revenue, if any. The amount was basically the result of a bargaining process between the trustee and the two parties. The *imam*s of Kasap İlyas usually took note of the sums that were being paid on these occasions.

On July 28, 1767, for instance, when a *vakıf* house in Kasap İlyas changed hands, a sum of 300 *kuruş* was paid to the foundation, and the *imam* approved and recorded the transaction.[12] On November 28, 1780, a payment of 500 *kuruş* was made when a *vakıf* "garden" in our neighborhood changed hands. This was certainly a vegetable garden, and its cultivation must have brought to the tenant a substantial income. About half a century later, on November 19, 1824, the transfer of the same garden was, this time, accompanied by a payment of 1,000 *kuruş*.[13] These were, in fact, quite large sums of money in the eighteenth and nineteenth centuries. But these were, obviously, only occasional payments, as the regular incomes controlled by the trustee consisted of the yearly or monthly rental incomes of the endowed property.

For instance, Hâfız Mehmed Efendi, *imam* of the Kasap İlyas mosque in the 1790s, disposed of a monthly rental income of about 300 *akçe*,[14] accruing from nine different local *vakıf*s that had been placed under his trusteeship. About half a century later Aziz Mahmud Efendi, another *imam* of our mosque, collected monthly rents amounting to a total of 235 *akçe*s.

In the seventeenth, eighteenth, and nineteenth centuries the usual financial arrangement involved in renting out a property item belonging to a *vakıf* was called *icareteyn* (two rents).[15] This type of arrangement meant that, from a practical point of view, two different types of rent had to be agreed upon in writing by the tenant of the *vakıf* property and by the trustee of the *vakıf*. The first kind of rent was the *icare-i muaccele* (the urgent, or immediate rent), an amount that was to be paid just once when the new tenant took over the *vakıf* property. The second kind of rent was called the *icare-i müeccele* (the postponed rent). This rent was to be paid from that moment on, on a regular (daily, monthly, or yearly) basis. Everything else being equal, the lower the "postponed" rent, the higher was likely to be the lump-sum required as an "urgent" rent. When, in 1663, for instance, the right of usufruct of an empty plot of land in the Kasap İlyas *mahalle* was given to one Mehmet Çelebi, an "immediate rent" of 3,300 *akçe*s was paid to the *imam*, trustee of the local *vakıf*. Besides, a "postponed rent" of 1 *akçe* a day was also agreed upon.[16] The *icare-i muaccele*, in this case, was the equivalent of about ten years of *icare-i müeccele*, and Mehmet Çelebi had made a down payment equivalent to ten years of the rent of that piece of land.

Obviously, there was also the option where a single type of rent (*icare-i vahide*) was applied, and only periodical payments were agreed upon. The double-rent option, however, seems to have constituted the basis of the overwhelming majority of agreements between trustees of a *vakıf* and tenants. It has been argued that the lump-sum payments involved in the first option constituted, especially in the inflationary periods of the late eighteenth and the nineteenth centuries, a much more substantial contribution to the repair and upkeep of various *vakıf* properties in Istanbul. Thanks to that option, many *vakıf*s are said to have had a much longer life span.[17]

However that may be, the end of the eighteenth and the first half of the nineteenth centuries were periods of high rates of inflation in the Ottoman Empire. The debasement of metallic currency, especially in the 1820s and 1830s, became a means of increasing fiscal revenues to which the government resorted more and more frequently.[18] Finally, in 1844, a monetary operation (*tashih i sikke*) redefined the gold and silver content of all of the coins in circulation and a new bimetallic system was established. In any event, toward the middle of the nineteenth century, the centuries-old asper (*akçe*) had already ceased to represent any significant purchasing power. Nominally 1 *kuruş* was still equivalent to 120 *akçe*s, but this last monetary denomination was maintained only as a unit of account for official transactions.

In the eighteenth and nineteenth centuries, therefore, "immediate rents" of 300, 500, or 1,000 *kuruş* did represent considerable sums of money, whereas the 20, 30, or 50 *akçe*s that the tenants of many *vakıf* property items in the Kasap İlyas *mahalle* were supposed to pay on a yearly basis, obviously only had a symbolic value. After all, in the late nineteenth century average-size houses in the Kasap İlyas *mahalle* were sold at prices ranging between 2,500 and 5,000 *kuruş*. When, in 1835, for instance, Aziz Mahmut Efendi, *imam* and trustee of the local *vakıf*s, let a "garden" in Kasap İlyas to a new tenant, he received the sum of 200 *kuruş* as an "immediate rent." This amount was the equivalent of no less than sixty years of "postponed rent" of the same piece of property. That garden was a "vegetable garden" on the products of which the tenant made his living. No wonder then that these symbolic and traditional amounts of periodical rents, always set down in *akçe* terms, were simply called *icare-i kadime* (old-time, or traditional rent). These symbolic monthly payments did not constitute a sufficient income for the *imam*s who, obviously, preferred to have recourse to the system of a double rent in times of inflation.

THE BENEFITS OF LOCAL POWER: THE CASE OF AZIZ MAHMUD EFENDI

Aziz Mahmud Efendi (d. ca. 1845) had a very long tenure as *imam* of the Kasap İlyas mosque. His signature appears on the local *vakıf* documents for the first time in 1821. In the course of his term of tenure, which lasted for about a quarter of a century, his signature appears, from 1827 on, as "*elhac* Aziz Mahmud,*"* indicating that he had accomplished the pilgrimage to Mecca shortly before that date. In the course of his long tenure of office as *imam* of the neighborhood mosque and as trustee of the *vakıf*s attached to it, some of his decisions and actions can be followed pretty closely.

We shall take here one example of a *vakıf* property situated in the Kasap İlyas *mahalle* and try to see how Aziz Mahmud Efendi "managed" it in his time of tenure as *imam* and as trustee. A number of transactions recorded by Aziz Mahmud Efendi himself clearly show how a piece of property belonging to a pious foundation could be used to his own convenience by the trustee of the foundation.

The property we take as an example here was named after its founder: Hurşide Hatun Vakfı. It consisted of ". . . a garden with, in it, lodgings with a single room, a covered area, a water-well, a kitchen, latrines, a pond, and fruit bearing trees, all surrounded by a wall of stone on four sides. . . ."[19] When this so-called garden was set up as a foundation, by a deed of trust dated April 24, 1770, it was described as having a circumference of 1140 *zira'*, that is, about 800 meters. With its water-well, its pond, and its "fruit-bearing trees" this was certainly a large vegetable garden, a *bostan*, as there existed many in and around Kasap İlyas, and that must have brought a substantial income to its manager. From time immemorial, the tenants of this garden used to pay to the trustee of the *vakıf* a monthly rent (an *icare-i kadime*, as the expression went) of just sixty *akçe*s, that is, just half a *kuruş*. This rent had apparently remained unchanged for more than half a century when Aziz Mahmud took over the post of *imam* of the Kasap İlyas mosque.

A few years after Aziz Mahmud's appointment to the *imam*hood, on September 14, 1829 (*15 Rebi' I 1245 a.h.*), Hediye Hatun binti Ismail, the woman who had been holding the right of usufruct to this large vegetable garden for the last eighteen years, returns it to the trustee of the *vakıf*. The reason for this act is not clear for, had Hediye Hatun died without a legal heir, the *vakıf* property would, first, have to be declared open or vacant (*mahlûl*). No payment seems to have been involved in the transaction, either.

Whatever the case may have been, only two days later, on September 16, 1829, Aziz Mahmud Efendi signs the document granting the transfer of the right of usufruct of this garden to another woman, probably also a local of the *mahalle*, Fatma Hatun binti Hasan. This woman made a payment of 1,000 *kuruş* for the transfer of the right of usufruct, and the sum was duly recorded with the transaction. The record itself makes interesting reading, but for quite another reason: ". . . Aziz Mahmud Efendi, holder of the right of usufruct to the garden with a monthly rent of sixty *akçe*s, has transfered this right to Fatma Hatun binti Hasan, wife of Ismail Ağa, and has received the sum of 1,000 *kuruş*, and I, as trustee, have allowed the transaction and recorded it in the *vakıf* book."[20]

The tone that prevails in this text does reflect the fact that Aziz Mahmud Efendi, in a transaction where he is personally involved, is both judge and party to the transaction. He is both holder of the right of usufruct, so he speaks of himself as if he were a third party (". . . Aziz Mahmud Efendi, holder of the right of usufruct. . . .") and, also, a trustee who agrees to and records the transaction, and therefore speaks of himself in the first-person singular (". . . I, as trustee, have allowed the transaction and recorded it. . . ."). It is noteworthy that all of the records concerning this particular vegetable garden bear an echo of this tone. They are all written in a style showing this mixture of personal enterprise and artificiality.

Just about a year later, on July 31, 1830, as recorded in a third transaction concerning the same property item, Fatma Hatun binti Hasan, who had taken over the vegetable garden from Aziz Mahmud Efendi eleven months ago, now returns it to him. The record reads: ". . . Fatma Hatun has taken back the received amount and returned the garden entirely to its first owner Aziz Mahmud Efendi and I, as trustee, have allowed the transaction and recorded it in the *vakıf* book." The wording of this record leaves two crucial points in the dark.

First of all, we are not told whether the "received amount" that Aziz Mahmud Efendi returns to Fatma Hatun is equal to the 1,000 *kuruş* that he had been paid, about a year ago, for granting to Fatma Hatun the right of usufruct to that garden. If the second amount was larger than the first, this means that the whole operation was in fact nothing more than a cover-up for a simple loan assorted with a rate of interest, an operation prohibited by Islamic law. What we see here is obviously a cumbersome method for concealing and transforming a prohibited operation, but from the point of view of Islamic jurisprudence, it was a fully sanctioned instrument.[21]

Second, and even if we assume that the two transactions were not a cover-up for what was, in reality, a loan assorted with a rate of interest (i.e., if the two sums were equal), we are still left in the dark as to the real nature of the whole operation. Was the garden transferred as a mortgage (a *ferağ bi'l vefâ* in Ottoman juridical parlance), or was it simply pawned (*ferağ bi'l istiglâl*) to Fatma Hatun as a security for money loaned by her to Aziz Mahmud Efendi? And, besides, what was it that prompted Aziz Mahmud Efendi, *imam* of a small neighborhood mosque in Istanbul, to borrow such a large amount of money for such a short period of time from a person belonging to his congregation? The answers to these questions are not clear. What is fairly obvious from these transactions of 1829 and 1830, however, is that Aziz Mahmud did not hesitate to use the *vakıf* properties entrusted to him, as and when he thought fit, for his own personal financial purposes.

Fourteen years then go by, during which this "garden" remains in the possession of Aziz Mahmut Efendi, to whom its nonnegligible revenues keep accruing. Then, on March 14, 1844, a last deed of transfer concerning the same vegetable garden provides another illustration of the *imam*'s arbitrary decisions. Here is the text: ". . . I have consented to transfer the right of usufruct of one half of the garden with a monthly rent of thirty *akçe*s, which had been at my disposal, to my daughter Hatice Huriye Hatun *binti* [daughter of] Aziz Mahmud, and that of the other half to my son-in-law Ahmed bey *bin* [son of] *elhac* İbrahim, so that they share it on a basis of equality, and have therefore agreed to record the transaction in the *vakıf* book...."[22] Aziz Mahmud Efendi has chosen not to hide anything in this record. What he has de facto done is simply this: he has divided this large *vakıf* garden into two equal parts and given one half to his daughter and the other half to his son-in-law. Here again Aziz Mahmud Efendi is obviously both judge and party. As trustee of the foundation he "consents" to the transfer of the endowment to "my daughter" [Hatice Huriye daughter of Aziz Mahmud] and to "my son-in-law." The record does not mention the payment of an "immediate rent," an *icare-i muaccele*. Besides, the monthly rent (*icare-i müeccele*) of this garden belonging to the Hurşide Hatun *vakfı*, had, for no apparent reason, been reduced from sixty to thirty *akçe*s.

As a principle, a trustee of a *vakıf* was supposed to lease the real estate property placed under his trusteeship at the highest possible rent. To that end, a number of well-known traditional "marketing techniques" (including consulting real estate "experts," and using town-criers and market auctioneers) were available to him. According to Ottoman law and to the common usage on *vakıf* real estate property in Istanbul, Aziz Mahmud Efendi should have first declared this garden to be *mahlûl* (open or vacant). Second, he should have informed all those likely to make an offer. Only then should he have put the *vakıf* property at the disposal of the highest bidder.[23] That is how the interests of the *vakıf* would have been safeguarded in the long run. Aziz Mahmud, however, had availed himself of none of these methods. Instead, on March 14, 1844, he had chosen, simply on his own initiative, to give the large *vakıf* garden that had been put under his care, to his daughter and son-in-law.

The successors and predecessors of Aziz Mahmud Efendi at the *imam*hood of the Kasap İlyas mosque and at the trusteeship of the *vakıf*s attached to it, often took the necessary precautionary steps to protect the long-run interests of their foundations. For instance, the newly vacated real estate properties were first advertised, that is, they were "... offered to the demanders, ..." and the trustees made up their mind on who the new tenant was to be only when "... no other demander offered a higher price...."[24] For some transfers of the right of disposal to *vakıf* property, it was made clear, for the record, that an auction had taken place ("... when the demand of the public has completely ceased after the market auction....")[25] Sometimes the records mention that, instead of having an auction, the trustee had recourse to the advice of experts in order to estimate real estate prices and rents.[26]

Obviously, all of the trustees of the many small local *vakıf*s of Istanbul could not always have had either the time, a sufficient margin of social initiative, or direct access to resources in order to perform all of these marketing operations. But, at least in Kasap İlyas, they usually took care to note that everything was done on a strictly legal basis and in the long-run interests of the foundation, that the *vakıf* records bore traces of their careful management of the endowed property, and that they contained no sloppiness likely to be picked up by inspectors.

Aziz Mahmud Efendi seems to have been an open exception to that state of affairs. For him, as a trustee, favoritism, flanked by a keen sense of his personal interest, seems to have been the habitual mode of operation. The same day as the case of the "garden" just described, that is, on March 14, 1844, the *imam* of the Kasap İlyas mosque also took a second initiative. This was quite similar to the first. Aziz Mahmud took another, but this time, a smaller "garden" that was under his trusteeship, split it into two and, again, put it at the disposal of the same two persons, his daughter and son-in-law.[27] Here, too, there is no trace in the records of any auction or advertisement of any sort. Besides, Aziz Mahmud Efendi reduces the monthly rent of the second garden, too. It was previously set at thirty *akçe*s, but Aziz Mahmud reduces it to ten *akçe*s. What was already a purely symbolic amount was thus reduced to almost nothing. Our trustee and *imam* had thus, the same day, transferred the right of disposal of two pieces of revenue-generating *vakıf* property to his daughter Hatice Huriye Hatun and to his son-in-law, and simultaneously further reduced the *vakıf*'s revenues.

We have been able to trace Aziz Mahmud's daughter forty years later in the 1885 census records.[28] She was then alive and well, a widow, and living with her eldest daughter in a house that belonged to her at 60 Samatya Street (formerly "Butchers' Road"). Hatice Huriye was then obviously a woman of some means, since she also owned another house in the Kasap İlyas *mahalle*, as well as a shop in the Grand Bazaar. The most interesting feature revealed by the 1885 census documents is that Hatice Huriye's eldest daughter, Fatma Ismet hanım, had been born in 1845, that is, just a year after her father had passed on the two *vakıf* "gardens" to her mother and to her father. Hatice Huriye was eighteen years old when her eldest daughter was born. We may surmise therefore that her marriage to Ahmed bey had taken place about a year before that date, perhaps in 1843 or 1844, that is, just about when Aziz Mahmut efendi transferred the rights of disposal to the two *vakıf* gardens to his newly married daughter and to his son-in-law. We do not know for sure whether there was a direct causal relationship between the two events. If, however, the two transfers made by Aziz Mahmud efendi on the same day were meant to be a dowry for his daughter who was just getting married, we would certainly have here a patent case of breach of trust, an open abuse of power.

The obvious questions that arise are the following: Was Aziz Mahmud efendi always as oblivious of the long-term interests and the perennity of the *vakıf*s put under his trusteeship? Was he always in the habit of making a disguised present of the real estate property he was supposed to oversee and protect? Did Aziz Mahmud treat all potential or effective tenants of this property with such tolerance and leniency? The answer is certainly negative. The case of his neighbor Mehmed Salih Efendi provides a good contrast.[29] In September 1825, Aziz Mahmut Efendi had let a *vakıf* "garden" in common to Mehmed Salih Efendi and to his wife Şerife Fatma hanım. Ten years later, Fatma Şerife hanım, who had no children, died. Her share of the right of usufruct of this "garden" did not revert to her husband, however, but to the foundation itself and to its trustee, Aziz Mahmud Efendi. Then, the *imam* of the Kasap İlyas mosque did not take into account Mehmet Salih efendi's past status as an honorable neighbor and as a good and trustworthy tenant of the *vakıf*. Mehmed Salih Efendi's and his wife's contributions to the upkeep of the *vakıf* property during the past ten years seemed not to carry any weight in his mind, either.

As a result, Aziz Mahmud Efendi agreed to the reversion of the right of usufruct that had belonged to the deceased Fatma Şerife hanım to her widowed husband only after Mehmed Salih had paid him in cash, on March 23, 1835, an "immediate rent" of two hundred *kuruş*. This amount was in fact the equivalent of more than ten years of "postponed rent" of the same garden. Indeed, there was more than one standard on our *imam*'s mind and, clearly, Aziz Mahmud's preferential treatment was addressed only to his daughter and to his son-in-law. Other considerations seem to have carried little weight for him.

To say that all of the *imam*s in Istanbul always used the real estate portfolio put under their trusteeship and management as a systematic instrument of oppression of the local populations and as a means of accumulating personal wealth would, of course, be an exaggeration. Nevertheless, the local power and influence that the *imam*s wielded, and the social leverage they acquired within their neighborhood by managing *vakıf* real estate properties can hardly be overestimated.

The example of Aziz Mahmud Efendi does show that local *imam*s in Istanbul could easily be tempted to enhance their own personal interests before dealing with those of the community or those of the *vakıf* that they were supposed to serve. Obviously, this was more likely to happen when the trusteeship of local *vakıf*s was the *imam*'s main source of income. To the extent that the long run objective of many local foundations in Istanbul was to generate a perpetual stream of income for the *imam* and for the *müezzin* of the local mosque, the interests of these two persons coincided with those of the *vakıf* itself. In that general context, Aziz Mahmud Efendi's free and reckless use of perpetual endowments and of *vakıf* real estate property, were, perhaps, far from being an exception.

We therefore have some reason to suppose that the complaints voiced by the Istanbulites about the mismanagement and the arbitrariness of their *imam*s were sometimes valid. When the administrative reformers of the Tanzimat instituted secular *muhtar*s as local headmen in lieu of the traditional *imam*s, the effect was to sever the religious and ritual functions of the minister from his traditional administrative powers and from its political extensions. "Westernization," as well as administrative and political recentralization, were the key ideas of the reforms and, at least in the strategic and sensitive capital-city of the empire, the new *muhtar*s were placed under the direct supervision of the political authority.

As to the process of the effective transfer of authority at the local level, it probably showed a large degree of variation from one *mahalle* to the other. What we know of the case of the Kasap İlyas *mahalle* through the personal notebooks that its *imam*s and *muhtar*s of the second half of the nineteenth century have left to us,[30] however, shows that, in our neighborhood at least, the transfer of authority and the progressive sharing of local initiatives went rather smoothly. As we shall see, the process was apparently devoid of conflict.

A Case of Peaceful Transition: *Imam* and *Muhtar* in Kasap İlyas

The precise mode of selection and/or appointment of the first *muhtar*s in the Istanbul *mahalle*s in the 1830s and 1840s is not well documented. It is highly improbable that a regular and really free election could have taken place at that time. Most probably, a well-known local figure, perhaps also approved and chaperoned by the *imam* of the local mosque, was presented to, and appointed by, the office responsible for order and security within Istanbul (Ihtisab Nezareti).[31] It is not to be excluded that the *imam* of the local mosque was appointed as the first *muhtar* in many of the Istanbul neighborhoods.

Duties and Powers

Religious duties and functions (daily mosque services, duties related to the celebration of marriages, trusteeship of *vakıf*s, etc.) put aside, the ordinary obligations of the new local headmen were more or less the same as those of their predecessors, the *imam*s. These duties were basically of two kinds: there were those connected with *security*, and those related to the *representation* of the neighborhood.

The functions of the *muhtar* related to security matters essentially involved keeping records on the inhabitants of the *mahalle*, and especially on the newcomers who wanted to set up house. This was a direct consequence of the Ottoman government's almost obsessive—but to some extent justified, given that many Istanbul revolts and uprisings had ended up by overturning rulers and governments in past centuries—preoccupation with the overcrowding of the capital-city of the empire and with the "quality" of its potential inhabitants. Poor single men of rural origin seeking temporary employment, and coming to the city from the faraway provinces were especially singled out for being filtered off.

The Tanzimat period saw the revival of a series of old regulations and practices, called *men'-i mürur* (prohibition of passage), that tried to reduce uncontrolled migration toward Istanbul.[32] Every person who moved from one place to another had to be in possession of a sort of internal passport called *mürur tezkeresi* (certificate of passage). The *muhtar*s were expected to refuse residence to all who came to their *mahalle* without this passport. As to those locals who were leaving the neighborhood, the *muhtar*s were to issue a bona fide sort of certificate of good behavior, which entitled them to acquire an internal passport from government authorities.

As to the *muhtar*'s duties of representation, they generally put him in the position of a mediator between the local population and the Ottoman executive or judiciary powers. The *muhtar* could testify in court in the name of his whole *mahalle*, of which he was the legal guarantor, collectively and, if need be, individually. For instance, he was almost systematically called to testify in cases of inheritance with litigation that directly involved inhabitants of his *mahalle*. He could also transmit to the authorities any collective wish or complaint of the locals and was asked to serve as a sort of mediator in quite a variety of instances.

A typical case is that of the "police station." In 1888 or 1889, Osman Efendi, then *muhtar* of Kasap İlyas, took the initiative of, or perhaps was asked to, inquire about the possibility of establishing a local police station within the neighborhood. He first looked for a suitable location within the neighborhood and, after consulting with the local inhabitants, found a centrally situated empty plot of land that apparently had no legal owner and seemed suitable for the building of a local police station. The inhabitants of the *mahalle* looked favorably on that initiative and supported their *muhtar*. On April 3, 1889, Osman Efendi wrote a long letter to the Police Department of Istanbul (Zaptiye Nezâreti) voicing the desire and the agreement of the locals, explaining the situation of the empty plot of land, and had his own letter countersigned by a number of inhabitants of his *mahalle*.[33]

As previously with the *imam*, the *muhtar* was also asked to help with taxes. He could not impose or apportion individually the taxes himself, as the *imam* used to do with the former *avârız* taxes, which were imposed collectively on the whole *mahalle*. The new taxes were now strictly personal. The *muhtar* of Kasap İlyas was asked, for instance, to help establish lists of taxpayers in his *mahalle* and to keep a copy of these lists. The incomes and real estate assets of the inhabitants were also collected by our *muhtar*. The taxes involved, in the case of Kasap İlyas, were the road tax (*tarik vergisi*) and the property tax (*musakkafat vergisi*).

Overlaps and Takeovers

After the 1885 Ottoman population census, new responsibilities were added to their list of duties, and the *muhtar*s were required to issue birth, death, and marriage certificates and record these demographic events.[34] The administrative setup for registering these events did not prove to be successful on the whole, and, right to the end of the Ottoman Empire, it remained incomplete.

The side effect on the Kasap İlyas *mahalle* of this obligation to record vital events was an overlap (apparently not a conflict, though) and a transfer of authority from the *imam* to the *muhtar*. This overlap concerns the marriage records in Kasap İlyas. According to Islamic Law marriage is not a sacrament and does not have to be religiously sanctified in any way. It is basically considered a contract of common law between two people, a contract having important personal and financial consequences.[35] The contract is deemed perfectly valid if a number of formal conditions are satisfied. The function of the religious authority, in our case the *imam* of Kasap İlyas, was simply one of supervision, and his presence was necessary to certify that all of the formal requirements had been fulfilled and that the marriage was legal.

From 1864 on, however, the local headman of Kasap İlyas had been recording the marriages celebrated by the *imam*, and a total of 654 marriages spanning the years between 1864 and 1907 are listed in the *muhtar*'s notebooks. What is noteworthy, however, is that the *muhtar* of Kasap İlyas took over from the *imam* a number of initiatives that went far beyond the simple and, perhaps, understandable zeal of listing the names and the dates of marriage of newlyweds in his neighborhood. The *muhtar* of Kasap İlyas was not content with a simple registration of marriages. As a matter-of-fact, he took it upon himself to deliver to acquaintances documents certifying that there was no hindrance to his or her marriage. This type of document was called an *izinname* and states that no legal barrier exists to the nuptial arrangements.[36]

These documents—the *muhtar* acting as a sort of moral guarantor—enabled the persons to whom they were given, to contract a lawful marriage in a neighborhood or an area where they were not personally well-known. On June 12, 1889, for instance, the *muhtar* of Kasap İlyas himself certifies that "As Ömer bin Raşit, living in number 25 Helvacı street, intends to get married, there is no impediment to it from the point of view of the *shari'a*. . . ."[37] In many other instances, the *muhtar* does not personally allow a marriage to take place but takes the testimony of third parties as sufficient evidence for the lawfulness of the marriage contract. Note is taken, with the marriage record itself, that "such and such a person has testified or guaranteed in writing that the bride, or the groom have no legal impediment to matrimony."

Here are three typical examples of such testimonies, all of them written in the *muhtar*'s notebooks as marginal notes to the relevant marriage records: "My daughter Fatma is not engaged to anyone and has no impediment of any sort to marriage. If any impediment appears later, I accept full responsibility. Signed and sealed, Ismail Hakkı, of the Justice department, 3 August 1889."[38] "Rıza bey has guaranteed that the bride has no legal impediment to matrimony, 5 March 1895."[39] "The bride has no impediment, as shown by the note from the Dizdariye neighborhood and the oral testimonies of Şeyh Halil Efendi, kahveci Hasan and muhallebici Kadri, June 1898."[40] As a matter-of-fact, more than one fourth of all of the marriages in the *muhtar*'s notebooks contain, in the margin, mention either of such a marriage permission or of the testimony of goodwill of a third party to the contract.

In all legality, however, only a person well versed in Islamic law, a person having full knowledge of both the formal and the substantive preconditions of marriage, a religious judge, a *kadı*, or an *imam* could evaluate the legal situation of the future spouses and could have the necessary authority to deliver such a certificate. Similarly, the legality of a marriage permission, or the validity of personal testimony on the matter could be fully evaluated and eventually accepted only by a religious authority, by a *kadı* or an *imam*, and not by a secular *muhtar*.

Clearly, in this matter of marriage registration and certification, the new local headman had trespassed a legal frontier and taken over part of the authority of the traditional local religious leader. This transfer of authority in our *mahalle* may well have been an exceptional situation in Istanbul, the result of a sui generis relationship of confidence between a highly prestigious *muhtar* and a rather complacent *imam*. In the absence of sources with a comparable variety of information for other Istanbul *mahalle*s, the question is bound to remain unanswered. This transfer of authority was not limited, in Kasap İlyas, to the sole issue of the recording and validation of marriages. A number of other duties that the *imam* had been traditionally performing for centuries were also taken over by the *muhtar*.

One of these traditional duties of the *imam* concerns the payments to be made to the *müezzin* of the Kasap İlyas mosque. In the 1880s the *müezzin* of the Kasap İlyas mosque was Ahmet Efendi. He was then living in a *vakıf* house at 52 Samatya Street, and was receiving a salary from another local pious foundation, the trustee of both of these *vakıf*s being the *imam*, Mehmet Necati Efendi. The payment of a salary to the *müezzin* out of the revenues of a local *vakıf* was a business which, in principle, concerned nobody but the trustee of the relevant foundation and the payee. In case of a conflict between them, the competent judicial authority was either the religious judge, the *kadı*, and his substitute (*naib*) or, in the second half of the nineteenth century, the newly established Ministry of Pious Foundations (*Evkaf Nezâreti*). No one else could have a say in the affairs concerning pious foundations.

What we see in the Kasap İlyas *mahalle*, however, runs contrary to this principle and reveals the existence of decisive interventions on the part of the *muhtar*. His notebooks contain traces of payments made by the *imam* of the Kasap İlyas mosque to the *müezzin* thereto attached. The *müezzin* of the mosque had, for a number of years, made and signed a statement of receipt in the *muhtar*'s notebooks. Here are two examples: "I hereby declare to have received from the Holy mosque my whole salary for the year 1304. Signed and sealed: Müezzin Ahmet, 27 February 1304 [March 11 1889]."[41] "I have received from the hand of the *imam* all my salary for the year 1307. Signed: Müezzin Ahmet, 1 March 1307 [13 March 1892]."[42] The *vakıf* of the Kasap İlyas mosque, by the hands of it trustee, the *imam* of the same mosque, was paying a salary to the person performing the office of *müezzin*, and this transaction was being recorded by the *muhtar*, a person who, in principle, should have had nothing to do with the transaction. Besides, the *muhtar* had also noted down the precise "address" of the transaction ("3 Cami-i Şerif Street") and this "address" was that of the mosque itself. The *imam*, as an employer of sorts, and the *müezzin*, his employee, got together in their usual "workplace" and the salary was paid in the presence of a witness, the *muhtar*, who kept the signed voucher of the paycheck.

If this had been an ordinary commercial transaction or a usual work contract between a firm and a worker, we would say that the *muhtar* had then fulfilled the function of a notary. And he often did so, as a matter-of-fact, in various financial agreements between two members of the local community. As we shall see, in the last quarter of the nineteenth century, the *muhtar* of Kasap İlyas did take upon himself the responsibility of performing a large number of public duties that turned him into a *community leader*, almost in the modern sense of the term. But in this precise case, there is clearly an encroachment of his secular power and authority into what is an otherwise strictly religious domain.

Contrary to all expectations, the trustee of a pious foundation and the *müezzin*, both of them clerics, did not choose, in order to register a transaction that obviously fell within the domain of the Islamic/Ottoman law of foundations, either the *sharia'* court or the Ministry of Pious Foundations. They selected somebody they knew personally well, the *muhtar*, that is, the newly established and strictly "secular" and "modern" local headman of Kasap İlyas. The *muhtar* of Kasap İlyas was both registering and authenticating marriages, and contributing to the regulation of the financial arrangements between the *imam* and the *müezzin*. The critical point here is that this restructuring of the *muhtar*'s field of authority seems to have involved no resistance on the part of the *imam* of Kasap İlyas. The whole picture is one of cooperation, not of competition or conflict.

The modernizing administrative reforms of the Tanzimat period, which tried to recentralize the Ottoman state apparatus had, as a corollary, the progressive elimination of the traditional local centers of authority.[43] As to the new and "secular" local administrative structures designed to replace them, they probably met with varied success. There were certainly many problems of local implementation; many conflicts of authority did occur, and so did functional overlaps and redundancies, gray areas with a conflictual potential. What we observe in Kasap İlyas, however, is a case in apparently peaceful and cooperative transition. The traditional local leader recognized the administrative authority of the newly appointed local headman and he managed to insert some of the religious functions of the traditional leader into a new and secularized administrative framework.

This final configuration may well have been the singularly exceptional product of the personalities of a succession of local protagonists, and of their very particular rapport. Was it the *imam* of Kasap İlyas who acquiesced to the "secularization" of some of his traditional functions, or was it the *muhtar* who acquired some religious functions? The question may lack an answer. What we can not exclude, at all events, is that what happened in Kasap İlyas might well have been a very special case, a sui generis instance of transition *cum* peaceful cohabitation.

THE ADMINISTERED BODY:
EARLY NINETEENTH-CENTURY PERSPECTIVES

There was neither a cadastral land survey nor a title-deed registry of any sort in the pre-nineteenth-century Ottoman cities. All items of real estate property, in Kasap İlyas as well as elsewhere in Istanbul, had to be described by reference to the nearest prominent geographic landmark or to the *mahalle* in which they were situated. As a second step, their precise location was defined by reference to the owner(s) of the adjoining pieces of property. Public buildings or utilities were also used for definitional purposes.

Here is a typical example of such a description, taken from a local deed of trust dated 1792: "In the city of Istanbul, in the Kasap İlyas *mahalle* near the Davudpaşa wharf... a plot of land bounded on one side by the house of the *imam* Mustafa Efendi, on the other by the house belonging to Atıf Efendi's vakıf, on another by Ahmed Efendi's house and by the public thoroughfare...."[44] For each piece of real estate property either sold to a private person, or donated to a pious foundation, the owners of the adjoining properties were named and recorded, respectively, in the deed of sale signed at the Davudpaşa Court or in the deed of trust of the local *vakıf.* Mosques, schools, fountains, walls, public baths, roads, and so forth were also frequently used as delimiters.

For empty plots of land, perimeter measurements were also given in a large number of instances. In a typical deed of sale, dated from 1802, a plot of land in Kasap İlyas is described as follows: ". . . In the city of Istanbul, in the Kasap İlyas *mahalle* . . . a plot of land whose perimeter is 214 *zira'* and is surrounded by the house of İbrahim Ağa, that of Halifezâde Mustafa Efendi, an empty plot of land belonging to Helvacı Ahmed and, on the fourth side, by the public thoroughfare. . . ."[45]

As shown by the local *vakıf* documents[46] for the eighteenth and nineteenth centuries, a profound modification in the basic pattern of settlement in the *mahalle* had occurred and this modification had preceded and accompanied the changes in its administrative setup, in the post-Tanzimat era. A closer look at these later *vakıf* documents and at the contemporary Davudpaşa Religious Courts records reveals the depth of the changes that had occurred in the configuration of streets and houses in the *mahalle*.

Streets and Houses

There was a fundamental change in the layout of the streets and in the distribution of the houses that had occurred in Kasap İlyas between the late sixteenth and the end of the eighteenth centuries.

For instance, of the ten pieces of *vakıf* property in Kasap İlyas described in their respective eighteenth- and nineteenth-century deeds of trust, seven were described as "bound by the public thoroughfare." In other words, they were overlooking a street. Only one of them was described as being accessed by a dead-end street (*tarîk-i hass*). Besides, *all* of the Kasap İlyas houses whose deeds of sale was, in the late eighteenth and in the early nineeenth centuries, recorded by the Davudpaşa Court of Justice were also described as "bound by the public thoroughfare."[47] Not a single one was situated in a dead-end street.

This is a stark contrast with the street layout and the usual housing pattern of the *mahalle* in the sixteenth and seventeenth centuries, when, as we saw, many of the houses in the *mahalle* were protected by dead-end streets and enclosed by large and walled "gardens." Now most of the houses in Kasap İlyas are simply overlooking a normal street and are contiguous to other houses. Two centuries ago there were at least as many semiprivate dead ends as there were public passageways in Kasap İlyas. Now the blind alleys have almost disappeared. So have the large walled "gardens" that were surrounding each and every house. Out of the ten Kasap İlyas houses donated to a foundation in the eighteenth and nineteenth centuries only one was situated in the middle of a walled "garden." And this house was the only one to have the extensions and outhouses that a majority of the houses in the neighborhood had, two centuries ago.

In other terms, most of the Kasap İlyas houses had become, in the early nineteenth century, unifunctional residential units. They were no more the topographical centers of an economic unit of production, that is, just the lodgings of the owner or of the manager of a large vegetable garden (*bostan*). The residential and the agricultural/commercial functions were clearly dissociated. Houses and *bostan*s were now clearly distinct, in location as well as in function. The *bostan*s were now just *bostan*s, not residences, and the majority of dwellings were monolithic units and had no gardens.

When and if the ordinary houses did have a garden, in the eighteenth and nineteenth centuries, it was nothing but a garden of a relatively small size. None of these gardens could boast either of "fruit-bearing trees" or of "large flower-beds" and "vegetable-beds." The *bostan*s were large, and the gardens that adjoined the houses were small. The two *bostan*s which, around the year 1800, had been set up as *vakıf*s within the Kasap İlyas *mahalle* had perimeters of 1,140 and 1,200 *zira'*. These were obviously large vegetable gardens, all part of the centuries' old cityscape of Kasap İlyas and of its environs.

As to the plots of land in the *mahalle* on which houses hade been, or were to be, built, those we have traced in the Davudpaşa Religious Court records in the late eighteenth and early nineteenth centuries had, for instance, perimeters of 214 *zira*s,[48] 130 *zira*s,[49] 136 *zira*s,[50] 430 *zira*s,[51] 80 *zira*s,[52] and so forth. Obviously these measurements represent enclosures just sufficient for an average-size house and, eventually, a miniscule garden. They are too small to constitute an agricultural and commercial asset in themselves.

The houses were built on smaller plots of land, and the facades were now more or less lined-up along the streets. The houses were all facing the street, and each other, thus giving to the public thoroughfare a sense of communication which, as we saw, it did not have back in the sixteenth century. The sixteenth century was a time when the "street" in Kasap İlyas was just a simple passageway, lacking both a form and a secondary social function. Things had greatly changed since then. Not surprisingly, of the ten houses that were part of eighteenth- and nineteenth-century *vakıf*s in Kasap İlyas, five had, as immediate neighbors, just another house or an odd shop. One of them was even surrounded by houses on three sides.[53]

We took a random sample of ten houses among those Kasap İlyas houses whose deeds of sale were recorded by the Davudpaşa Court of Justice between 1785 and 1825. We found, first, that exactly forty immediate neighbors to these houses were cited in the deeds' detailed descriptions. Among these neighbors, there was, first, the anonymous "public thoroughfare" along which all of the ten houses were aligned (10 instances). Then, there were other houses (18 instances) and, finally, gardens and empty plots of land were cited as neighbors (12 instances).[54] In contrast to the generally irregular (sometimes polygonal or triangular) shape of the plots of land in the sixteenth-century Kasap İlyas *mahalle* (see chapter 1) almost all of the late eighteenth- and early nineteenth-century Kasap İlyas houses had exactly four neighbors each. These houses had quadrangular surfaces, and they occupied quadrangular plots of land.

A typical Kasap İlyas house was therefore immediate neighbor to two other houses, on the average. That house had a facade that directly overlooked the street, and occasionally had a garden. Houses in the *mahalle* were more and more surrounded by other houses and buildings, and not by "gardens." And, obviously, this meant that there were now, everything else being equal, more houses in the *mahalle* as compared to two centuries ago.

Moreover, and again in sharp contrast to the sixteenth and seventeenth centuries, the houses in Kasap İlyas now generally had more than one floor. In the random sample of the ten houses drawn from among all of those real estate property items from Kasap İlyas whose deeds of sale were recorded by the Davudpaşa Court of Justice between 1785 and 1825, six houses were described as having two floors. The lower one contained, more often than not, a hall, a kitchen, a lavatory, a storage place for wood and coal, stables, and so forth,[55] and the upper floor(s) a variable number of rooms. A typical description could be ". . . three rooms, a hall and a lavatory in the upper floor and, in the lower one, a kitchen, latrines, a bathroom, a storage place for coal, a water well, a courtyard, and a gate to the street. . . ."[56] Though more exceptionally, some later deeds of sale also occasionally mention the existence of houses with a shop or a workshop on their ground floor.[57]

Not only had Kasap İlyas a larger number of houses in the late eighteenth than in the sixteenth and seventeenth centuries, but there were now also more floors to each house. This meant that the *mahalle* had a larger population, which was spread over an area that had not considerably changed in the preceding centuries. Kasap İlyas was therefore less sparsely populated in the nineteenth century. There is, however, no meaningful way in which either the size or the rate of growth of the population of Kasap İlyas in the eighteenth and nineteenth centuries could be measured.

The number of houses in Kasap İlyas, back in the sixteenth century, could not, as we saw, have much exceeded fifty or sixty, given the basic pattern of settlement and land use (see Chapter 1). As to the late Ottoman Census and Population Register of 1885, it recorded a total of 153 houses, small and large (denominated *hane*s and *konak*s, respectively) in Kasap İlyas,[58] plus a small number of inhabited "rooms." The definition of a *konak* is rather vague and problematic. How large must an Istanbul house (*hane*) have been to deserve to be called a *konak*? Or was it the wealth and status of the occupants that were determinant? The evaluation seems to have been prone to change. For instance, the 1885 census had listed four *konak*s situated within the Kasap İlyas *mahalle*. Osman efendi, the *muhtar* of Kasap İlyas thought differently and, in his own list of real estate property of the neighborhood, had counted only three *konak*s. He had chosen to call the fourth a simple *hane*. Whatever the case may have been, the number of dwellings had almost grown threefold during the intervening centuries.

Our *mahalle* contained, according to the census of 1885, around 1,100 people. This is lower than 1,550, the average population of the 251 intramural Istanbul *mahalle*s, according to the same census returns.[59] As Kasap İlyas had a larger area than most of the centrally situated neighborhoods of Istanbul, its population figure definitely point to a generally lower density of settlement. As to the total population of Istanbul, it had been on a rising trend throughout the nineteenth century, passing from an estimated 400,000 inhabitants in the 1840s to more than twice that figure in 1885.[60] The population of the Kasap İlyas *mahalle* simply followed suit.

Had then the traditional semirural and peripheral character of Kasap İlyas totally disappeared during the nineteenth century? Certainly not. The *bostan*s were there, as they are still now,[61] and there is no indication that their overall size was considerably reduced either in the eighteenth or in the nineteenth centuries. These large extents of uninhabited greenery situated within the city walls continued to put their stamp on the whole area. While taking a stroll right in our neighborhood, that is, "between Samatya and Langa" in 1874, the Italian traveler Edmondo de Amicis took note of ". . . large areas scarred by recent fires, the city resembling a village, dervish convents. . . ."[62] The Davudpaşa vegetable gardens, which extended right into our neighborhood, have always remained part and parcel of the map of the capital-city of the empire.[63]

What had happened was not that the gardens and the greenery of this semiperipheral neighborhood had disappeared just before the nineteenth century. It was simply, first, that the "streets" of Kasap İlyas had acquired a certain topographical stability and an urban function that they did not have two centuries ago. Now the houses had to adapt their positioning to these streets, and not the opposite, as was the case in the formative sixteenth century. The destructive fires of the end of the eighteenth century had certainly erased to a great extent the former irregular grid of "streets." As to the increasing population pressure of the nineteenth century, it resulted, as elsewhere in the capital-city of the empire, in a more localized but denser web of streets, houses, and inhabitants.

At the beginning of the nineteenth century the streets of Kasap İlyas had already acquired more or less the shapes and configurations that were to appear on the first detailed street-map of traditional Istanbul, dating from 1875.[64] Some of these streets already had names, although not yet official ones. Apart from the neighborhood's "high street," the centuries-old Butchers' Road, there was that winding street leading to the seaside, the Davudpaşa wharf, and the nearby wood and coal sellers, Wharf Street (*İskele Sokağı*), alias Davudpaşa Wharf Street (Davudpaşa İskelesi Sokağı). The two streets which, from the "Butchers' Road," climbed up the hill toward the Davudpaşa mosque, were already well defined: Yokuşçeşme Street, with, in the middle, its eponymous old public fountain, and Çavuşzade Street, leading to the small Çavuşzade mosque, at the north-westernly border of Kasap İlyas. The streets of Istanbul were given official names in the 1860s, but the official denominations were not immediately adopted and really used by the locals. As late as the 1890s the "addresses" of plaintiffs and witnesses living in the Kasap İlyas *mahalle* were set down in the Davudpaşa Court records as the Coal Sellers' Street (Kömürcüler Sokağı), the Street of the Arabs (Araplar Sokağı), or in the Haysellers' Street (Samancılar Sokağı).[65] These were all names that never had any official existence, and many of the official names given by the municipality had to wait for the end of the century before being generally recognized.

As to the small market area across from the Kasap İlyas mosque and around the public bath, it had kept its location for centuries, despite numerous fires and devastation. In the late eighteenth and early nineteenth centuries this small group of shops consisted of[66] among others, a barbershop, a tailor, a seller of glassware and a maker and seller of *boza*.[67] Most, though not all, of the shops in Kasap İlyas were independent, detached, small, and shabby structures. Houses with shops on their ground floor were quite exceptional. The commercial and residential areas of Ottoman Istanbul (just as in Byzantine times, for that matter) were set apart from each other and the shops and workshops situated in residential areas were generally small in size and in number and were all meant to meet the small-scale daily needs of the local inhabitants.

As for the houses themselves, wood was, of course, still the main building material. The mostly two- or three-story wooden houses of Kasap İlyas, with their latticed bay windows overlooking the street, their large tiled eaves extending over the street, and their various overhangs, were now in a contiguous row, lined along the narrow, winding, and mostly unpaved or barely cobbled streets. They had then come to conform to what is nowadays almost canonically perceived to have been the "typical traditional Istanbul housing pattern." This pattern—the typical postcard-view of a street of Ottoman Istanbul—however, was the product of very particular circumstances dating from the end of the eighteenth and the nineteenth centuries.

Pictures from a Neighborhood

The *mahalle*s of Istanbul were mixed in terms of wealth, social class, and status. Residential patterns usually ran along lines of ethnicity and religion, though ethnically mixed neighborhoods were not infrequent either. The *mahalle*s were either predominantly Muslim, Armenian, Jewish, or Greek Orthodox. The class-based differentiation of the urban fabric was a product of the twentieth century, and it took hold only after the First World War.[68] Before that, within the same *mahalle*, the large mansions of the rich and powerful neighbored on the shanty lodgings of beggars and street-porters. These groups were not usually clustered in different segments of the same neighborhood, either. This was so in the sixteenth as well as in the nineteenth centuries.

There had indeed always been *mahalle*s where, on the whole, the inhabitants fared better than other neighborhoods, but really "exclusive" areas, particularly well-off or uniformly destitute ones were quite exceptional in Ottoman Istanbul. Some areas were more prestigious, and especially those situated in the vicinity of the center of political power, the Palace. So were *semt*s such as Vefa, Zeyrek, Koska, and Fatih, where many of the large mansions of the high-ranking bureaucrats and the *ulema'* were mostly concentrated. By contrast, the *mahalle*s that were too far away form the urban commercial and political centers of activity, just as those situated close to the city-walls, were never considered as prestigious or "posh." Take the example of our neighborhood. The Cerrahpaşa District, situated up the hill, whose "air" was reputably better and whose houses had a more scenic view of the Sea of Marmara, was held, at least in the nineteenth century, in higher esteem, as compared to its immediate neighbors. Supposedly, it contained a larger number of mansions. Among Cerrahpaşa's immediate neighbors were the Davudpaşa *semt* and its constituent part Kasap İlyas, situated downhill and bordering on the ramparts. Nevertheless, our neighborhood housed, in the eighteenth and nineteenth centuries, a wide variety of people, rich and poor. Any a posteriori attempt at defining a local homogeneity seems doomed to failure.

The series of later deeds of trust belonging to the late eighteenth and nineteenth centuries do provide a short glimpse of the unsurprisingly variegated group that inhabited our *mahalle* in those centuries.[69] First of all, of these ten local *vakıf*s, eight had been founded by a woman. Among these, Hurşide hatun stands out. She had endowed no less than three different local foundations with real estate property (a house and two rather large "gardens") situated in Kasap İlyas and had appointed the *imam* of the mosque as beneficiary and trustee of all three *vakıf*s. All we know about Hurşide hatun is that she had died before 1770. A transaction dated from 1770 mentions "the late Hurşide hatun" as founder of the *vakıf*. She was most probably a convert to Islam and/or a manumitted slave, the clue being that, in all of the three *vakıf* documents, her name occurs as Hurşide Hatun binti Abdullah (Hurşide Hatun, daughter of Abdullah). So was, perhaps, Sakine Hatun, benefactor of her own foundation and also "daughter of Abdullah." Of the other female local benefactors, we know only the names: Gülendam Hatun, Hanife Hatun, and Hasibe Hatun (d. before 1771). Besides, among the 140 names mentioned in the documents as effective users or holders of the right of usufruct of *vakıf* property situated in Kasap İlyas, at some time during the late eighteenth and nineteenth centuries, thirty nine, that is twenty-eight percent, were women. In six other instances a husband and a wife were mentioned in the *vakıf* records as partners in the use of the same *vakıf* property. As in the sixteenth century, Kasap İlyas women were much involved in the rent and use of real estate property in the neighborhood.

The documents list the occupations for only twenty of the one hundred and fourty occupants of property belonging to Kasap İlyas *vakıf*s. Artisans and shopkeepers, however, seem to have been the more numerous of the social categories represented. Between 1770 and 1780 Mustafa Ağa, the owner of a *hamam* and a prosperous tradesman, was living in Kasap İlyas. So was Hacı Halil Efendi, a maker and seller of handkerchiefs (*yağlıkçı*), a more modest shopkeeper, who had rented a *vakıf* shop in Kasap İlyas. In the same decade, a barber, Tahir occupied a *vakıf* house situated on Çavuşzade Street. In 1807 Mustafa Ağa, a seller of perfume and herbs (*aktar*), was living in a *vakıf* house in Kasap İlyas. Between 1788 and 1792 Molla Mustafa bin Mehmed Efendi, a member of the *'ulema* class, had rented a house in the neighborhood and had been part of the community for four years.

The successive tenants of a particular house in Kasap İlyas belonging to the *vakıf* of Amine hatun[70] provide a good picture of the variety of local inhabitants, and of their rate of turnover. The deed of trust gives no details about the house itself, except that it was bounded by one of the streets of Kasap İlyas. The variety of people who used this house suggests, however, that it was an ordinary dwelling, rather than an exceptionally large one, a mansion. On July 26, 1797 Ahmet Ağa, a butcher, rents this house from the trustee (the rent was of one *akçe* a day, or thirty *akçe*s monthly) and lives there with his family for the next twenty-two years. We do not know whether, between 1797 and 1819, Ahmet Ağa had practiced his profession within Kasap İlyas or not. It is, however, certain that he had, in the interval, undertaken the pilgrimage to Mecca. After the death, in 1819, of the butcher, the right of disposal of this *vakıf* house was inherited by his son, also named Ahmet. On October 25 of the same year, this son sold his right of usufruct to *Hacı* Ahmet bin Ibrahim, a slave-trader (*esirci*). The slave-trader lived in this Kasap İlyas house for about two and a half years and then, on May 22, 1822, transferred it to Seyyid Mehmed Ağa, who was the chief musician of the Janissaries' Military Band (*mehterbaşı*). Five years went by. In the meantime, in June 1826, the centuries' old Janissary Corps was crushed and suppressed by Sultan Mahmud II. With the Janissaries, the Military Band attached thereto (the *mehter*) was also abolished. Seyyid Mehmet ağa therefore lost his job, and was perhaps even persecuted, as was the case with many former Janissaries. About a year after the event, on August 5, 1827, the former *mehterbaşı* transfers his right of use to the former occupant of the house, the slave-trader Hacı Ahmet bin Ibrahim, who was now married to Fatma Şerife hanım, with whom he shared the house. Four years go by. The last transaction concerning this house and mentioned in the *vakıf* documents tells us that early in July 1831 Ahmet bin Ibrahim left the house to a new tenant, Seyyid Mustafa ağa. This new tenant was a "civil servant," a *tatar*, that is, an official in charge of carrying messages from one branch of the government to another, or from the capital-city to the provinces.

The *mahalle* also housed a number of other bureaucrats and civil servants. In 1813 Ali ağa, a *kapıcıbaşı*, one of the higher-ranking officials of the imperial Palace, took over a garden in Kasap İlyas. In 1802, a *vakıf* house in the neighborhood was rented by Ahmet efendi, who was a *beytülmal kâtibi*, an official attached to the Janissary corps, and whose duty was to apportion the estate of deceased members of the corps.[71] In July 1796 a *ruznamçeci*, that is, an official in charge of the financial responsibility of the daily expenses of a branch of government, had rented a "garden" from a *vakıf* in Kasap İlyas. Another important official of the financial administration of the empire also lived in Kasap İlyas between 1807 and 1822. Kethüdazâde Mustafa Efendi was indeed one of the senior bureaucrats of one of the central tax offices, and his official title was "*Mevkufat kalemi hulefâsından.*"

After the 1840s, a few members of the newly established bureaucratic apparatus of the Tanzimat, all of them products of the administrative reforms of the day, also chose to reside in the *mahalle*. Their names are cited in the local *vakıf* documents preceded by the official modes of address that the Tanzimat had instituted. Izzetlû Mehmed Esrar efendi was an undersecretary for official correspondence in the Administrative Court (*Meclis-i vâlâ evrak müdür muavini*), and Fütüvvetlû Mehmed Şevket bey was a higher official attached to the Cabinet (*Hacegân-ı Divan-ı Hümayundan*).

Alongside these high-ranking bureaucrats, the Kasap İlyas *mahalle* continued to harbor many members of some of the less-favored professional groups of the city throughout the nineteenth century. For instance, in 1834 Yusuf, who was a simple street-porter (*hammal*), rented a shop from one of the local *vakıf*s in association with Mustafa, who was a hayseller (*samancı*). In 1855, Seyyit Süleyman, a seller of charcoal (*kömürcü*), rented a garden in Kasap İlyas. In this case, the *vakıf* document openly specifies that Seyyit Süleyman was an "inhabitant of the Kasap İlyas neighborhood."[72] The witnesses coming from the Kasap İlyas *mahalle,* and whose testimonies were registered in the Davudpaşa Court records during the first half of the nineteenth century, were also mostly artisans and shopkeepers (sellers of wood and charcoal,[73] barbers,[74] grocers,[75] water-carriers, street-porters,[76] etc.). The sellers of wood (whether for burning or for construction) and charcoal (*tahtacı*s, *keresteci*s, and *kömürcü*s) constitute together the single largest occupational category appearing as plaintiffs or as witnesses in the Davudpaşa Court records of the nineteenth century. This is no doubt a reflection of the role that the Davudpaşa wharf and the shops for wood and coal continued to play in Kasap İlyas.

As many of the traditional intramural Istanbul mosques, Kasap İlyas also has a small burial-ground (*hazire*) just next to it. This small cemetery adjoining the mosque also bears witness to the social diversity of the inhabitants of the *mahalle* in the late eighteenth and early nineteenth centuries. There are about forty tombstones in this small burial ground. Except for that of the legendary Kasap İlyas himself (his own tombstone is dated 1494—a.h. 900), all of them have been erected between 1780 and 1867. In 1868, a government order forbade the use of the small intramural burial grounds in Istanbul and ordered all burials to take place outside the city walls.[77]

The Ottoman tombstones, by the inscriptions that they bear as well as by their very shape and the elaboration of their design, give some information on the occupation, the official positions, the social status, and the family of the deceased.[78] They always indicate the dates of death/burial, but very seldom contain any information as to the age of the deceased. Some of the names and dates of death that appear on the Kasap İlyas tombstones that have survived are as follows: Hacı Mustafa ağa, *müezzin* of the Kasap İlyas mosque (1819); Rukiye hanım, wife of Çuhadar (footman) Ali ağa (1805); Mustafa Çavuş, an officer of a mounted brigade (Sipahi Ocağı Çavuşlarından) (1809); Zeliha hanım, daughter of Hacı İbrahim efendi (1810); Mehmet Sadık efendi, a silversmith (*gümüşçü*) (1849); Ahmet Muhtar efendi, a Customs official (Gümrük memurlarından) (1863); and Mehmet Cemil ağa, a seller of charcoal (*kömürcü*) (1865). No grandee of the empire appears. Neither does any high-ranking bureaucrat or military.

As to the inscription on Ahmet Vehbi efendi's tombstone, it describes the origin and occupation of the deceased in exceptional detail. Ahmet Vehbi Efendi had died in 1860. The fact that he had been living in the Kasap İlyas *mahalle* must have been very important for him and for his family. Just as his official position and function in the Ottoman administration, the simple fact of his neighborhood of residence was also used as a basic item defining his identity and social status and, as such, was made to appear on the inscription engraved on the marble tombstone: "Ahmet Vehbi Efendi, inhabitant of Kasap İlyas and scribe in the bureau of the *mahalle*s of the Istanbul Municipality—A prayer for his soul—1276 [1860 a.d.]."[79]

Ever since the sixteenth century, the Kasap İlyas *mahalle* had always been a basically Muslim neighborhood. What small non-Muslim minority there may have been in our neighborhood hardly ever appears in the late eighteenth- and nineteenth-century documents. Among the one hundred and forty inhabitants of the neighborhood whose names appear in the local *vakıf* documents of this period, we came across the name of only one non-Muslim. This person had, in 1807, rented a shop selling wood and timber from one of the local *vakıf*s.[80] The names of hundreds of inhabitants of Kasap İlyas occur in the nineteenth-century Davudpaşa Court records. Only three non-Muslims are ever mentioned. These are Orthodox Greeks who, in 1807 and again in 1823, had applied to the court on a matter concerning the ownership of a garden situated in Kasap İlyas.[81] It appears that the Kasap İlyas *mahalle*, which had been an essentially Muslim neighborhood in the sixteenth century, had kept this character right to the end of the nineteenth century.

3

Migration and Urban Integration
The Arapkir Connection

As is the case with all economic and political capital-cities, Istanbul has always been a city which, over the centuries, attracted a large number of newcomers and migrants of various types and origins. Notwithstanding the nostalgic protests of the natives or the governmental efforts to repel the newcomers, the Ottoman city accepted and, eventually integrated them. Obviously, social and political upward mobility in the Ottoman Empire entailed a passage through Istanbul. The city always supported a substantial number of migrant workers, a labor supply pool for unskilled or nonguild work of various kinds.[1] Some areas of Anatolia are frequently mentioned as sources of migrant labor.[2] Being the center of political power of such a large empire, the city's population was no doubt very disparate.[3]

But migration to the capital was not always necessarily voluntary. The *devşirme* process that forcibly brought to Istanbul children from the provinces to be trained as soldiers (Janissaries) or as servants for the Palace in the fifteenth and sixteenth centuries is one instance. What was more important, quantitatively at least, were the consequences of warfare, of territorial losses, and of the frequent border changes that ensued. These provoked, especially in the nineteenth century, a massive flocking of mostly Muslim refugees toward the capital and its Anatolian hinterland, which progressively became the heartland of the shrinking empire.

Ottoman Istanbul was the end point of the politically motivated occasional, sudden, and massive migration-wave. But, as we shall see, it was also the final destination of a continuous trickle of newcomers, rural migrants in search of work and economic and social opportunities. To use more modern terminology, there was both *mass-migration* and *chain-migration* toward

Ottoman Istanbul in the eighteenth and nineteenth centuries. As a matter-of-fact, Kasap İlyas provides us with a centuries-old instance of a well-organized, established, almost institutionalized chain of migration. Men of working age and their kin originating from a small locality in eastern Anatolia moved to our small Istanbul neighborhood, were welcomed there by their already established co-locals, and these "patrons" helped the newcomers to settle, find a job, and officialize their stay in the city.

However the case may have been, the Ottoman governments often saw this flow of migrants as a potential danger to security within the capital-city. Uncontrolled migration to Istanbul was always a politically sensitive issue and migrants were perceived, first and foremost, as a potential threat to political stability in the sensitive and "protected" imperial capital (*mahmiye-i Konstantiniye*). Uprisings and various real or imaginary urban disorders (of a physical as well as of a moral sort) were often attributed to the presence of uncontrolled elements in the capital, and especially of groups of provincial and unsettled younger males who came seeking employment.

The authorities tried to control the flow of migrants, and often took forceful measures designed to curb the number of newcomers and to limit their possibilities of residence in the city. For instance, single migrant males were for centuries confined to living in special bachelor's quarters (*bekârodaları* or *bekâr hanları*) and their numbers and whereabouts were often the subject of official inquiries and reports.[4] Strict regulations concerning the issue and the holding of a sort of internal passport called *mürur tezkeresi* (certificate of passage) for those who were moving, either permanently or temporarily, within the territory of the empire were revived toward the middle of the nineteenth century.[5] In previous centuries various types of "suspicious" men were not infrequently rounded up in Istanbul and either driven out of the city or sent back to their place of origin.[6]

However, judging from the number of edicts and regulations issued on this matter over the centuries, it seems that, on the whole, these efforts have been of no avail and that the flow could not be reversed. The flow of migrants, mainly depending on the economic and political fortunes of the empire, could neither be stopped, nor was it ever effectively controlled. We shall see how the migrants who came to settle in the Kasap İlyas *mahalle* in the nineteenth century succeeded in circumventing these strict residence regulations.

There is no precise method and no historical documents that could allow us to give realistic estimates of the number of migrants to Istanbul in the periods preceding the nineteenth century. None of the early nineteenth-century Ottoman population counts contain any information on the geographic origin of the Istanbulites. We do know, however, that the nineteenth century witnessed a permanent trickle of migrants in search of work, income, and security, and that the population of Istanbul grew more than twofold during this century. The speed of this trickle is hard to estimate, and the first trustworthy figures on the demographic composition and geographic origin of Istanbul's population are those of 1885.[7] A five percent sample drawn from the population of the central districts of Istanbul in the 1885 Ottoman census, show us that fifty two percent of the Muslim inhabitants of Istanbul had not been born in the capital of the Ottoman Empire.[8] More than half of the capital's population had come from elsewhere. The percentage of the non-Istanbul born among the Muslim inhabitants of the Kasap İlyas *mahalle*, was equal to 49 percent, at the same date.[9]

A period of relative political calm and stability followed the disastrous Russian War of 1877–1878. This was a period that lasted for about a quarter of a century, with no large-scale wars, no significant losses of territory, and no subsequent massive influx of Muslim refugees from the former territories of the disintegrating empire. This long period devoid of international conflict—which coincided more or less with the reign of Abdülhamid II—slightly reduced the proportion of the province-born within the Istanbul population. According to the last Ottoman census of 1907, 57 percent of the Muslim residents of Istanbul had been born in the capital, and 43 percent in the rest of the empire.[10] In the Kasap İlyas *mahalle* the proportion of non-Istanbul-born Muslim inhabitants had, between 1885 and 1907, slightly declined, from 49 to 47 percent.[11]

The Formation of a Migrant Shelter in Kasap İlyas: *Ispanakçi Viranesi* and the *Arapkirlis*

The non-Istanbul-born Muslim residents of Kasap İlyas at the end of the nineteenth century had come from a wide variety of places within the empire, and some of them even from abroad. The largest single group of migrants to the Kasap İlyas *mahalle*, however, had come, according to the 1885 census documents, from the city of Arapkir and its surroundings, in east-central Anatolia. To those migrants originating from Arapkir must be added those coming from the neighboring small towns of Arguvan, Keban, Ağın, Divriği, Akçadağ, and Malatya. These were all small towns situated within a circle with a radius of about fifty kilometers having Arapkir at its center. All of them were, at the time, part of the Ottoman Province of Mamuretülâziz.[12] It is well documented that there were people from Arapkir and from its surroundings living in Kasap İlyas as early as the last quarter of the eighteenth century. We shall examine the structures and the processes of urban integration of this group of migrants in greater detail. For reasons of practicality we shall call them all "the Arapkirlis" and shall, when necessary, specify the precise place of birth of a particular person.

The Arapkir-born migrants in Kasap İlyas, especially in the second half of the nineteenth century, provide an exceptional case where the historical background and detailed documentation of an Ottoman urban migration process, albeit on very small scale, becomes possible. The mechanics of migration and integration into city-life (approximate dates of arrival to the city, particular household and family structures and living arrangements, acquisition of legal documents of residence in the city, relationships with the rest of the *mahalle*, occupational integration and social mobility, etc.) which applied to the Arapkirlis arriving to our neighborhood can be followed through documentary evidence. The chain-migration of the Arapkirlis to Istanbul and their quick integration into city-life is probably not a sui generis process and may perhaps be taken to constitute, in a nutshell, a sort of archetype for rural migration from Anatolia toward the Ottoman capital.

Ispanakçı Viranesi: Family Connections

Prior to that, however, some attention must be given to the historical background of a precise location situated within Kasap İlyas. There was indeed, in the *mahalle*, a particular area that was very densely populated by people originating from Arapkir and its surroundings toward the end of the nineteenth century. This site had, as a matter-of-fact, served as a well-defined and localized migrant-shelter to this group of people ever since the last decades of the eighteenth century. The formation process and the evolution of this migrant-shelter might possibly point toward a particular and interesting Istanbul/Ottoman model of rural migration, social mobility, and integration in urban life.

This portion of the Kasap İlyas *mahalle* where these Arapkirlis were concentrated was known as *Ispanakçı Viranesi*. The existence of this name is documented from the middle of the nineteenth century, and it appears as such in the official 1885 census documents. Elderly inhabitants still remember it today, and the location is still associated with the migrants from Arapkir. The area called *Ispanakçı Viranesi* was neither a particular street, nor a group of streets or a square but an irregular conglomerate of rather run-down houses that occupied a very large plot of land. This plot of land, situated at the nothernmost tip of our *mahalle*, was connected to Yokuşçeşme Street by a short and narrow passageway, the homonymous Ispanakçı Viranesi Street (Fig. 3.1).

According to the 1885 census, Ispanakçı Viranesi and Ispanakçı Viranesi streets together contained about thirty-five houses in which a total of 272 people, that is, about twenty-nine percent of the Muslim population of the neighborhood, was then living.[13] More than half of these residents of *Ispanakçı*

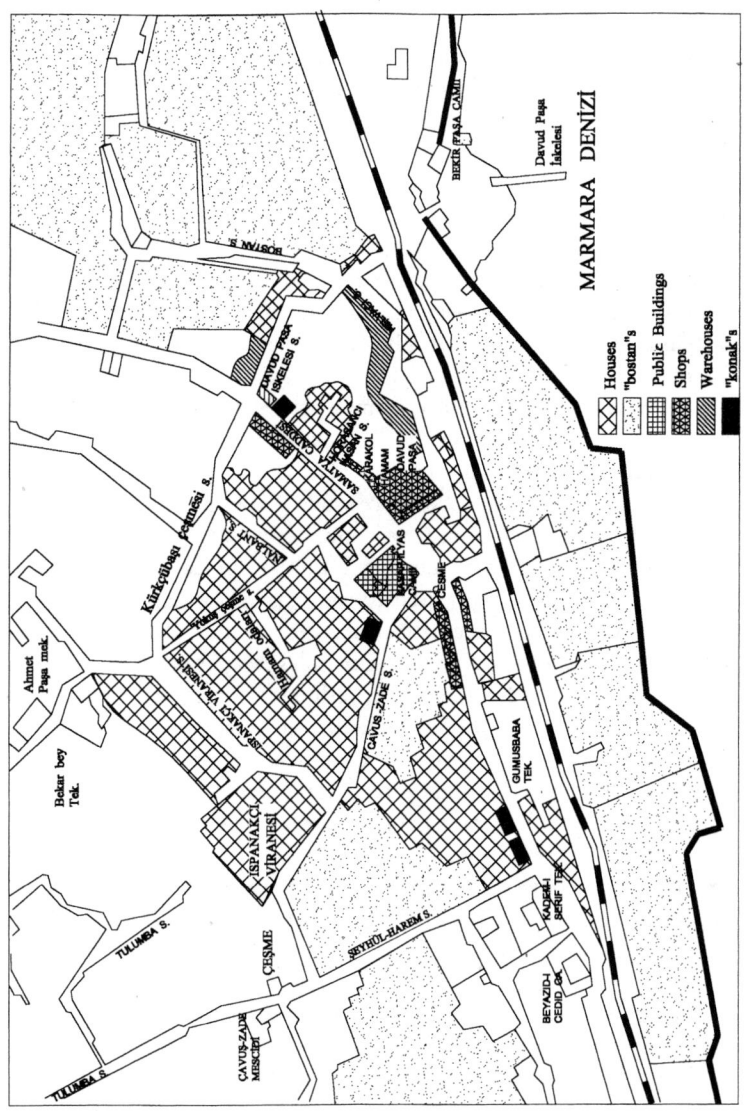

FIGURE 3.1 The Kasap İlyas Neighborhood in 1885

Viranesi had been born in or around Arapkir. Besides, in 1885, more than two thirds of the total number of Arapkirlis (i.e., those who were born in or around Arapkir) officially residing in the Kasap İlyas *mahalle* were living within *Ispanakçı Viranesi*. Rural migrants from a particular geographic region of the Ottoman Empire were therefore clustered in a portion of our neighborhood.

In Ottoman Istanbul, the term *Virane* (literally, ruins) usually designated a plot of land on which a house had been partly or totally destroyed by fire. The long-run implication of the usage of this term is that the burned-out plot of land has been thereafter either neglected, or completely abandoned by its legal owners. With the passage of time, this plot of land becomes eligible for parceling out, if not for outright and illegal occupation by a squatter settlement, and thus is a candidate for progressive slummification.

On the Ispanakçı Viranesi had formerly stood a mansion (*konak*) known as Ispanakçı Konağı that belonged to the Ispanakçı family, from which it had got its name. Some members of this family had close connections with Arapkir and its region. Ispanakçızâde Hâfız Mustafa Paşa (d. 1779) was the first owner of the Ispanakçı mansion. It was him, perhaps, who built or purchased it. Born in Erzurum, this high-ranking Ottoman official served first in the Topkapı Palace where he was raised to the rank of *kapıcıbaşı*. He was then named Paşa and was appointed superintendent of the silver mines (*maden emini*) of Ergani and Keban, barely twenty miles away from Arapkir. It is this last city that he chose as his permanent residence during his tenure of office in the silver mines. He was made a vizier in 1768 and appointed governor of Erzurum the next year. Governor of Damascus in 1773 and of Konya in 1774, he was dismissed the same year. Appointed governor of Bagdad in 1776, he was called back from his post a year later and was ordered to reside in Diyarbakır.

Ispanakçızâde Hâfız Mustafa Paşa must in some way have strongly displeased the imperial authorities of the capital, for he was executed in Diyarbakır in 1779. His body was brought to Istanbul and buried in the Kasap İlyas *mahalle*,[14] just a few paces from his own *konak*. His body was laid to rest in the garden of the small Abacızâde mosque and dervish convent (*tekke*), both of which were later completely destroyed by fire. This small convent, belonging to the Rufâî order of dervishes, was situated toward the upper end of Yokuşçeşme Street, at the northeasternly tip of the *mahalle*. In his exhaustive compendium of Istanbul mosques and shrines written in the 1770s, Ayvansarâyî Hâfız Hüseyin Efendi describes the location of the small Abacızâde *tekke* and *mescid* simply as "next to the Ispanakçızâde *konak*."[15] This means that the family house of the *Ispanakçızâde*s was already so well-known within Istanbul around 1770, that it could be used as a topographical landmark for describing the location of neighboring, and probably less prestigious, public and private buildings. Mustafa Paşa had therefore most certainly acquired the mansion that came to be known by his family name before his appointments to the provinces, perhaps in the 1750s or 1760s, while still a *kapıcıbaşı* at the Topkapı Palace. Ispanakçızâde Mustafa Paşa's family and dependents were indeed living in the *konak* at the time of his death.

It is Ispanakçızâde Hâfız Mustafa Paşa himself who provides the missing link between the Ispanakçı mansion and the migrant shelter peopled by the Arapkirlis that later took shape in the same location. What we know of Mustafa Paşa's career gives us clues as to the inception of the long-lasting connection between Kasap İlyas and the waves of migrants from Arapkir.

First of all, while on duty there, this high-ranking Ottoman official seems to have taken a liking to Arapkir and to its inhabitants. He undertook to act as a public benefactor of sorts, and, as some of the governors and grandees of the empire posted in the provinces used to do, tried to leave a lasting imprint on his town of residence. After the governor of the province of Sivas, whose seat of government, however was situated about a hundred miles away, he was the most powerful man in Arapkir. At the time when he was a superintendent of the silver mines of Ergani and Keban (certainly a very lucrative job), and a resident of the neighboring Arapkir, Ispanakçızâde Mustafa Paşa built a public library in this town. He also established and endowed a philanthropic foundation, again in Arapkir. The revenues of this *vakıf* were to be spent for the needs and the upkeep of the "Ispanakçızâde public library," as it later came to be known. This public library was, for some time, also used as a mosque, or rather as a prayer room, during the nineteenth century.[16]

Second, during his residence in Arapkir it is highly probable that Ispanakçızâde Mustafa Paşa surrounded himself with an immediate entourage composed of locals. His retinue, servants, followers, and workers of various sorts, were locally recruited. In fact, every vizier, governor, or grandee of the empire invariably had with him at the time such a retinue. This was a largely non-kin group of followers, a "large household" composed of servants, attendants, and personnel of various kinds. For a vizier or a governor, having such a large retinue was a necessity in the exercise of his official functions. It was obviously an outward sign of his social status too, as they helped him in both his public and his private affairs. With men of his retinue, the high-ranking Ottoman official acted both as an employer and as a promoter, a protector, and often as a lifelong patron.

In the seventeenth and eighteenth centuries many people sought such employment and for the protection that supposedly went with it. In a political body largely devoid of a land-based hereditary aristocracy like the Ottoman Empire, these patronage relationships were particularly crucial. Entering the service of a high-ranking official constituted, among other things, one of the main avenues for upward social mobility as well as for geographic mobility from the provincial centers to the capital. This was the case before the

Tanzimat reforms, which tried to centralize and standardize accession and promotion procedures within the state bureaucracy. In the pre-Tanzimat period, being part of a vizier's household was quite an enviable position.

The canonical model of the whole process was, obviously, the Imperial Palace, the Sultan's household, and the royal road to political power. This is reflected in the vocabulary used to describe such a widespread web of patronage relationships. People who were part of a high-ranking official's retinue were collectively called the the people at [the/his] gate (*kapı halkı*). The act of passing through that real and symbolic gate that led to being part of his household was, then, designated by a verb meaning to be affiliated to a gate (*kapılanmak*). Similarly, those who had already passed through the most prestigious of all of the symbolic gates, that which led to the imperial Palace and to being a modest member of the imperial household, were called the servants/slaves of the gate (*kapıkulu*).

This was the web of relationships in which Ispanakçızâde Hâfız Mustafa Paşa, vizier, governor of many Ottoman provinces, and owner of a large *konak* in Istanbul, found himself. It is more than probable that Mustafa Paşa, surrounded on all sides by Arapkirlis, exercised his patronage to promote their social and geographic mobility. Arapkir was, as we shall see, a city that had a long-standing local tradition of migration. Mustafa Paşa, as the benefactor of this town, also exercised his benevolence by encouraging or helping some of the citizens to move to the imperial capital. While in official duty and residence in Arapkir, some of his local protégés were brought or sent, either as butlers, lackeys, stablemen, gardeners, caretakers, or as servants of various kinds, to Mustafa Paşa's real and permanent household, that is, to the familial Ispanakçı *konak* in Kasap İlyas.

Those Arapkirlis who thus got to be "affiliated to Mustafa Paşa's gate" were housed either in his *konak* in Istanbul, or in its immediate vicinity. The first nucleus of migrants from Arapkir to the Kasap İlyas *mahalle* came to settle in or around the Ispanakçızâde mansion during the third quarter of the eighteenth century. They thus constituted a first small local center of attraction for a succession of migratory movements that were to last for more than a century and a half.

As to the Ispanakçızâde family *konak* itself, it did not survive its first owner for very long, as it was totally destroyed in the large Istanbul fire that wrought havoc in our neighborhood in 1782, just three years after Mustafa Paşa' execution. The existing documents strongly suggest that Ispanakçızâde Hâfız Mustafa Paşa's family left the *mahalle* after the fire, and that the family mansion was never rebuilt. The records have kept a few traces of his son and of some of his grandsons. One of his sons, İbrahim Yümnî Paşa had a military career and died in Van in 1819. A younger son and two grandsons Tahir Mehmet bey (d. 1843), Mustafa İzzet Efendi (d.1862), and Cemaleddin

İbrahim Efendi (d. 1888) became *ulema*s,[17] that is, they were members of the official religious hierarchy. We do not know for certain whether any of the descendants continued to live in or around Kasap İlyas. If they did, there are no traces. None of the members of the Ispanakçızâde family were buried in or anywhere near the Kasap İlyas *mahalle*, anyway.

Besides, there is no trace in the local documents of another *konak* having ever been built in the same location. A court case dated November 1809, for instance, mentions the existence of "a plot of land belonging to the inheritors of Ispanakçıbaşı" in the *mahalle*.[18] Thirty years after his death, the family name of the first owner of the *konak* had been almost forgotten by the locals (Ispanakçıbaşı instead of Ispanakçızâde). But the plot of land on which the Ispanakçızâde Mustafa Paşa's mansion had formerly stood had not yet been totally neglected or abandoned by his descendants, who still claimed ownership. Indeed, the term *virane*, bearing the connotation of a general neglect, does not appear in the records before the middle of the nineteenth century. The migrants from Arapkir were already in the *mahalle*, though, and long before the census of 1885, the records bear traces of their presence.

The Arapkirlis—A Migratory Tradition in the Nineteenth Century

From the end of the eighteenth century on, the presence of Arapkirlis in Kasap İlyas is abundantly recorded in official documents. The death of Ispanakçızâde Mustafa Paşa, the destruction of his *konak* in the fire of 1782, and the subsequent dispersal of his family did not deter migrant Arapkirlis from coming to our neighborhood. Their effective concentration within the Ispanakçı Viranesi cannot be documented before the 1885 census, but the Davudpaşa court records refers to many of these Arapkirlis who appealed to the court or were called to testify in their capacity of inhabitants of Kasap İlyas throughout the nineteenth century.

As early as 1785, for instance, the inheritance of a native of Ağın living in Kasap İlyas is the object of litigation and was brought to the Davudpaşa Court. The way in which the deceased person is mentioned in the *Sicil* (religious court record) is typical: "... Hüseyin beşe bin Abdullah, a seller of charcoal, originating from the village of Pezenka(?), a dependance of Ağın, who died a while ago as a resident of the Kasap İlyas *mahalle*...."[19] A few years later, in 1792, the court recorded a deed of sale concerning a piece of agricultural land. This field, situated in a village called Bostancık near Arapkir was being sold for the sum of forty-eight *kuruş*. The buyer and the seller were residents of Kasap İlyas, and they were both Arapkirlis.[20] The manner in which these two Arapkirlis are recorded in the *Sicil* stresses equally their place of residence and their place of origin. This 1792 record tells us that the seller of the field was "... Kara Ahmet bin Mehmet, from the village named Bostancık, a dependance of Arapkir in Anatolia, and a resident of the Kasap İlyas mahalle near the Davudpaşa wharf, ..." and the buyer "... İbrahim beşe bin Abdurrahman, from the same village...."[21]

Throughout the nineteenth century, the Davudpaşa Religious Court records contain many more instances where residents of the Kasap İlyas *mahalle*, qualified as people from Arapkir (*Arapkir ahâlisinden*) appear either as plaintiffs or as witnesses.[22] In all of them, the Arapkirlis are designated by their place of origin. The records include cases of divorce, of inheritance with litigation, registrations of powers of attorney as well as a number of registrations of deeds of sale of land in or around Arapkir, and so forth. Toward the end of the nineteenth century, approximately one inhabitant of Kasap İlyas out of four was born in or around Arapkir and about two thirds of these Arapkirlis were located in the Ispanakçı Viranesi.

The French Orientalist and geographer Vital Cuinet, in his monumental four-volume work on the economic, social, and human geography of the Asian part of the Ottoman Empire published in the 1890s, devotes a whole chapter to the province of Mamuretülaziz, of which Arapkir was a district (*kazâ*). One of his comments on the inhabitants of the district of Arapkir is another confirmation of our observations in the small Kasap İlyas *mahalle*:

> Immigration—Most of the inhabitants of the rural areas of Arapkir, either because of the prevailing low level of wages and of frequent unemployment, or perhaps because they prefer to have other kinds of occupations, often migrate to Constantinople or to other large cities, so that there are practically no important urban centers where one does not meet a few *Arapkirlis*.[23]

Arapkir and the surrounding area were the point of departure of a real migratory tradition. Quite a few of the migrants from Arapkir and from its surroundings became prominent political, artistic, and literary figures in the Ottoman Empire and in republican Turkey. Yusuf Kâmil Paşa (1808–1876), Grand Vizier in 1862, was born in Arapkir. So was Dr. Abdullah Cevdet (1869-1932), one of the founders of the Party for Union and Progress. Such important republican political figures as Refik Koraltan (1889–1974) and Şemsettin Günaltay (1883–1961), prime minister in the late 1940s, had moved from Arapkir to Istanbul just before the end of the nineteenth century.

Such well-known Arapkirlis as Osman Nuri Ergin (1883–1961), Ismail Saib Sencer (1873–1940), and Sedat Çetintaş (1889–1965) became an integral part of Istanbul's artistic and intellectual scenery, on which each left a particular imprint. Osman Nuri Ergin was born in Malatya and came to Istanbul when he was ten years old. He worked all his life in the Istanbul municipality, and became the Secretary General, a post that he occupied for twenty-two years. His numerous works and publications on Istanbul are a very substantial contribution to the history of the city, and they are still very widely referred to by urban historians. Ismail Saib Sencer also had been born into a family of Arapkirlis. A very cultured individual, he served for more than twenty years as head librarian of the largest public library of Istanbul. As for Sedat Çetintaş, another native of Arapkir, he was an architect and worked as a restorator of historical monuments. He planned the repair, conservation, and restoration of many historical sites and monuments of his city of adoption. Except for Ismail Saib Sencer, however, we have no evidence as to whether any of these figures lived in or anywhere near Kasap İlyas.[24] Kasap İlyas was probably not the only point of landing in Istanbul for the newcoming Arapkirlis.

Arapkir's rural hinterland was probably not very prosperous in the eighteenth and nineteenth centuries. As to the town itself, Cuinet estimates its population at 20,000 in 1892. Arapkir does not seem to have grown much during the nineteenth century, although its cotton cloth manufacturing industry was expanding. An estimate for the 1830s had put the population of the city at about 15,000 people.[25] In 1930 Arapkir became a district of the Turkish republican province of Malatya. Its population had by then fallen to only 8,000, according to the first republican census of 1927.

The city of Arapkir itself was, in the nineteenth century, best known for its production of two particular types of thick cotton cloth called *manusa* and *kezi*. Weaving developed in Arapkir after the 1820s and 1830s and mostly used imported British cotton yarn.[26] Cuinet tells us that there were no large-scale manufacturers in town and that the production of these local cottonades was put out by local traders to hundreds of spinners, dyers, and weavers who worked at home. The final product was then exported, mostly to Iraq, Syria, Lebanon, and to other cities of the eastern Mediterranean, through the ports of Beirut and Alexandretta. Arapkir is said to have contained up to a thousand looms in the late nineteenth century. Cuinet gives 75,000 meters as being the total yearly output of *manusa* cotton cloth in Arapkir.[27] Forty years after Cuinet, a local historian from Malatya complained in the 1930s: "Most of the male inhabitants of Arapkir frequently leave their home town in order to earn a living and help the families left behind."[28] In the meantime, local textile products had been isolated from their traditional eastern and southern outlets by the First World War and by the border changes that followed. The import of British cotton yarn had ceased for the same reason, and production had greatly declined.

As for the neighboring town of Keban, the town with the silver mines—one of the superintendents of which, in the second half of the eighteenth century, had been Ispanakçızâde Hâfız Mustafa Paşa—it did not fare much better. The extraction of silver was totally abandoned in the early 1870s, the inhabitants progressively left and, as Cuinet indicates in 1892, the prosperous town "which contained 3,000 houses has today only 300."[29]

To summarize, during the third quarter of the eighteenth century, the retinue of an Ottoman Paşa and a governor of the provinces posted in Arapkir, and the personnel of his *konak* in the capital had made up the first nucleus of the large group of migrants whose descendants, more than a century later, came to be counted as residents of Kasap İlyas in the 1885 census. The flow of migrants from that small district of east-central Anatolia to the small Kasap İlyas *mahalle* in Istanbul continued, for all we know, for almost two centuries.

Notwithstanding their progressive and successful integration into urban life, their being Arapkirlis remained part of the identity of the migrants and of their descendents. Whether these Arapkirlis ever met with reactions of resistance or of rejection coming from the urbanites of Kasap İlyas or from those of Istanbul at large, has not transpired into the documents. However, it is highly unlikely that such a specific cultural "urbanite-peasant" rift could have been part of the urban culture of eighteenth- and nineteenth-century Istanbul. "Urban problems" were then perceived as almost exclusively connected with security, political troubles, and deviant morals. And on all of these counts, the group of migrant Arapkirlis who settled in Kasap İlyas performed quite well. Besides, it is not in a peripheral, almost semirural neighborhood of Istanbul such as the Kasap İlyas *mahalle* that this sociological duality, if any, would have first been felt and voiced.

Fruit Vendors and Civil Servants: Provincials and Arapkirlis in 1885

The residential and occupational patterns of the Arapkirlis living in Kasap İlyas can best be documented through the information provided by the late Ottoman census of 1885. Most of these Arapkirlis were of rural origin. Together with that of the district, the name of the village from which the migrants came is also often mentioned in the census documents or in the Sharia' court records. Precise village names like Bostancık, Saldak, Mutmur, Alıçlı, and Hasdek often occur in the *muhtar*'s notebooks as well. Once in the city, and with the help of networks established by their Arapkirli co-locals, many of them went directly into a "semi-agricultural" occupation, the itinerant vending of fruits and vegetables. Clearly, the sources of approvisioning for their merchandise, the Langa vegetable gardens, and their extensions into the *mahalle*, were within reach.

A Case in Chain-Migration

One important feature of the Arapkirli migrants to Kasap İlyas, that concerning their duration of stay, must be made clear. The Arapkirlis did not migrate to Istanbul as seasonal workers or just for a limited short period of time. They did not come with the idea of a certain return to the home town or village with their accumulated savings. First of all, traveling all the way from the region of Arapkir to Istanbul was a long and complicated affair. At least until about the end of the nineteenth century, it involved first a trek northward through unpaved, mountainous, and difficult roads to one of the Black Sea ports, and then a trip by boat to the capital. The whole trip from Arapkir to Istanbul (ten to twelve hours by coach, today) used to take no less than three weeks.

For instance, when, in 1833, Yusuf bin Hüseyin, a rather well-to-do Arapkirli living in the Kasap İlyas *mahalle* planned a visit to the family, back in the Ömeran village near Arapkir, he correctly predicted a pretty long absence. He therefore left the *imam* Aziz Mahmud efendi in charge of all of his business in Istanbul and gave him a wide-ranging power of attorney, which he regularly registered with the Davudpaşa Court.[30] Obviously, short-term "commuting," or undertaking the whole travel for a relatively short period of time—say, just a summer season—was almost unthinkable at the time.

In fact, the Arapkirlis in Kasap İlyas constituted a typical case of *chain-migration*—as opposed to the mass-migrations caused by wars and by the shrinking empire in the nineteenth century—and they shared the main characteristics of that migration pattern.

With chain-migration, potential migrants first acquire information about their destination and then, upon arrival, are supported by their kin or by their co-locals who preceded them. This leads to clustering of kin and co-locals within the city. Besides, it implies that relations with the place of origin will continue. If urban opportunities do not prove promising, a return is always possible, especially if the migrants still possess a claim to land in the village of origin. If prospects are good, then the settler will constitute a new link in the chain. Chain-migration may also increase the interdependence between city and country by making migration more sensitive to economic conditions, both at the point of departure and at the point of arrival.

Unlike mass-migration, chain-migration also leads to a greater density of relations between those sharing a similar position in the city. The migration chain being based on kinship and/or co-locality, once in the city these webs of relations breed informal networks, since preexisting urban formal structures fail to provide the minimum necessities of survival. Not surprisingly, chain-migration also results in co-locals concentrating in similar professional groups. In the late nineteenth century, just as a century later, place of origin was the most effective marker determining the composition of informal networks in the Istanbul.[31] Each Arapkirli who came to Kasap İlyas as part of this co-local network could then settle without experiencing a sense of alienation. The Arapkirli newcomers had "patrons" who had previously migrated from the same town or village, and this cushion helped to avoid the competition and the resistance, if any, of the Istanbulites.

Family and kinship relations are one of the most important assets that the rural migrants bring with them. Contrary to mass-migration, chain-migration is by nature selective. Therefore kinship structures and relations cannot be transplanted intact from the village to the city. Not surprisingly, the kinship relations of the Arapkirlis settled in Istanbul exhibit different forms and densities as compared to that in their place of origin. The size and kin-composition of the Arapkirli households are indeed quite particular and resemble neither that of the sedentary Istanbulites nor that of other groups of immigrants in Kasap İlyas (see chapter 4).

The Arapkirlis of Kasap İlyas did not sever their links with their place of origin. Apart from the support that the newcomers received from their fellow-citizens already settled in Kasap İlyas, many of them maintained, at least for some time, strong links with Arapkir, despite the distance. For instance, they bought and sold pieces of land in their town or village of origin. At least four such deeds of sale were recorded by the Davudpaşa Court in the first half of the nineteenth century. Some Arapkirlis had their family back home arrange a marriage with someone from the same town or village, brought their wife to Istanbul, and perhaps went back to visit the family once or twice. And this tightly knit migrant community (they still showed, toward the end of the nineteenth century, a surprisingly high level of local endogamy) lived in close proximity within our *mahalle*.

Neighborhood Localization

Contrary to other groups of rural migrants to the Ottoman capital,[32] the Arapkirlis were not transient, temporary, or seasonal migrants. They brought with them their family—mostly of a nuclear type (see chapter 4). Using the data of the 1885 census in Kasap İlyas, we have looked at the birth dates and birthplaces of various family members of Arapkirli households in order to approximate the date of arrival in Istanbul of each and every Arapkirli living in the neighborhood. What we found was that their average length of stay was very long indeed. We were able to approximate the dates of arrival to Istanbul (though, of course, not always and not necessarily to Kasap İlyas) of only seventy-two natives of Arapkir living in 1885 in the Kasap İlyas *mahalle*. Twenty-seven of these seventy-two Arapkirlis (i.e., about 37.5 percent) had arrived before 1875 and had therefore spent, at the time of the census, more than ten years in the capital-city. The flow of Arapkirlis continued well into the twentieth century. Using the data of the last Ottoman population census of 1907 we found the approximate date of arrival to the capital of thirteen household heads born in Arapkir or its environs. Ten of them had been residing in Istanbul for eight years or more.

In 1885, 470 of the 925 (50.8 percent) Muslim inhabitants of Kasap İlyas had been born in Istanbul. The rate is lower for household heads, adult males for the most part. Sixty-two percent of the household heads living in Kasap İlyas had been born in the provinces (see table 3.1). In 1885 about one Muslim resident of Kasap İlyas out of five, and almost one household head out of three had migrated from Arapkir and from its immediate surroundings. In the last Ottoman population census of 1907, 14.7 percent of the *mahalle*'s population and 22.2 percent of its household heads were born in or around Arapkir.

Kasap İlyas was, and in a sense still is, deeply marked by the presence of these migrants from Arapkir and from its surroundings. This was always acknowledged in our interviews with elderly people from the *mahalle*. A second-generation migrant from Arapkir was elected headman (*muhtar*), served for more than twenty years and is still remembered as the best headman the neighborhood had in the twentieth century (see the appendix).

As far as we can judge from the oral testimony of their children and grandchildren and of other elderly people who lived in the *mahalle* in the first half of the twentieth century, it appears that the first-generation Arapkir migrants who came to settle in our neighborhood belonged, for the most part, to the heterodox and liberal muslim *Alevi* sect, at that time (pejoratively)

TABLE 3.1
Birthplaces of Muslim Population and
Household Heads in Kasap İlyas (1885)

Birthplace	Population		Household Heads	
	N	%	N	%
Istanbul	470	50.8	88	36.4
Rumelia	104	11.2	26	10.7
Arapkir	140	15.1	56	23.1
Malatya, Arguvan, etc.	31	3.4	14	5.8
Anatolia (other)	50	5.4	29	12.0
"Circassia"	36	3.9	4	1.7
"Arabia," "Sudan," and "Ethiopia"	50	5.4	11	4.5
Other	18	1.9	7	2.9
Unknown	26	2.8	7	2.9
TOTAL	925	100.0	242	100.0

qualified as *Kızılbaş*. These Alevis, who were not mainstream Sunni Muslims, were spread over a large portion of central and eastern Anatolia. Cuinet estimates that, toward the end of the nineteenth century, the population of the district (*kazâ*) of Arapkir, as well as that of the neighboring districts of Eğin, Malatya, and Keban contained about one third of Alevis (Kizil-Bach, as he names them) and about 10 percent of ethnic Kurds, which he classifies apart from other Muslims, be they Sunni or Alevi.[33]

Just like their rural/peasant origins, however, neither the religious beliefs nor the ethnic origin of the Arapkirli seem to have caused friction or raised any serious problems of cohabitation within the Kasap İlyas *mahalle*. The aforementioned elected *muhtar*, for instance, was an Alevî whose father had migrated from Arapkir, probably in the 1870s or 1880s.[34] The *muhtar* himself had been born in Kasap İlyas—in *Ispanakçı Viranesi*, to be more precise. "*The Arapkirlis and my husband's family had been living in this mahalle and in the Ispanakçı Viranesi for three centuries*," declared his widow in an interview in an attempt at bridging the gap between the assumed provincialism of her husband's family, and a well-justified sense of local identity within Istanbul.[35]

> Kasap İlyas was a neighborhood where we lived with the Alevis in perfect harmony, especially when you think of the Ispanakçı Viranesi.... We had excellent relationships with them, and never called them Kızılbaş.... My mother had given help to many women that lived in the Virane... they were poor and honest people... the men there sold fruits, melons and watermelons with a cart... later, some of them became taxi drivers," declared another of our elderly local informants.

Clearly, the suggestion is that life in Istanbul, and the tolerance shown to them in Kasap İlyas had somehow redeemed the provincialism and the religious heterodoxy of the Arapkirlis of his childhood years.[36] "They all came from the East but they nevertheless lived in perfect harmony with the neighborhood... most of them were fruit and vegetable sellers, they worked in the vegetable gardens down there and gathered and sold the products of the bostans" another elderly former inhabitant of Kasap İlyas told us.[37] All of these informants were referring to the situation prevailing in the 1930s and 1940s as personal eyewitnesses, and to even earlier periods, of which they were informed by hearsay.

The Arapkir-born population of the Kasap İlyas *mahalle* in 1885 was almost evenly divided between males and females (72 men and 68 women). This is yet another indication about the type of migrants who had been coming from the region of Arapkir. Males of working age were not the only ones involved. The high rate of regional endogamy that prevailed suggests that family and permanent migration had always been prevalent. That couples were formed or reunited after the initial move of one of the members to Istanbul is not to be ignored. The group of Arapkirlis living in Kasap İlyas in 1885 includes cases of single men who had married women born in Istanbul after having settled down in Kasap İlyas as well as cases of men who had married a fellow-citizen and had their children once in Istanbul.

There were in all 62 Arapkir-born and married male household heads living in the Kasap İlyas *mahalle* in 1885. Forty-six of these male Arapkirlis (74.2%) were married to women born in the same town/village, and the rest, that is, 16 of them, had been wed to women born in Istanbul. The picture is reversed, however, when we look at the children born to these couples. Among the forty six regionally endogamous Arapkirli couples living in Kasap İlyas in 1885, thirty five had children. The majority of the children, however, had been born in Istanbul. Only nine of these thirty five couples had moved from Arapkir with their children whereas in twenty six cases the Arapkirli wives had given birth to their children in the capital.

We shall examine more closely the family structures that prevailed among this group of migrants. Intermarriage seems to have been rather unusual, at least for the first- and second-generation migrants from Arapkir. This is further exemplified by the table showing the distribution of the birthplaces of spouses living in Kasap İlyas in 1885 (see chapter 4), and confirmed by oral testimonies.

As we have already stressed, the Arapkirlis of the Kasap İlyas *mahalle* had another very important characteristic in 1885: they all lived very close to each other. The *mahalle* covered an area crossed by a total of fourteen streets and blind alleys. 117 out of a total of 140 people born in Arapkir (i.e., 83.5%) were packed into a single location, the Ispanakçı Viranesi and into the small street leading to it (Ispanakçı Viranesi *sokağı*). The same street and plot also housed 10 of the 31 people who were born in the districts surrounding Arapkir (see table 3.1). Three quarters of all of the Arapkirlis living in the Kasap İlyas *mahalle* were settled in the land where the charred remnants of Ispanakçızâde Mustafa Paşa's *konak* had stood just about a century ago (see the map).

The *Virane*, as it was often called, was a rather crowded area. Two hundred seventy two people lived there in 1885, that is, almost 30 percent of the neighborhood population. More than half of the *Virane*'s inhabitants had been born in or around Arapkir. There was, to our knowledge, no other community of the same type within the Kasap İlyas *mahalle*, that is, no other identifiable group of co-locals sharing an identical religious/ethnic background and living in close proximity within the neighborhood. Of the 56 household heads who had been born in Arapkir (see table 3.1), no less than 47 lived in the *Virane* in 1885, which contained in all 75 households. Four other households were headed by men born in districts near Arapkir. More than two thirds of household heads established in this specific area (51 out of 75) were therefore Arapkirlis.

Besides, some of the houses situated in the Ispanakçı Viranesi were apparently functioning almost exclusively as a sort of home for the newcomers from Arapkir. In the house at 3 Ispanakçı Viranesi, for instance, lived no less than 15 people in 1885, among which were a few single males but also some small nuclear households. These people had all been born in or around Arapkir. Some of them had moved in this house upon their arrival to the *mahalle*, and then moved out within a short period of time, which induces us to conclude that this house must have functioned as a sort of transiting premise, a temporary welcoming area for the poorest or most destitute of the Arapkirlis who came to Kasap İlyas. Other houses in the same area were also being rented to the Arapkirlis alone.

A patent example is provided by the houses in Ispanakçı Viranesi that belonged to one Yeşilin Mehmet Efendi.[38] This person did not reside in the neighborhood, as he does not appear in the 1885 census documents, but, according to the *muhtar*'s property lists, he owned no less than ten houses, large and small, all of them situated within the Ispanakçı Viranesi. In these ten houses lived, at the time of the census, no less than 45 people, all of them Arapkirlis. One third of the migrants from Arapkir living in the Virane were therefore paying rent to Yeşilin Mehmed Efendi, the absentee landlord who made a living by renting out his run-down houses to the poor and needy migrants.[39]

The Arapkirli community living in the Ispanakçı Viranesi showed, not surprisingly, a very high degree of regional endogamy. Eighty-five percent (40 out of 47) of the Arapkir-born male household heads living in the Virane were married to women also born in Arapkir. This rate of endogamy was only fifty nine percent for the province-born household heads of the *mahalle* in general.

It is certainly the presence of so many migrant Arapkirlis that gave Ispanakçı Viranesi its poor and highly provincial character within the *mahalle*. 61.4 percent of the inhabitants of the Virane had indeed been born in the provinces of the empire, as opposed to only 49 percent for the population of Kasap İlyas as a whole, as well as more than 80 percent of its household heads (63.8 percent for the whole of Kasap İlyas). The Istanbul born were a small minority in the Virane, and most of these were children of the Arapkirlis anyway, second-generation Arapkirlis themselves. Another of our elderly informants from Kasap İlyas gave us a colorful description of what the Ispanakçı Viranesi and its migrant settlers must have meant for the *mahalle* toward the end of the nineteenth century:

> ... They were all poor people ... they sold vegetables, worked as street-porters here and there, or carried sand and gravel on their

backs from the wharf... not only single young men, but also whole families were living in the Ispanakçı Viranesi, whole families that had been there for more than ten or twenty years... the houses in the Virane were all small, single storey and run down... people had come there from places in the East such as Malatya, Arapkir...."[40]

Occupations and Integration: "Nonguild Labor"

According to the census returns, 259 people in the *mahalle* had regular occupations in 1885 (see table 3.2). Of these, 254 were men. Of the 5 women whose occupation was clearly specified, 4 were living as "servants" within various households in the neighborhood. As to Fatma Şerife hanım (aged sixty, and living at 15 Hamam Odaları Street), she was a midwife, a *kabile*.

Artisans and shopkeepers were a majority in Kasap İlyas (52.9 % of all declared occupations). The next largest group was that of civil servants. Most of these were lower- and middle-echelon scribes and bureaucrats, as seen from their official position, put down in the census register in most cases as *kâtip* (scribe) or *ketebeden* (one of the scribes). But in 1885 some really high-echelon military bureaucrats also lived in their *konak*s on Samatya Avenue (formerly "Butchers' Road"). At 64 Samatya Avenue Şevket Paşa (1824–1890), a *şeyhülharem* (guardian of Mecca and Medina) and former cabinet minister, lived with his family, and 5 Samatya Avenue was the residence of Ahmet Faik Paşa, a retired army general, aged seventy-five at the time of the census. Sadettin Bey (later Paşa), a colonel on duty with the General Staff of the Ottoman army, lived with his family in the mansion at 62 Kasap İlyas' main street.

TABLE 3.2
Occupations of the Residents in the Kasap İlyas *Mahalle* (1885)

Military	10
Civil Servants	49
High-ranking Bureaucrats	3
Clergy	3
Wage Earners	15
Artisans/Shopkeepers	137
Trade and Commerce	1
Retired	10
Other	31
TOTAL	259

Source: 1885 Census Roster for the Kasap İlyas *mahalle* [Atik Defter 14]

The "wage earners" category in this table includes all those who were paid wages but who, apparently, did not work for the government. As to the "others" category, it includes such undefined and unclassifiable statuses and occupations as *teb'asından, mensubatından,* and *çavuş*. Ten people in the *mahalle* were classified as *sa'il, se'eleden,* or *fukara*. These were apparently making a living by begging. They all lived either in the Virane or in one of the streets between Samatya Avenue and the Davudpaşa wharf. They have been included in the "others" category.

Within the large and heterogenous category of artisans/shopkeepers, the numerically most important subgroup was that of the *küfeci* or *manav küfecisi*. There were 51 of them in Kasap İlyas, making up 37.2 percent of the total occupational category. A *küfe* is a large and deep basket, usually to be carried on the back. *Küfeci* is the person who carries this basket for a living. That person might be either a street-porter or an ambulant vendor of various goods. A *manav küfecisi* would be the person who carries and sells fruits and vegetables with the *küfe*. The Kasap İlyas listings, however, always clearly differentiate itinerant fresh fruit and vegetable vendors (*manav küfecisi*s) from ordinary street-porters (*hamal küfecisi*s). Not surprisingly, given the proximity of the *bostan*s, the *küfeci*s in Kasap İlyas were almost all street vendors of fresh fruits and vegetables. Almost one out of every five adult male resident whose occupation was known earned his living as an itinerant fruit vendor.

In 1885, next to this large number of street peddlers of fruits and vegetables there lived in Kasap İlyas only one single fruit shop owner (*manav*) and one wholesaler of fruits and vegetables (*kabzımal*). The owner of the fruit shop (a native of Arapkir), however, must have had his shop elsewhere, since there was no such greengrocer in our neighborhood at the time. The proximity of the large *bostan*s would indeed have made such a shop redundant. As to the wholesaler of fruits and vegetables, his warehouse was near Yemiş İskelesi, the wharf on the Golden Horn where imported fresh or dried fruits and vegetables were usually brought.

After the ambulant fruit and vegetable vendors, the next two largest groups of street peddlers living in Kasap İlyas were the porters (*hamal* or *hamal küfecisi*), with 10 members, and the old-clothes-men (*koltukçu*), with 9. The itinerant fruit and vegetable vendors (51), plus the street-porters (10) and the old-clothes-men (9) thus made up more than half of the artisan/tradesmen/shopkeepers category. This group, the backbone of the non-wage-earning population of Kasap İlyas in 1885, was clearly neither well educated nor well-off.

An "Informal Sector" Activity: Ambulant Fruit Vending

Communications were slow and scarce at the time and most of the fresh fruits and vegetables consumed within the city of Istanbul necessarily came from the many local vegetable gardens and orchards due to the absence of appropriate means of conservation. These were all within the walled city itself, or in its immediate surroundings. One of the largest *bostan*s within Istanbul was that of Langa, just to the east of Kasap İlyas. In the city, most of the fruit and vegetable sellers were of an itinerant type, and it is they who carried and marketed fresh fruits and vegetables to the areas where there were no nearby *bostan*s. Stable vegetable and fruit shops were relatively few. Besides, the job of itinerant peddling of fresh fruits and vegetables was not a seasonal job. In the *bostan*s, some of which could specialize in the cultivation of a particular product, usually every fruit and vegetable for which there was a demand was planted and reaped in its own season. The marketing and sales activities could therefore proceed all-year-round.

The itinerant vending of fresh fruits and vegetables was neither a difficult, specialized occupation, nor one that required a special or formal training, or a permit or a license. To sell vegetables and fruits in the streets of Istanbul there was no need to go through a particular apprenticeship. Carrying and/or selling ordinary merchandise was the simplest thing any newly arriving and nonqualified rural migrant could expect to do once settled in the capital, with a bit of luck, or thanks to the help of his connections and network. The irregular and ambulant peddling of some well-known and easily sellable consumption goods at a small profit was, and still is, an easily accessible "poor man's trade." In the less-developed countries of the twenty-first century, street trading still remains a preferential point of entry for rural migrants into the working life of the big city, but it is also a lifetime activity for many of the urban working poor.[41]

Contrary to the stable greengrocers, the itinerant fruit vendors of Ottoman Istanbul had no particular guild organization. The total number of these itinerant vendors have therefore never been limited by municipal regulations, or by the practice of *gedik*.[42] The practice of *gedik* designates the existence of a *numerus clausus* in the right to set up a particular kind of shop in a given locality.[43] To exercise the profession of ambulant vending of fruits and vegetables did not require a considerable amount of initial capital endowment either. Obviously, no insuperable technological barriers were involved. These fruit and vegetable vendors lived, understandably, not very far from their sources of provisioning. Then, they either bought their goods on credit from the owner or manager of the *bostan*, whom they paid after cashing the proceeds of their trade, or had the necessary connections to obtain a sufficient amount of initial investment finance.

What the occupation of itinerant vending of fresh fruits and vegetables in Istanbul certainly did require, however, was the possession of one crucial asset: a solid network of personal relations. This was probably a sine qua non condition that compensated for the apparent relative ease of entry to the trade and sealed it off to "outsiders" or to any other type of nondesirables. There certainly existed a web of partnership deals and arrangements by which the various trading routes, market outlets, and potential customer neighborhoods in Istanbul were already shared and apportioned between different groups of itinerant vendors. Established credit and payment deals, pricing arrangements between the sellers (*küfeci*s) and the producers (the *bostancı*s, "the owners or managers of vegetable gardens") were also setting precedents for future pricing and distribution practices. It is also likely that fresh fruits and vegetables were sold at a lower price by these informal sector itinerant sellers, as compared to their competitors, the formal segment of the trade, that is, the stable-and tax- and rent-paying greengrocer shops.

Such a thing as an absolutely free entry to the trade of itinerant fresh fruit and vegetable vending could not have existed in Istanbul. Entry into the trade was dependent upon access to some nonprofessional, informal, and primary networks such as kinship or fellow-citizenship. This type of a solidarity network, if strongly based on fellow-citizenship, would obviously function in the long run as a means of encouraging and facilitating migration to the city and of easing the urban insertion and integration of newcomers. That is precisely how a chain-migration process functions in the long run.

And this is precisely the kind of network that the fellow-citizens coming from Arapkir and from its environs who settled in Kasap İlyas *mahalle* were forming in 1885. Of the fifty eight natives of Arapkir whose occupations were clearly specified in the census documents, forty five were classified as *küfeci* (77.5 percent). Forty-five out of the fifty one fruit and vegetable vendors living in Kasap İlyas in 1885 had therefore been born in Arapkir. Two others were natives of the neighboring district of Arguvan. Besides, almost all of them were living within the Ispanakçi Viranesi.

All of this cannot, obviously, be just coincidental. All too clearly, coresidence in a subunit of a neighborhood and the practice of an identical trade constituted, for the poor and mostly Alevî migrants from Arapkir and its surroundings, a preferential mode of insertion and integration into city life. This was not new in 1885, and the chain-migration process had certainly been going on for a number of generations. Understandably, the "soft landing" opportunities and the support system provided by the already established fellow-citizens in Kasap İlyas encouraged the migrants from Arapkir to bring their families with them, or to establish a new one in Istanbul. As it still is the case today, migration to Istanbul and settlements in the city in past centuries could and did follow patterns of regional or religious allegiances and solidarities. Co-locality and kinship were, then as now, the guiding principles.

The economic activities of the Arapkirlis in Kasap İlyas are indeed a recognizable ancestor of what later came to be called the "informal sector" in the less-developed countries of the late twentieth century. In the economic development literature, belonging to the "informal"—or "marginal"—sector is defined as a way of doing things characterized by ease of entry, reliance on family-owned and indigenous resources, small scale of operation, use of labor intensive technologies with skills acquired outside the formal schooling system, and unregulated and competitive markets.[44] Besides, the primary objective of informal sector activities is to generate employment for the participants rather than to maximize profits. Some of these characteristics of informality may have to be qualified with the adverb "relatively" but, clearly, the definition broadly applies to the migrant Arapkirli network in Kasap İlyas in the nineteenth century.

The legal and social status of the itinerant vending of fresh fruits and vegetables in nineteenth-century Istanbul had apparently not greatly changed from what it was back in the second half of the seventeenth century, as described by Robert Mantran.[45] The "informality" we have observed in the second half of the nineteenth century had in fact been there for at least two centuries. According to Mantran, some members of the Janissary corps based in Istanbul were at that time actively helping some of their fellow citizens to start a trade of street vending, mostly of fruits, vegetables, yogurt, and water. These Janissaries were apparently also keeping "nondesirables" from exercising the same trade. The absence of legal barriers to entry to the trade was, in the seventeenth century as in the middle of the nineteenth, more than compensated by other, nonlegal—but certainly as efficient—screening procedures.

Once settled in the city, other avenues for urban integration were obviously also open. Among the natives of Arapkir living in Kasap İlyas in 1885 there were five households where both father and son(s) were working as *küfeci*s. In one of these households, located in the Ispanakçi Viranesi, both the father, aged 44, and the three sons, all born in Arapkir and aged respectively 19, 17, and 11, were listed as *küfeci*s.

It is noteworthy that none of the natives of Arapkir and of its environs, most of whom were of rural origin, had been qualified as a *rençber* (a day laborer or a farmhand—a denomination that necessarily implies agricultural work) in the 1885 census documents. There were two *rençber*s in the 1885 census listings of Kasap İlyas, and both were working in the nearby *bostan*s. None of them, however, had been born anywhere near Arapkir. This can be considered a sure indication of the pretty rapid occupational integration of the Arapkirlis into the urban economic tissue. The well-established *küfeci* network, which distributed fruits and vegetables in the urban economy, provided to the newcoming Arapkirli a means of fast economic insertion. The Arapkirli rural migrant was indeed a *rençber* himself. Besides, the transportation and itinerant selling of fresh fruits and vegetables obviously was an occupation not too removed from direct agricultural work. Nevertheless, the fruit-vending Arapkirlis had become part of an urban economic network. They were now officially identified by their new urban professional status and their agricultural origins were easily forgotten or disregarded.

The itinerant vending of fresh fruits and vegetables was far from being the universal predicament of the Arapkirlis in our *mahalle*. In 1885, many of them had already moved on to other occupations and, perhaps, to other neighborhoods. There were still five Arapkirli household heads who continued to reside in the Kasap İlyas *mahalle* although they had already moved to a different occupation. Among them, two had entered the civil service. Two others had also risen in their respective guild's hierarchy and had become wardens (*kethüda*s) of their respective trade guilds. As to the last Arapkirli, he was not an itinerant vendor of fruits and vegetables anymore, but had become the owner of a greengrocer shop (*manav*). He had transcended his precarious itinerant position and acquired one of the rare greengrocer *gedik*s. He had thus moved from the "informal" to the strictly legal and formal sector and become integrated into the official and socially accepted segment of his trade. He was not a fruit vendor but a fruit merchant now.

Of the two natives of Arapkir who had already entered the Ottoman civil service before the 1885 census, the first, Abdullah bey, had become a scribe in the Customs Office.[46] This Arapkirli had lived in Istanbul for more than twenty years. In 1885, Abdullah bey already had a son who was 21, who had been born in Istanbul, and who had followed in his father's footsteps and had also entered the Ottoman civil service. This son was a scribe at the central Post Office.[47] The second Arapkir-born resident of Kasap İlyas who had gone to the public sector was a summoner (*muhzır*) at the Mahmudpaşa Court. The two Arapkirlis who had become wardens of their respective guilds were also certainly not recent rural migrants. It is unimaginable that these two wardens had only recently been recruited to their respective occupations in Istanbul. Coincidentally, neither of these wardens was a *küfeci*, but both worked in occupations that were widely practiced within the Kasap İlyas *mahalle*. One of these Arapkirlis had become *kethüda* of the guild of street-porters (*hamal*s) and the other was warden of that of the sellers of coal (*kömürcü*s).

The second half of the nineteenth century was a time when most of the traditional craft and trade guilds of Istanbul were losing their monopoly and much of their importance and influence.[48] In general, nonguild labor, such as the itinerant fruit and vegetable vendors, scarcely found its way into the records, although it had its importance in Istanbul. Its significance, its magnitude, and its contribution to the urban labor market is often overlooked, especially for periods preceding the nineteenth century. Much of the debate on labor and manufacturing in the Ottoman Empire has focused so far on the craft guilds, on their restrictive and monopolistic practices, and on their final demise. Relatively little attention has been paid to the status and function of nonguild labor in cities. In Istanbul nonguild labor and nonguild activities have often constituted a pool of cheap and unqualified labor, as well as a possible avenue for the integration of rural migrants, a transitional stage on their way to being part of a regular guild. The Istanbul labor market may not have been as strictly segmented as is suggested by traditional interpretations of usual guild practices. Besides, as there never was a centrally imposed pattern of guild organization in Ottoman cities, local arrangements could and did diverge considerably.

The itinerant fruit vendors of Kasap İlyas constitute a case in point. Except perhaps for the water-carriers (*saka*s), ambulant vendors were not, in the Ottoman Empire, generally part of a guild.[49] Merchant guilds, such as that of greengrocers, however, were well represented in Istanbul. In the early nineteenth century, stable fruit and vegetable shops did have their own guild in the capital, headed by a *kethüda*. They were relatively few, and had the privilege of *gedik*. They might indeed have had good reason to complain about unfair competition on the part of the ambulant *küfeci*s, who, after all, sold more or less the same merchandise but had no guild regulation and paid no taxes. If they did complain, however, they were certainly not heard, judging from the perennity of their competitors.

Many of the guilds were apparently just loosely organized associations with few privileges to offer to, and almost no effective power of, control over their members. In these, membership probably did not mean much more than having a common commercial activity. Such seems to have been the case of the stable greengrocer shop owners (*manav*s) of Istanbul. Besides, the activity of the stable greengrocer shops was obviously not of strategic importance, and their plea was not heard by the authorities. Theirs must have been a "soft" trade monopoly that apparently could not help allowing market penetration by newcomers and the survival and reproduction of a permanent pool of potential competitors.

The guild of the *manav*s was therefore neither powerful, nor rigid or closed, which may explain how and why, in the face of these established and apparently well-organized *manav*s, the poor provincial *küfeci*s, these premodern "marginal sector" workers just went on with their trade and their unfair competition generation after generation, deregulating the market. Some of these "informal sector" workers even crossed over to the "formal" segment of the same line of activity, and simply set up shop in the capital. Though we have no solid documentation on this, a sort of symbiotic relationship may have existed between ambulant fruit vendors and stable, "formal sector" greengrocers. The symbiosis could take a number of forms, ranging from a cartel-like partnership involving a sharing of trading routes, outlets, and markets to a straightforward relationship of employment for purposes of transportation and delivery of goods.

In any case, retail activities and markets for consumption goods, and especially for fruits and vegetables, in Istanbul, were perhaps more fluid than is generally construed, and guild and nonguild activities of a similar kind were far from being totally impermeable to each other. This permeability finds an illustration in the ambulant fruit and vegetable vendors who had migrated from Arapkir and were living in Kasap İlyas.

Legal Residence: Regionalism and Nepotism

The Arapkirlis who migrated to Kasap İlyas knew that they would be facing a "soft landing" upon their arrival. This was true in terms of housing, thanks to the presence of a community of fellow-citizens and of specialized housing units that welcomed them in the Ispanakçı Viranesi. The Virane, this plot of land of dubious ownership, as we saw, functioned in the second half of the nineteenth century as an informal housing unit, a remote ancestor of the present-day *gecekondu* settlements of peripheral Istanbul.

The newcomers from Arapkir also received preferential treatment in their urban professional activity, as they could expect to be quickly integrated into one of the networks of ambulant fruit and vegetable sellers. As to their acquisition of legal residence in Istanbul, the notebooks of Osman Efendi, the *muhtar* of Kasap İlyas in the 1880s and 1890s, does provide important clues about the details of the process. The legal means by which the Arapkirlis managed to secure official residence in the Kasap İlyas *mahalle* and in Istanbul deserve closer scrutiny. The migrant Arapkirli community of the nineteenth century largely managed to avoid complying with the very strict migration and residence requirements that the Tanzimat administration, for security reasons, tried very hard to implement in the capital of the empire. The inquiry into how religious/ethnic/regional solidarities secured a relatively easy circumvention of these regulations requires a short detour.

Migration Records

The notebooks of the *muhtar* of Kasap İlyas contain a total of about three hundred records of people having entered or left the *mahalle* in the years between 1885 and 1895. One hundred and ten were records of incoming people and one hundred and ninety concerned persons moving from the *mahalle*. However, the records of only about forty cases of birth and just about twenty five deaths that occurred in the *mahalle* had found their way into Osman Efendi's notebooks, during the same ten-year period.[50]

The registration of such vital events was very far from being complete in Istanbul, anyway. In this matter, coverage was not due to attain exhaustivity for a long time to come yet.[51] Obviously, the pressure exerted by the central government on the *muhtar*s concerning the control and registration of migrants within the empire had been much more effective. The official regulations making the registration of vital events compulsory were, after all, quite new. The first of these had been promulgated only in 1883.[52] Besides, in the Ottoman population at large, be it Muslim or not, there was no widespread habit of, and incentive to, declare births or deaths to the authorities. Nor had there ever existed any administrative setup designed to record and/or to centralize information on demographic occurrences. By contrast, the laws and regulations on internal population movements were well-known in Istanbul and, at the time of the 1885 census, had been in full force for more than fifty years. Moving and migrating within the Ottoman Empire had been strictly defined and put under control by two different regulations, issued in 1826 and again in 1841.[53]

Basically, these laws stated that all persons who were temporarily or permanently moving from one place to the other within the bounds of the Ottoman Empire had to be in possession of a sort of internal passport called *mürur tezkeresi*. To it was attached a control system that worked both at the point of departure and at the point of arrival of the traveler or of the migrant. This *mürur tezkeresi* was delivered by the local authority in charge of Law and Order upon presentation of a certificate or note (an *ilmühaber* or *pusula*) delivered by the *muhtar* of the migrant's neighborhood or village of departure. This *ilmühaber* or *pusula* was to be given only to persons of good conduct and good reputation. As to the certificate of passage carried by the traveler or migrant, it was to be presented upon request to all authorities and was to function as a basic identity paper. At the points of arrival of eventual migrants, the *muhtar*s were requested not to allow newcomers who were not in possession of this *mürur tezkeresi* to settle in their *mahalle*. They were not to put them down in their register and therefore not grant them a signed *pusula* upon their eventual departure from their neighborhood. This was the most important duty of the *muhtar*, and it was perceived to be of basic importance for urban security, especially in the capital.

These strict regulations were meant to apply even to people who were moving within the same city, although the urban and settled inhabitants were less of a jeopardy to security in general. At all events, these intracity migrants had to present the *pusula* duly signed and stamped by the *muhtar* of their neighborhood of departure to that of their neighborhood of destination. This system of internal passport and local registration remained in operation for the rest of the nineteenth century and was abolished only after the 1908

Young Turk Revolution. Small wonder, then, that the notebooks of the *muhtar*s of Kasap İlyas *mahalle* contained five times more entries concerning geographic movements of population than entries of births and deaths for the period between 1885 and 1895.

This migration control system provided for checks at points of departure and of arrival and had built-in sanctions for trespassers. In theory the system seems to be watertight. In practice, however, things did not go as smoothly as the regulations intended. Not even in a relatively small and relatively stable *mahalle* such as Kasap İlyas could a dutiful and zealous *muhtar* ever manage to keep track of everybody. For instance, Osman Efendi, a longtime *muhtar*, signed quite a large number of personal notes and certificates stating that such and such a person "had lost his *mürur tezkeresi*." The "loss" of these certificates of passage eventually became habitual. So much so that Osman Efendi ended up by giving a particular heading to a portion of his personal notebooks: "Those who had not registered and have moved to other places." Under this title, which was obviously in perfect contradiction with the laws and regulations on the matter, he took note of the *pusula*s he had given to migrants who had come to Kasap İlyas without a *mürur tezkeresi*, when these migrants had to leave the neighborhood.[54]

Who, then, in the second half of the nineteenth century, came to our neighborhood with, and who came without proper identification documents? There were indeed some well-defined groups that fit into both of these categories.

It appears from the *muhtar*'s notebooks that those who came to Kasap İlyas with proper documents were coming, first and foremost, from other neighborhoods of the capital. It was the Istanbulites themselves who were showing the greatest care in acquiring a note from the muhtar of their *mahalle* of origin before moving to Kasap İlyas. Of the 110 instances of newcomers' registrations *(kuyudat*s) in the *muhtar*'s notebooks, 87 (i.e., almost 80 percent of the total) concerned persons who had changed residence within Istanbul and had moved from one *mahalle* to the other.

The local headman of Kasap İlyas had often put down an indication as to the area, the neighborhood, or the district of Istanbul from which these people had come. These indications are more or less detailed, but they invariably point out at the precise Istanbul *mahalle* from which the newcomers to Kasap İlyas had moved. Indeed, the notes that these people carried with them bore the seal of the *muhtar* of their neighborhood of origin. Here are a few examples of these indications of location within Istanbul: "From the Sahhaf Muhiddin *mahalle* in Kasımpaşa,"[55] "From number one in the Seyyid Ömer *mahalle*, near Molla Gürani,"[56] "Seven people from Langa avenue, number 156, in the Kürkçübaşı *mahalle*,"[57] "From number 22 in the Hacı Piri *mahalle* near the Saturday Market,"[58] and so forth.

Paradoxically, maximum compliance with the regulations had been shown by people who, in the eyes of the Ottoman authorities, carried minimum risk, and to whom, in the same line of logic, the very strict security regulations had the least reason to be applied. The *muhtar*'s powers of control and the contribution he was thereby presumed to make to urban "security" never really discouraged the migration of "undesirables" to the capital. The figures tell us that the apparently strict population movement control system that had been put in place in the nineteenth century, as far as we can judge from the Kasap İlyas *mahalle*, had not been efficient. It had not worked as a proper instrument of control of migrants, nor did it constitute a serious deterrent to rural migration to Istanbul.

Indeed, the overwhelming majority of people who came to Kasap İlyas from outside Istanbul in the 1880s and 1890s were not holding legal travel documents. Therefore, if they wanted to be officially registered in the *mahalle* or to obtain regular travel documents (either the *pusula* or *mürur tezkeresi*) when they left the *mahalle*, they needed a sponsor/guarantor (*kefil*). Somebody the *muhtar* knew and trusted had to authenticate that person's statement of identity. By contrast, those who had come to Kasap İlyas from other parts of the capital never needed that sort of an authentification. As we pointed out, they had all come with a regular *pusula* from the headman of their *mahalle* of origin and, when and if they left Kasap İlyas, our *muhtar* simply gave them, as a matter of routine, another certificate addressed to the muhtar of their *mahalle* or village of destination. Only those who had arrived in Kasap İlyas without regular travel documents would have needed the authentification of a *kefil* when they left.

All of this was obviously true not only for the Kasap İlyas *mahalle*, but for all of the two hundred and fifty one traditional neighborhoods that existed in Istanbul in the late nineteenth century.[59] Indeed, our *muhtar*'s notebooks show that about half the 87 people who had moved to Kasap İlyas from another Istanbul *mahalle* with all legal documents in hand were, as a matter-of-fact, people who had not been born in the capital. They, too, had been rural migrants some time ago. Simply, the Kasap İlyas *mahalle* was not their first but their second (third, fourth?) neighborhood of residence within the capital. They, too, had managed to comply with the regulations after having settled first somewhere else in Istanbul.

In sum, despite some apparently very strict rules and regulations, it was not that difficult for a rural migrant to legally become a resident of Istanbul. That such a large-scale bypassing of these regulations occur at a specific period when, for some external reason, there is a sudden and massive flow of migrants/refugees toward Istanbul would be understandable. For instance, in the aftermath of the 1877–1878 war with Russia or as a result of the Balkan wars of 1912–1914 there had been an uncontrollable massive flow of Muslim refugees toward the heartland of the empire. Istanbul and parts of Anatolia received large numbers of refugees. But there was nothing of the sort in the 1880s and 1890s, decades of relative calm and political stability. Still, the implementation of the laws on migration left much to be desired. Our sample of migrants to a small locality within Istanbul provides a glimpse of the relative ease of entry to, and settlement in, the capital of the Ottoman Empire.

In 1885, Kasap İlyas had a population of around 1,000 people. During the ten-year period from 1885 to 1895, the *muhtar* of our neighborhood noted down in his book more than three hundred entries to, or exits from, the *mahalle*. This figure can be taken as a rough approximation of horizontal, geographic mobility. Three hundred entries and exits during a period of ten years for a population of about 1,000 people means an average rate of turnover of about 3 percent yearly ([300:10]/1000). This is a very high rate of population turnover indeed. Clearly, with such a rapid circulation, within about thirty years the *mahalle*'s composition will have completely changed.

To this turnover by simple geographic mobility should be added the (very incompletely recorded) births and deaths that occurred within the neighborhood itself. Besides, a record of entry or of exit by the *muhtar* often comprised more than one person, sometimes a whole family, and there were more persons moving to and from the neighborhood than entries in the *muhtar*'s notebook. These movements obviously entailed a rapid change in the overall composition of the neighborhood's residents. Twenty years later, in the last Ottoman census of 1907, almost none of the former inhabitants of the *mahalle* are to be found. The population of Istanbul in the second half of the nineteenth century was certainly more mobile than is commonly thought, and almost none of the individuals and households present in Kasap İlyas in the 1885 census can be traced twenty years later.

Fellow-Citizens and Guarantors—The Arapkirlis Legally Settle in Kasap İlyas

The majority of people who came to Kasap İlyas from outside Istanbul in the 1880s and 1890s came without holding legal travel documents. Therefore, if they wanted to be officially registered in the *mahalle* or to obtain regular travel documents when they left the neighborhood (they needed to have, as we saw, either the *pusula* to move within Istanbul or the *mürur tezkeresi* for moving over longer distances), they had to have a sponsor/guarantor. Somebody the *muhtar* knew and trusted had to witness and authenticate that person's statement of identity. Put another way, the presence of a guarantor was necessary for the migrants in order to legalize their residence in the capital. The identity of the guarantors who put their signature in the *muhtar*'s books is therefore significant for tracing eventual networks of solidarity and patronage linking residents of Kasap İlyas to newcomers.

It appears that the identity-guaranteeing signature of these *kefil*s was in fact nothing but a sort of subsidiary procedure that allowed for the bypassing of the passport laws. The Arapkirlis of our neighborhood had arrived in Istanbul thanks to the help of a network of primary relationships that provided them with a place to live (mostly in and around the Ispanakçı Viranesi) and a job (for the largest number, the ambulant vending of fresh fruits and vegetables). What they lacked were the official travel documents, and therefore the certificate of official residence in Istanbul, signed by the local headman of a *mahalle*. But this was really no problem. For there always seems to have been in the *mahalle* a fellow citizen from Arapkir ready to act as a legal sponsor/guarantor and a *muhtar* complacent enough to accept this sponsorship and to produce the necessary residence certificate. Basically the Arapkir-based regional network of support that provided both housing and work to the newcomers was at work to secure official papers as well. In a way, this three-tiered support and solidarity system for rural migrants is not fundamentally different from that which functioned in republican Turkey and that helped many groups of rural migrants in a metropolis like Istanbul.[60]

Every time the *muhtar* of Kasap İlyas gave an Arapkirli one of these certificates, the local *kefil* was asked to stamp with his own seal (*mühür*) the relevant page of the *muhtar*'s notebook.[61] All of these were obviously cases of people *leaving* the neighborhood, because only those people who had moved to the neighborhood without the required official documentation would need the presence and the seal of a guarantor in order to obtain the *pusula* when they left Kasap İlyas. There were no less than 190 cases of people who left the *mahalle* and were recorded as such in the *muhtar*'s notebooks, in the 1885–1895 period. More than two thirds of these records are accompanied by the seal of the guarantor. The material state of the documents, however, have allowed for the decipherment of 79 of the *kefil* seals only, and we shall try to have a closer look at them.

First of all, the *muhtar* of Kasap İlyas personally knew most of these guarantors. On top of their seals in his notebook the *muhtar* often jotted down a remark that designated these *kefil*s in terms that are indicative of a certain degree of familiarity. "The guarantor is Ali," or "the guarantor is Yusuf, from the coffeehouse," is the most frequent type of remark. The *muhtar* did not care to give any detailed information on the identity of these persons, their occupation, or their whereabouts within the neighborhood.[62] There was no need for it, since he knew them well and trusted them. The *muhtar* acted therefore, in a sense, as a guarantor for these guarantors.

Among the 79 legible guarantor seals in the notebooks of the *muhtar* of Kasap İlyas, some names appear much more frequently than a random distribution of guarantorships among the residents could ever warrant. For instance, the name of Kahveci Ibrahim (Ibrahim the coffeehouse keeper) occurs no less than thirteen times in the *muhtar*'s notebooks. Kahveci Arapkirli Yusuf (Yusuf the coffeehouse keeper from Arapkir) appears as guarantor in twelve instances. The name of Süleyman Kâhya appears six times, that of Halil Kâhya four, and that of Bekir three times. Therefore only two people (Ibrahim and Yusuf), two coffeehouse owners (or perhaps managers), had signed as guarantors in more than one third of the cases, and almost half the guarantor seals belonged to just five people. As to the remaining forty one legible seals, none appears more than twice.

Some of these *kefil*s can easily be traced within the neighborhood. In 1885, there were three coffeehouses in the Kasap İlyas *mahalle*.[63] Like most of the coffeehouses in Istanbul at the time, these were simple single-story wooden buildings with few amenities inside. The small local coffeehouses situated in the residential neighborhoods of Istanbul could not compare with the larger and more showy ones in the central and commercial areas of the city. A dirt floor, a stove in the middle, some kitchen utensils in one corner, perhaps a few chairs and low tables, and some wooden benches (*peyke*s) along the walls were the lot of most of them. They were frequented exclusively by men.[64] Two of the coffeehouses were situated on the *mahalle*'s main thoroughfare. The first was at 29 Samatya Street and the other at 40 Samatya Street. The third was on the seaside, across from the landing of the Davudpaşa wharf, and was known as the Wharf coffeehouse (Iskele Kahvesi).

The proprietor of the coffeehouse at 29 Samatya Street was one Hayri ağa who was living in the house just next to the coffeehouse, at 29B Samatya Street. The name of Hayri ağa, who was born in Istanbul in 1843, however, occurs only once as a guarantor in the *muhtar*'s notebooks. As to the coffeeshop at 40 Samatya Street, it belonged to Ibrahim, precisely the Ibrahim whose name appeared as sponsor no less than thirteen times in the *muhtar*'s notebooks. Ibrahim, the coffeehouse owner, had been born in Divriği in 1840 and was living with his wife and daughter at 6 Horasancı Street, one of the small streets situated between the public bath and the Davudpaşa wharf. Süleyman Kâhya, whose name appears six times as guarantor, was living in Kasap İlyas as well. He had been born in Arapkir in 1844, was a warden of the guild of street porters (*hammallar kethüdası*) and was living in 1885 with his two wives and his son in a house at 23 Davudpaşa Wharf Street. As to Yusuf, his name does not appear among the residents of the *mahalle* in 1885. He might simply have been working in one of the coffeehouses of the neighborhood. One thing we know about him, however, is that he was also an Arapkirli, and that the *muhtar* of Kasap İlyas trusted him as well.[65]

These three Arapkirlis living in 1885 in Kasap İlyas (Kahveci Ibrahim, Kahveci Yusuf, and Süleyman Kâhya) had signed as guarantors in the *muhtar*'s notebooks for thirty one different people between 1885 and 1895. These thirty one people were all Arapkirlis. Clearly, they had sponsored thirty one of their fellow-citizens who had come to Istanbul without the necessary legal documents.

Obviously, in 1885, Kasap İlyas did not only have immigrants from Arapkir (see table 3.1). There were many people from other parts of the empire who came without a proper *mürur tezkeresi* and who needed a guarantor after having settled in the *mahalle*. It is only the Arapkirlis, however, who were sponsored exclusively by their own fellow-citizens already established in the neighborhood. For none of those who had come from various areas of Rumelia (the European parts of the empire), for instance, was there such a well-established configuration of solidarity and sponsorship based on geographic proximity. These Rumelia-born people were, after the Arapkirlis, the largest single group of provincials living in Kasap İlyas and made up more than 10 percent of its population. The sheer quantity of co-locals migrating to Istanbul was apparently not sufficient to create such a permanent solidarity network. Except for the Arapkirlis, the equivalent of such a strong pattern of regionalism and favoritism is discernible for no other group living in the *mahalle* in the second half of the nineteenth century.

The Arapkirlis living in the Kasap İlyas *mahalle* were systematically acting as sponsors/guarantors for their fellow-citizens who were newly coming to the capital and were helping them to acquire legal residence. As we saw, this pattern of solidarity was not new. In 1885, it had been operating for at least a century and had been perpetuated generation after generation. The tradition of migration had, in time, created its own mechanisms of attraction and particular avenues for integration. This snowballing effect had indeed been in operation ever since Ispanakçızâde Mustafa Paşa, the Ottoman provincial governor of the 1760s, brought from Arapkir servants to work in his *konak* in the capital. After the Tanzimat, the system became effective not only for securing housing and employment for the newcomers but also for getting them legal residence papers.

The two *kahveci*s and the warden of street-porters from Arapkir, for instance, were settled there for a long time and were well-known in the neighborhood. They too had also been sponsored by other fellow-citizens. It is likely that these two coffeehouses in the *mahalle* owned or run by Ibrahim and Yusuf, the two well-established Arapkirlis, were not only ordinary locales for the recreation of fellow villagers in Istanbul. They also served a real professional need, bringing together co-locals from Arapkir and thus creating a kind of soft guild solidarity by promoting the exchange and dissemination of information on employment and business opportunities. Thus, these coffeehouses (and their owners or managers) were an important link in the chain of migration of Arapkirlis.

Clientelistic relations and networks may also have appeared in Kasap İlyas, leading to inequalities and positions of local power.⁶⁶ Those that had helped their co-locals in the initial process of settlement may have attained positions of power vis-à-vis those who became clients. Under conditions of urban life, solidarity relations with kin or with co-locals may well have been transformed into relations of power. In a single little *mahalle*, though, the stakes were too small and, besides, the data do not allow us to follow closely the spatial and social trajectory of all Arapkirli migrants.

As to the *muhtar* of Kasap İlyas, he was perfectly aware of the existence of this regional solidarity network. He knew well the insuperable practical difficulties involved in the full implementation of the very stringent migration regulations. What could he then do but give the required legal backing to whole sequences of Arapkirlis' mutual sponsorships? At the end of the nineteenth century, Osman Efendi filled the post of *muhtar* of Kasap İlyas for almost twenty-five years (see the appendix). Knowing full well that the Arapkirlis were bypassing the law, he often felt the need to put down in writing a sort of a posteriori justification for the certificates he kept giving to those who left the neighborhood.

On April 30, 1888, for instance, Ali bin Sadullah, a native of Divriği, left the *mahalle* with a regular residence certificate signed by the *muhtar* Osman Efendi, who noted that "he had lost his Certificate of Passage *(mürur tezkeresi)*."⁶⁷ In 1889, when Ismail bin Ali, who was a native of Arapkir and a professional woodchopper was leaving the neighborhood, Osman Efendi took note of the fact that ". . . he had come from his village a couple of years ago, and he is now returning to his village. . . ."⁶⁸ The same year our *muhtar* took note that Sadık bin Mehmed, a native of Arguvan, ". . . had come from his province six years ago, had not registered and is now leaving for Izmir. . . ."⁶⁹ Another Arapkirli might have a justification such as, ". . . he had come three years ago, but had lost his documents of identity. . . ."⁷⁰ Needless to say, the guarantors in all of these cases were either one of the two coffeehouse keepers, Ibrahim and Yusuf, or Süleyman Kâhya the warden of the guild of streetporters. All three, as we saw, were Arapkirlis.

Whether, in this solidarity network of fellow-citizens from Arapkir, kinship also had its role to play unfortunately cannot be documented. The *muhtar*'s notebooks contain only information on the birthplaces of the migrants and on their last addresses within the neighborhood, and nothing on their kin relationship, if any. There were a few cases of a whole Arapkirli family being sponsored by a co-local living in the *mahalle*. But no more is known on the proximity of the sponsors and his protégés. Among the birthplaces of migrants, however, not only districts but precise villages of birth are very frequently referred to. In fifteen out of the thirty-one cases of sponsorship bearing the seal of Ibrahim, Yusuf, and Süleyman Kâhya, the precise village of origin of the migrant is mentioned in the record. Saldak and Bostancık (villages situated within the district of Arapkir) are the two recognizable village names.

As to the local addresses of the Arapkirlis who applied to the *muhtar* for a certificate, their pattern of settlement within the *mahalle* was pretty much as expected. Before they left Kasap İlyas, about half of them were living in Ispanakçi Viranesi. The other half were residents of Helvacı and Davudpaşa Iskelesi Streets, two of the narrow and winding alleys that went from Samatya Street to the Davudpaşa wharf. None of them resided on Samatya Street itself or on Çavuşzade Street or on Yokuşçeşme Street, the two streets that went north from it. These were considered, as we shall see, the more prestigious parts of the neighborhood, the "upper *mahalle*."

4

"End of Empire"
Portrait of a Neighborhood Community in the Late Nineteenth Century

Thank God, the terrible earthquake was over. Facing the tombstone that stood in the small cemetery behind the Kasap İlyas mosque, Osman efendi, the *muhtar*, addressed a prayer (*fâtiha*) to the soul of Kasap İlyas, founder of the mosque and of his neighborhood. As every morning, he had just left his house situated just behind the mosque and was on his way to his haberdasher's shop in the Great Bazaar. Large parts of that large and central commercial complex were left in ruins, as well. By an extraordinary coincidence, the seismic catastrophe had hit Istanbul on July 10, 1894, a year that marked the quadricentennial anniversary of the death of Kasap İlyas. The wooden houses of the neighborhood in which, rich or poor, almost everybody in the *mahalle* lived, had not suffered much and, fortunately, there were few casualties.

But the stone buildings of the neighborhood were in a pitiful state, and, naturally, these were buildings of public utility. The tiled roof of the four-centuries-old Kasap İlyas mosque had caved in and what was left of the walls was rather shaky. The pointed upper part of the slender minaret had crumbled down. Services could not be held and the believers had to climb up the road and pray in the Davudpaşa mosque. The public bath, the only other large stone building of the neighborhood, was in need of heavy repair as well. All this caused Osman Efendi genuine concern.

His concern had grown after his conversation with Ahmet Necati Efendi, the *imam* of the Kasap İlyas mosque and the trustee of the local foundations attached thereto. Ahmet Necati Efendi had made it clear that what was left of the pious foundations (*vakıfs*) attached to the Kasap İlyas mosque, of their endowments and revenues, was insufficient to cover the expenses that the extensive repair work required. Osman Efendi was not really surprised. He had been helping the *imam* of Kasap İlyas with his book-keeping for some years and he knew that the *vakıf* revenues that now accrued were barely sufficient to cover running expenses, to pay for the *müezzin*'s wages, and for operating costs and maintenance.

So, what was to be done? How were they to collect the large sums of money necessary to do the repair work? There appeared to be no other way but to try to raise funds from the wealthier inhabitants of Kasap İlyas. And that was something that only he, Osman Efendi, could do. Though a direct stakeholder in the repair work, it was unlikely that Necati Efendi, the *imam* of the ruined mosque, could ever muster sufficient support alone. After all, Necati Efendi was not a local of Kasap İlyas. He was a native of the faraway eastern Anatolian city of Merzifon and he had been posted in the neighborhood only a short time ago. Besides, he was too young.

Necati Efendi had recently been asking for Osman Efendi's help in many instances. So much so that Necati Efendi had come to relinquish part of his traditional *imam*'s prerogatives to the benefit of the *muhtar*. It was now Osman Efendi who was keeping track of the marriages that the *imam* had celebrated. Osman Efendi had also come to check whether these nuptials were being celebrated in accordance with the shari'a law. Osman Efendi had also helped to settle a small financial disagreement that had occurred a few years ago between the *imam* and Ahmet, the *müezzin* of the Kasap İlyas mosque. Although the obvious legal recourse was the Davutpaşa *shari'a* court, the parties had come to him instead, further proof of the confidence that the neighborhood as a whole placed in him. There had occurred a de facto transfer of local prestige and authority. Authority had been transferred from the traditional religious to the new and secular local leadership, that is, from the *imam* to him, Osman Efendi, *muhtar* of the Kasap İlyas *mahalle*.

Osman Efendi therefore thought that his own personal status, position, and prestige within the *mahalle* was the only thing that could warrant the success of such an extensive fund-raising operation. Hadn't he been a muhtar of the Kasap İlyas mahalle for more than ten years now? Hadn't he occupied, before that, the post of first assistant to the previous headman for three years? Hadn't the confidence that the residents of Kasap İlyas had put in him been openly manifest during all these years? Besides, he personally knew almost everybody in the neighborhood, from the richest and most powerful to the poorest and most destitute. Everybody was within his reach. He had easily access to Şevket Paşa, the former cabinet minister who lived with his family in the large *konak* on Samatya Street, as well as to Abdullah, the poor ambulant street vendor of fruits and vegetables who had come only last year from his faraway Arapkir and was temporarily sharing with a couple of fellow-citizens some shoddy lodgings in the Ispanakçı Viranesi.

Osman Efendi therefore felt he would be successful in mustering enough financial support. He first planned to knock on Şevket Paşa's door. Şevket Paşa, who had served for many years as Şeyhülharem, the official responsible for the security of the holy cities of Mecca and Medina, would certainly agree to contribute. And Şevket Paşa would be the obvious example to show to the rest of the neighborhood. Then Osman Efendi could follow with the other grandees who lived in the *mahalle*: Ahmet Faik Paşa, the retired army general; Nebil bey, the high-ranking foreign affairs bureaucrat; and Sadeddin bey, the colonel who was now posted with the General Staff in Istanbul. The others would certainly follow suit. But it wasn't going to be easy, and he would certainly have to knock on many doors.

Then the *imam* Necati Efendi, in his usual Friday sermons, would also encourage the Kasap İlyas population at large to contribute. Whether this would be really efficient, however, Osman Efendi was not so sure. First of all, the inhabitants of the *mahalle* were not generally opulent, to say the least. True, Kasap İlyas was one of the oldest and most glorious of the traditional muslim Istanbul neighborhoods. But it was not anywhere near the centers of economic and political power, and had never become a prosperous area. The rich were few in this semiperipheral and semirural area surrounded by city-walls and vegetable gardens. Most residents were small artisans and shopkeepers and the few civil servants who lived here were mostly of lower rank. So, Necati Efendi would certainly have difficulty in convincing the residents to make substantial financial contributions. But still, the *imam* could raise contributions in kind; he could convince many to do a charitable act by working on the construction site of the mosque.

Besides, the neighborhood housed a large number of poor rural migrants, most of them coming from Arapkir and from its surroundings. Not only were they poor, but they belonged for the greatest part to the *Alevî* sect, and they formed a closed and tightly knit subcommunity within the *mahalle*. They were modest and honest people, but they never showed a high rate of attendance to prayers and services in the mosque, to say the least. How could they be convinced to contribute to the repair of a place of worship they did not frequently attend?

Osman Efendi had an idea. He suddenly remembered that he did have some leverage on this group of people. As a *muhtar* he had rendered all of these migrants from Arapkir some sort of service or other in the past. He had facilitated the settlement of many of them in Kasap İlyas and in Istanbul, and two of the *kahveci*s of the neighborhood had often been instrumental in the process. Ibrahim and Yusuf, old-time migrants from Arapkir, were both well established and were managing two of the coffeehouses in Kasap İlyas. Each time an Arapkirli needed some sort of official paper, one of these coffeehouse owners was ready to act as a witness and a sponsor in support of their fellow-citizens who had newly migrated to Istanbul. This solidarity should now work the other way around, thought Osman Efendi. It was only fair that these two *kahveci*s who had come from Arapkir should demand a small contribution to the reconstruction of the mosque from each one of their fellow-citizens. The *mahalle* had contributed to their well-being. Now it was their turn. These coffeehouse owners would certainly comply, and their fund-raising efforts would no doubt be crowned by greater success than those of the *imam* Necati Efendi.

Osman Efendi felt greatly relieved by this brilliant idea. He addressed a last prayer of thanks to the founder and patron of his *mahalle*, and calmly walked to work....

The 1885 Census Population Roster for the Kasap İlyas *mahalle* shows a total of 925 Muslim inhabitants (498 women and 427 men).[1] A second register that contained the non-Muslim population of the neighborhood has unfortunately been lost. It seems reasonable to assume that the proportion of non-Muslims was the same as in the count of 1907 (10.2 percent). Kasap

İlyas had a total of around 1,100 inhabitants in 1885. One also has to allow for some underregistration of children, women, and also of men, for military service and tax evasion reasons. We had previously estimated the rate of underregistration for children in the late Ottoman censuses at around 15 percent.[2] Even after due correction, however, the irregularity in the age-groups from 20 to 40 remains. Though the sample is small and subject to random variations, that irregularity is certainly due to the presence of a considerable number of migrants (see table 4.1). There is also a considerable degree of rounding-off in age declarations.

That Kasap İlyas was smallish (in terms of population only, though, and not of geographic area) is confirmed by the overall results of the 1885 census itself. The city of Istanbul within the old ramparts had a total population of 389,545 people.[3] As to the total number of *mahalle*s in Istanbul, it is given as 251 in a listing of houses and neighborhoods dating from 1877, which was established in preparation for parliamentary elections. The listing shows an average number of 163 houses per *mahalle*.[4] The variance in the number of houses per quarter was very large, however, with the smallest neighborhood containing as little as 8 houses, and the largest 477. As to the average population per Istanbul *mahalle*, it was around 1,550, about 50 percent above that of Kasap İlyas, which contained 149 houses in all.

The median age of the Kasap İlyas population in 1885 was 27.2.[5] The age below which half the population happens to be at the time of the census, is the median age. As to the mean age, it was equal to 29.2. Considering the fact that the median age was only about 22 for the whole of Turkey according to the 1990 census, it is clear that we are not dealing with a population having a young age-structure. Correction for the underreporting of children would decrease the figure by one or one and a half years at most.

TABLE 4.1
Age Composition of the Muslim Population of Kasap İlyas (1885)

Age — Group	*Number*
0–4	88
5–9	92
10–19	152
20–29	163
30–39	154
40–49	117
50–59	65
60–69	62
70+	31
Unknown	1
TOTAL	925

Families and Households

A total of 242 households were living in Kasap İlyas in 1885. This gives us an *average household size of 3.82* for the whole *mahalle*. The average household size in Istanbul was 4.1, at the time.[6] In the last Ottoman census of 1907 the mean household size in Istanbul was 4.2, but only 3.68 in Kasap İlyas. The difference between average household size in the capital and in Kasap İlyas is far from being negligible and is directly related to the fact that Kasap İlyas was then receiving a nonnegligible number of migrants (see table 4.2). The difference in mean size between households headed by Istanbul-born people and those headed by migrants is also truly considerable, and will need some explanation.[7] According to the latest Turkish population census of 1990, the average household size was 4.9 for the whole of Turkey. It was still equal to 4.1 in the metropolitan area of Istanbul, despite a long-standing fertility decline, a radical change in kinship cohabitation trends, and a progressive nucleation of families.[8]

The largest household in Kasap İlyas in 1885 was that headed by retired army general Ahmet Faik Paşa (b. in Istanbul in 1815). His household, settled in a mansion (*konak*) at 19 Şimendifer Street, contained a total of 20 family and nonfamily residents. There were also households in Kasap İlyas containing more than 10 permanent residents at the time of the census. The heads of 6 of them had been born in Istanbul. The next largest household was that of Nebil bey (b. Istanbul in 1835), who was a high-ranking foreign affairs bureaucrat. His *konak* at 5 Samatya Street housed a total of 12 people.

In 1885, only 12 of the 242 Kasap İlyas households consisted of solitaries, that is, they were composed of a single person. One of these "solitaries" was Ahmet efendi, the young *müezzin* of the Kasap İlyas mosque. He was living not far from the mosque itself, at 52 Samatya Street in a small house that belonged to a local *vakıf* whose trustee was the *imam*, Ahmet Necati efendi.

TABLE 4.2
Household Size in Kasap İlyas by Birthplace of Head of Household (1885)

Birthplace of Head	Number	Average Size
Istanbul	88	4.48
Arapkir (1)	67	3.70
Rumelia (2)	25	3.28
Other places (3)	59	3.27
Non-Istanbul (1+2+3)	151	3.46

The Demographics of Household Composition

What sort of households were these? The size of the sample does not allow us to go into a very detailed analysis, for the census listings give us only a cross-sectional snapshot and almost no clues as to the dynamics of families and households in the neighborhood. Besides, such an analysis might not even be meaningful when done on the basis of a single Istanbul *mahalle*. It is highly unlikely that families and households in Kasap İlyas (or those in any other Istanbul *mahalle* of similar size, for that matter) could have had dynamic and structural characteristics singular enough to clearly differentiate them from those of other areas of late Ottoman Istanbul.

In the absence of comparable data sets for other neighborhoods, we will therefore underline a few salient features of these 242 Kasap İlyas households, and exclude all attempts at generalization as well as claims of representativity. The analysis for the whole of Istanbul has been done elsewhere.[9] We shall see that there are noteworthy differences between the households of the Istanbulites and those of the migrants (Arapkirlis and others) living in Kasap İlyas, and that the contrast deserves special emphasis.

There were only 15 female-headed households in Kasap İlyas, that is, 6.2 percent of all households. The percentage was around 15 percent for the whole of Istanbul. Only 5 percent of Kasap İlyas households consisted of "solitaries," compared to no less than 18 percent for the whole of the city.[10] One hundred twenty-one households of Kasap İlyas (exactly 50 percent) were "simple family households," or "nuclear" households. That is, they consisted of a married couple and of their offspring, if any. The corresponding percentage was 25.1 percent for Istanbul as a whole at that time.[11] These features are directly related to the type of migrants that the *mahalle* had been receiving for some time.

One hundred sixty-four households in the *mahalle* out of 242 (67.8 percent) were two-generation households, that is, they contained kin from two generations. Thirty-three (13.6 percent) were "three-generation households," and they contained a grandfather and/or a grandmother and one or more grandsons and/or granddaughters. The "no-family households," that is, those households that contained people with no apparent kinship relationship, were but a small minority (only 10 households). These structural characteristics show a marked difference when viewed against the geographic origin of the household heads (see tables 4.2 and 4.5).

Out of the nearly 200 married men living in Kasap İlyas in 1885, only 4 were polygynously married, and each had two wives. The general rate of polygyny for married Muslim men was around a low 2.5 percent for the whole of Istanbul at the time.[12] It was therefore even slightly lower for the Kasap İlyas *mahalle*. Wealth and the existence of a religious connection were the main factors which, in late Ottoman Istanbul, accompanied or enhanced the propensity to marry polygynously. And Kasap İlyas was neither particularly well-off, nor did it contain (contrary to the *mahalle*s which, especially in the Fatih District, surrounded the traditional theological schools, the *medrese*s) men having prominent positions within the Ottoman religious hierarchy.

Besides, citywide data have shown that Ottoman men born in the capital were, in general, less prone to enter into polygynous unions than their provincial counterparts. Not surprisingly, in Kasap İlyas, three out of the four polygynous men and six out of their eight wives had been born in the provinces. One of these men, Hasan Efendi, aged 42 in 1885, was a weigher (*kantar memuru*) and had been born in the northeastern Anatolian town of Gümüşhane. Two of the polygynous husbands of Kasap İlyas were straightforward Arapkirlis: Hüseyin Efendi the street-porter (*küfeci*), aged 40 and living at 38 Ispanakçı Viranesi, and Ömer Efendi, aged 35, made a living by hiring out his horse (*beygirci*). The four spouses related to Hüseyin and Ömer had all been born in Arapkir, just like their husbands. As to the fourth polygynous husband, Abdülkadir Efendi, he was a retired civil servant and was living in his house at 54 Samatya Street. Abdülkadir Efendi was 61 in 1885 and had been born in Istanbul. His two wives, Nefise, age 70, and Sıdıka, age 35, were both of Circassian origin, conceivably manumitted slaves.

Classifying the male and female Kasap İlyas inhabitants in 1885 according to age and marital status, we calculated that the Singulate Mean Age at Marriage (SMAM) in 1885 was 20.0 for women and 30.4 for men. The Singulate Mean Age at Marriage (SMAM) is a cross-sectional nuptiality index calculated from census or survey data. It pertains only to the year in which the census or the survey was taken. It is an approximation used by demographers to replace the usual mean age at marriage when time-series or cohort data on male and female marriage ages are not available. This SMAM of 20.0 for women living in Kasap İlyas was slightly—though not necessarily very significantly, from a statistical viewpoint—higher than that for Istanbul as a whole in the same census (19.1). The mean age for men, however, as well as the age-difference between spouses, matches fairly well the average figure for Istanbul.[13]

A significant difference appears here between those couples who had been born in Istanbul and those who were not. The average age-difference between spouses was 11.5 years for the Kasap İlyas couples in which the wife was born in Istanbul and only 7.4 years for those where she was born in the provinces. In Istanbul, marriages followed—demographically speaking—a so-called Mediterranean age-pattern, with men marrying, on the average, rather late and women quite early. Therefore, couples had a larger age gap than in traditional peasant societies, such as much of the rural areas of the nineteenth-century Ottoman Empire. The figures for Kasap İlyas confirm what we know of the marriage patterns in Istanbul and of its differences with its Anatolian counterpart.

In 1885 there were 190 married couples in Kasap İlyas for which the exact birthplaces of both spouses were known. Table 4.3 gives their cross-distribution.

The distribution in table 4.3 tells us that in 61 percent (43 + 73/66 + 124) of the married couples living in Kasap İlyas, husbands and wives had been born in the same locality. The proportion is 65 percent (43/66) for Istanbul-born husbands and 59 percent (73/124) for the province-born married men. On the whole, married women had been born in the provinces in a smaller proportion than their husbands. Otherwise stated, a few men (5, to be precise [124–119]) born in the provinces had married women from the capital. This fact, plus the high rate of regional endogamy, confirms that migration to Kasap İlyas had not been of a temporary or seasonal type. On the contrary, permanent familial migration was the prevalent type. That couples and families could have been formed or reunited after the initial move to Istanbul of one of its members is, of course, not to be excluded.

Migrants and Family Structures

There had been a significant flow of Muslim refugees from the European parts of the empire and from the Caucasus after the 1877–1878 Russian War. The population of Istanbul had suddenly greatly increased as a consequence.[14] These war refugees (probably containing many single-parent and truncated

TABLE 4.3
Cross-Distributional Chart of Spouses in Kasap İlyas (1885) according to Their Birthplaces

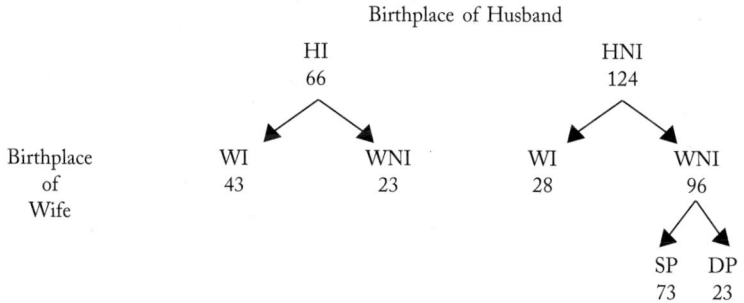

HI/WI = Husband/wife born in Istanbul; HNI/WNI = Husband/wife not born in Istanbul; SP/DP = Same/different place)

families), however, were relatively few in our neighborhood. We figured out an indirect evaluation of the approximate date of arrival to Istanbul of some of the province-born inhabitants of Kasap İlyas by using the census information on the birthplaces of heads of households, of their spouses and, eventually, of successive children. Taking the 1877–1878 war as a benchmark, it appears that more than half of those whose date of arrival to Istanbul we were able to approximate had in fact arrived before the onset of that war. The migrants originating from the regions most affected by the war were, at all events, but a minority of the migrants living in the neighborhood in 1885.

About 50 percent of the Kasap İlyas inhabitants had been born in the provinces. This proportion is only of 16 percent for the children who were less than 10 years old. This difference can be considered as another indication on the average length of time that must have elapsed since their parents' arrival to the city. What we see therefore in Kasap İlyas is the presence of groups of migrants that had come to Istanbul neither as war refugees nor as seasonal migrants but in order to work and settle down, and who eventually brought with them a stable family and kinship network.

The Arapkirlis and their young children provide another illustration. Out of the 88 children who were less than 5 years old and were recorded in the 1885 census, only 6 had been born in Arapkir. Needless to say, so were all of their fathers. 78 out of these 88 children of Kasap İlyas (i.e., almost 90 percent) had been born in Istanbul. But the fathers of one third of them were Arapkirlis. This pattern is also clearly visible when we look at the Arapkirli male household heads and their children's birthplaces. Table 4.4 includes children of all ages and the Arapkirlis are compared to other migrant groups living in Kasap İlyas in 1885. Two thirds of the children of the Arapkirli male heads of household had been born in the capital. It is there that the migrant Arapkirlis had been setting up a family. The corresponding proportion was only 45 percent for the children of male migrants from other parts of the empire. This is indicative both of a longer duration of stay and of a different overall pattern of migration.

TABLE 4.4
Birthplaces of Migrant Fathers and Their Children

Child's Birthplace	Father's Birthplace	
	Arapkir	Other non-Istanbul
Same as Father's	9	9
Istanbul	42	27
Not Specified/No Child	11	24
TOTAL	62	60

The structure of Arapkirli households set them apart from those of other migrant groups. They nevertheless still showed a marked difference with respect to longtime settled Istanbul families (see table 4.5). This table includes only those households in which the kinship relationships of the various members to the head of household was clearly specified in the census listings. The solitaries have naturally been excluded.

Three-generation households composed of a couple and their children plus one or more grandparents, make up a significantly greater proportion of the Kasap İlyas resident households whose head had been born in the capital. By opposition, the sum of single-generation households composed of only a married couple or only of co-resident siblings, plus "nuclear," form a large majority of the households whose head had migrated from the provinces.

In a traditional society, multigenerational coresidence of kin-groups can, conceivably, be considered a function or a rough indicator of the geographic stability over time of the family unit as a whole. In the absence of significant differences in the mortality levels of household members according to the place of birth of the head of household (and there is absolutely no demographically or historically justifiable reason why significant urban/rural, Anatolia/Rumelia, or Arapkirli/other migrants mortality differentials should be posited for the Ottoman Empire in the nineteenth century), past mobility is the only factor that could explain such blatant differences in generations-wise household structures as are observed in our neighborhood. Obviously, the precise type of spatial mobility involved (seasonal, temporary, permanent, familial, etc.) did influence the resulting household structures at the point of arrival.

What is also striking in table 4.5 is that the generational structure of the Arapkirli households stands somewhere between that of the settled Istanbulite families and that of the migrants from other regions of the empire, with whom they could be a priori expected to share many more features. That is not the case, however. These Arapkirli families were very strongly nucleated and the proportion of single- and triple-generation households that they contained likened them more to the settled Istanbulites than to their fellow-migrants. If we take only those 1885 Kasap İlyas inhabitants aged 60 and above, we see that 77 percent of those born in Istanbul lived within three-generation households. The corresponding percentage is 32 percent for the Arapkir-born elderly, but only 11 percent for those who had come from other parts of the empire. The Arapkirlis of Kasap İlyas were migrants, that is certain, but they were either bringing their families with them, or reconstituting them upon arrival.

The migrants from Arapkir and from its surroundings did exhibit particular household features that set them apart both from locals and from other types of migrants to Kasap İlyas. We have reordered the 1885 family

TABLE 4.5
Number and Percentage of Households Containing Kin from 1, 2, and 3 Generations in Kasap İlyas by Birthplace of Head (1885)

		Birthplace of Head	
Generations	Istanbul	Arapkir	Other Places
1	6 (8.4)	11 (16.2)	20 (26.3)
2	37 (52.1)	50 (73.5)	53 (69.7)
3	28 (39.5)	7 (10.3)	3 (4.0)
	71 (100.0)	68 (100.0)	76 (100.0)

listings by birthplace of household head in accordance with the household and family classification system devised by the Cambridge Group for the History of Population and Social Structure.[15] Table 4.6 confirms that the Arapkirlis of Kasap İlyas were mostly living in households containing only a couple and their children, if any (category 3).

More than three quarters of the Arapkirli household heads of Kasap İlyas had constituted simple, "nuclear" families. Neither "solitaries" (category 1) or households with no married couple (category 2), nor those containing more than one married couple (category 5) made a significant proportion of the Arapkirli households. The contrast with households having an Istanbul-born head is really striking. These exhibit a much greater structural variety. The settled and stable Istanbulites lived, in a much larger proportion, in extended and three-generation households (category 4), as well as in families containing more than one conjugual unit (category 5). Not so with the Arapkirlis of Kasap İlyas. A married couple and their children was the standard form of

TABLE 4.6
Households in Kasap İlyas and Numbers and Percentages of Types of Households by Birthplace of Head (1885)

	Birthplace of Household Head			
Household Types	Istanbul	Arapkir	Other Places	Total
1	7 (8.3)	2 (2.9)	5 (6.0)	14 (6.0)
2	10 (11.9)	2 (2.9)	15 (17.9)	27 (11.4)
3	21 (25.0)	52 (75.4)	48 (57.1)	121 (51.0)
4	36 (42.9)	12 (17.4)	13 (15.5)	61 (25.7)
5	10 (11.9)	1 (1.4)	3 (3.5)	14 (5.9)
Total	84 (100.0)	69 (100.0)	84 (100.0)	237 (100.0)

Solitaries (1); no-family households (2); simple-family households (3); extended family units (4); multiple-family households (5)

the Arapkirli coresidential pattern. There was a permanent trickle of people moving in from Arapkir to Kasap İlyas ever since the middle of the eighteenth century. The cross-sectional snapshot of 1885 tells us that these Arapkirlis attained their standard residential pattern quickly and methodically—to judge from the high rate of regional endogamy (see table 4.3).

Arapkirlis came to stay, settle down, find some work, and start a family. By contrast, migrants from other regions of the empire (e.g., those coming from Rumelia, which was the part of the empire most affected by the demographic consequences of the 1877–1878 war) lived in a much greater proportion (almost 1 out of 4) in truncated and dislocated families (categories 1 and 2) containing no central conjugal unit. True, average household size was largest for the Istanbulites (see table 4.2). Among the province-born heads, however, the Arapkirlis stand out with a distinctly larger size compared to other provincials, again, a possible indicator of a greater geographic and familial stability within Istanbul.

All of these characteristics pertaining to the Arapkirli families and households living in Kasap İlyas that we have underlined are obviously valid for the period under consideration, that is, roughly, the last quarter of the nineteenth century. There are no comparable data for other *mahalle*s. There is no way of following the geographic and professional mobility of migrants within the capital, either. Moreover, that the Kasap İlyas *mahalle*, or the Virane within it, might have been used as a temporary first landing-ground for Arapkirli families on their parallel itinerary toward both permanent settlement and increase in size, cannot be totally ignored, in which case, what we have observed in Kasap İlyas might well be but the outward signs of a transitional stage in the centuries-old urban integration process of the Arapkirlis arriving to the capital.

Variety: Pashas, Manumitted Slaves, and Beggars

The migrant Arapkirlis were certainly not the only social group worthy of note living in our modest and peripheral neighborhood. The Arapkirlis were the largest but not the only group of migrants living in Kasap İlyas. The population of the *mahalle* was a microcosm that did reflect to a certain extent the wide social and occupational variety that was manifest in the capital-city of such a large and motley empire. There were also some other microcommunities that lived in our neighborhood.

The most striking example is that of the black inhabitants of the *mahalle*. In 1885 Kasap İlyas contained a nonnegligible number (38, to be precise, and only 6 of which were men) of black people, denoted as *arap*, *zenci*, or *zenciye* in the census listings. Their birthplace was indicated as either Arabia (Arabistan),

Sudan, or Ethiopia (Habeş), and few of them had any declared occupation. All of them were either manumitted slaves (*mütteka*) or the offspring of former slaves. The African slave trade in the Ottoman Empire, strictly forbidden by an imperial Edict of 1857, had, although slowed, continued well into the 1860s and 1870s.[16] Most of the black slaves whose arrival predated the edict, however, had kept their initial status.

Most of these black inhabitants of Kasap İlyas were living in independent households, and a few were married and had children. Four of them were still listed as cooks or as "servants" and were living within various households of the neighborhood. Ahmet efendi, the *müezzin*, had one such servant. The listing was at times even more explicit than that. In a few cases, the relationship to the head of the household was put down in the census listings as his slave (*kölesi*) and, in one instance, as his female slave/concubine (*cariyesi*). The reasons why so many of these manumitted black slaves had chosen precisely this neighborhood for a residence may be related, first, to the fact that Kasap İlyas was neither a central nor an expensive one and, second, because of the presence of one of their community leaders.

Neş'et Kadın was aged 50 in 1885 and was living with her son and seven other women also born in "Arabia" in the house at 22/24 Hamam Odaları Street. She is qualified as *Kolbaşı* in the census listing. These seven females living with her were of various ages, the youngest being only 15 and the oldest about 80. *Kolbaşı* was the name given to the head of each of the informal solidarity and support networks established by manumitted black female slaves in late-nineteenth-century Ottoman Istanbul.

These exclusively female informal networks of support obviously provided minimal food and shelter to those former slaves left without a "home." They also provided shelters against the tyranny of masters, sickness, and other accidents of life. Before the nineteenth century, the *kolbaşı* would also intervene to purchase the freedom of black slaves who were on bad terms with their masters. They housed the unemployed manumitted female slaves and occasionally served as informal placement offices for cooks and servants in large *konak*s. But, in many instances, the *Kolbaşı* also seems to have provided a location for the meetings and semireligious ceremonies and rituals of African origin that many of these manumitted slaves continued to perform long after their arrival to Istanbul and after their conversion to Islam. In these exclusively female ecstatic rituals the *kolbaşı* acted as a sort of priestess, a mediator of the imported African pagan deity. These unorthodox rituals of vodoo-like possession in which only women were allowed to participate were called *Arap düğünü* (Arab wedding) in popular parlance. These pagan rites were sometimes the object of complaints.[17]

Neş'et Kadın was apparently the *kolbaşı* of such an informal group, both priestess of a religious cult and union leader. She owned two houses in the *mahalle*, one of which was probably rented out. A share in one of her two houses was sold by Neş'et Kadın in 1885 to another manumitted female slave living in the neighboring area of Etyemez. In three other neighboring houses, all situated within a radius of about a hundred meters from the house belonging to Neş'et Kadın, lived together a total of nine manumitted black female slaves. Two other natives of "Arabia" lived together in yet another house, situated in the same street as Neş'et Kadın.

It appears that Neş'et Kadın was the wealthiest of the lot and that her presence had constituted a center of attraction for a wider peer group that came to live in her vicinity and all of them in close proximity within Kasap İlyas. Hakan Erdem qualifies these groups as "local lodges" of manumitted slaves, but whether the organization ever acquired that degree of formalism and permanence is far from being certain.[18] A total of five houses in Kasap İlyas belonged to the members of the same group, all women. One of these, Şirin Kadın, whose status is clearly specified as being a manumitted slave (*Çorlulu Eyüp Ağa'nın müttekâsı*) is recorded as having sold her house situated at 8 Horasancı Street in 1883.

According to the last Ottoman population census of 1907 Kasap İlyas contained only twenty-five such manumitted slaves. The slave trade had effectively stopped in the 1880s and death had taken its toll. Neş'et kadın, the *kolbaşı*, was not there anymore and the twenty-five natives of Arabia, Sudan, or Ethiopia were now more randomly distributed within the *mahalle* and were not concentrated in just a few households.

The category "Çerkes" was indicated as being the birthplace of thirty six people living in the neighborhood in 1885 (see table 3.1). Although the name of a specific ethnic and linguistic group from the northern Caucasus, this denomination was then used to denote a much wider area and included in fact all Muslims originating from the Caucasus and from Transcaucasia. The traditional Ottoman slave trade also involved the import of (mostly female) slaves from the area.[19] The empire had however witnessed, in the 1850s and 1860s, an inflow of immigrants and war refugees from this area, so that it is difficult to say whether we are in the presence of manumitted slaves or not in 1885. Thirty of the natives of "Çerkes" living in our neighborhood (including Fatma Şöhret hanım, the wife of Osman Efendi, the *muhtar*) were women. Only six are listed as servants or "dependents" living within various households. Only four male household heads were natives of "Çerkes."

That nineteenth-century Kasap İlyas was a variegated but not a particularly prosperous *mahalle* has already been underlined. The most destitute of the inhabitants, however, were neither the community of Arapkirli migrants nor the members of the small group of manumitted black slaves. Obviously, none of these two groups were living in opulence but both communities had, after all, some sort of internal organization, a more or less efficient network that supported and housed those in need, took care of the sick and most destitute, found them jobs, and so forth.

Comparing rather badly with these two groups, there also was a small number of people in the *mahalle* whose only occupation was begging and who were apparently living exclusively out of public alms. In 1885 ten people living in the neighborhood were officially classified as *sa'il* (beggars) or *se'eleden* (one of the beggars), and one person as *fukara* (poor) in the census listings. There were two married couples among them, in which both husband and wife were officially classified as beggars. Apart from their being elderly people for the most part, no other particular pattern (as to sex, birthplace, family structure, or location within the neighborhood) is discernible within this small group of beggars. Where they did their begging, or which group of public benefactors, whether on a strictly local scale or otherwise, contributed to the living expenses of these poverty-stricken people living in Kasap İlyas is also not known.

We have noted that the census register that contained the non-Muslim population of the neighborhood has unfortunately been lost and we have assumed that the proportion of non-Muslims was the same in 1885 as in the later count of 1907 (10.2 percent). This proportion does not hold, however, as to property-ownership in the *mahalle*. According to the *muhtar*'s notebooks, of the approximately 250 privately owned pieces of real estate in the neighborhood, only eight or ten were recorded as belonging to non-Muslims.[20] All of these property-owners, to judge by their name, were Greek Orthodox. Kasap İlyas was a basically Muslim neighborhood with but a small minority of non-muslims. This was so in the sixteenth as well as in the nineteenth centuries.

Streets, Houses, Warehouses, and Shops: Residential and Commercial Areas in Kasap İlyas

In 1885 there was a total of 242 Muslim households in Kasap İlyas. However, the *mahalle* did not contain that many dwellings. The census documents only show a total of 149 houses. We can surmise that the total number of houses in the *mahalle* must not have exceeded 160. Whatever the case may be, it is clear that in many cases the same house was shared by two or more coresidential units. Households were listed in the census by address (by street name and street number), and to many of these addresses was appended the word *mükerrer* (repeated), followed by the relevant street number. This clearly signifies that more than one household shared the same dwelling unit bearing an identical street number.

Households and Dwellings

The simple comparison of the number of houses and of households (149 and 242, respectively) clearly tells us that more than half of the houses in our neighborhood must have contained at least two households. There must have been approximately 150 households in the *mahalle* that had to share the same dwelling-unit with another family. Although shareholding of the same dwelling-unit by kin or non-kin households was certainly not uncommon at the time, a nonnegligible proportion of these coresiding households must clearly have been *tenants*. This must have been particularly the case for migrants to the *mahalle*. Each household, therefore, did not necessarily correspond to a houseful of people. Each house contained on average more than one household, more than one family-unit. The average household size was 3.82 in Kasap İlyas in 1885. Had each of the households lived in a separate house, this same figure would have also represented the average number of people living in each of the dwelling-units of the *mahalle*. Dividing the total population by the number of dwelling-units in the neighborhood, however, we obtain a much larger figure: 5.53. This is the average number of people living in each of the Kasap İlyas houses, a figure that is 45 percent higher than the mean size of familial units. The corresponding figure is even considerably higher (6.32) for the Ispanakçı Viranesi, the area with the highest concentration of migrants. Most of the run-down houses in the Virane were inhabited by more than one household, and some of them, as we saw, accommodated four or five of them.

Do these raw figures, however, constitute sufficient evidence for speaking of a *wohnungsprobleme* in the Kasap İlyas *mahalle* at the end of the nineteenth century? Are we entitled to say that Kasap İlyas was, generally speaking, "overcrowded"? That is difficult to assert. We know that some of the migrants, especially the bachelors, were, in all probability, living in small, cramped, shoddy, overcrowded, and relatively uncomfortable lodgings, but it is difficult to say more. First of all, a comparative housing standard for the whole city does not exist, nor are any comparable data sets for other parts of the city available, and it is highly doubtful whether such a standard could be devised at all. Second, and in the absence of any detailed cadastral maps, we do not have detailed information on the property and houses in Kasap İlyas itself. For instance, we know little about how many floors each of these houses in Kasap İlyas had. We have an insufficient knowledge of the number, type, and size of their rooms and of the various amenities that they might have contained, the size of the gardens, if any, and so forth.

Judging from the wealth, social status, and occupations of its inhabitants, what we can only dimly guess is that, despite the few *konak*s (mansions) that

FIGURE 4.1 A Typical Street in Late Nineteenth Century Istanbul

it contained, the Kasap İlyas houses were in general neither particularly large nor comfortable, in relation to the standards of the time. Here is how, for instance, a mansion sold in the neighborhood in the 1840s is described in the Davudpaşa Religious Court records :

> ... A privately owned *konak* with, in the upper floor three rooms, a water-closet, a pantry and a hall, in the middle floor three rooms, a bathroom and water-closet and a hall, in the lower floor a kitchen, a toilet and a storage place for coal plus, in the men's quarters (*selâmlık*), a room, a bathroom and water-closet in the top floor, a room and a bathroom and water-closet in the middle-floor, plus stables, a water-well, a garden and garden gates. . . ."[21]

There were, however, all in all just four such *konak*s in the neighborhood in 1885 (see table 4.7). Here is how one of the more modest houses of Kasap İlyas was described in a deed of sale recorded by the Davudpaşa Court of Justice in the 1850s. Part of the ground floor of this house was apparently occupied by a barbershop : ". . . on the upper floor two rooms and a hall, and on the ground floor two rooms, a bathroom, and a barber with a shop. . . ."[22] This was the lot of most of the ordinary houses in Kasap İlyas. A few deeds of sale of the early nineteenth century also record even smaller dwellings that contained, for instance, just ". . . a room in the ground floor, a hall, a courtyard, a kitchen and a garden. . . ."

Besides, a number of people lived in various kinds of premises (a coffeehouse, a shop, a stables, or a warehouse) that were not designed to be proper houses and that probably lacked the minimum level of comfort and privacy that even those who lived in the Ispanakçı Viranesi were entitled to. According to the later population census of 1907, these people were more numerous

TABLE 4.7
List of Property and Buildings in Kasap İlyas (1885)

House (*hane*)	149	Bakery (*fırın*)	2
Mansion (*konak*)	4	Public fountain (*çeşme*)	2
Shop (*dükkân*)	24	Dervish convent (*tekke*)	2
Warehouse (*mağaza*)	24	Public bath (*hamam*)	1
Room (*oda*)	4	Police station (*karakol*)	1
Vacant lot (*arsa*)	29	Boathouse (*kayıkhane*)	1
Mosque (*cami*)	2	Mausoleum (*türbe*)	1
Vegetable garden (*bostan*)	1	Mosque fountain (*şadırvan*)	1
Garden (*bahçe*)	7	Storage for coffins (*tabutluk*)	1
Coffeehouse (*kahvehane*)	2	Stable (*ahır*)	2
Unspecified	11		

than in 1885. In 1907 twelve people were recorded as residing in shops (*dükkân*s) and eight others in coffeehouses (*kahvehane*s). Twenty other people (mostly Arapkirli bachelors) were living in six different warehouses (*mağaza*s).[23]

During the 1885 census a complete listing was made by Osman Efendi of all private property and buildings in the *mahalle* (see table 4.7). Every single item that was given a street number was put down in this list, whether built or unbuilt, whether public, private, or belonging to a foundation, whether inhabited or not.[24]

It appears that houses (*hane*s) and mansions were not the only type of premises used as dwelling units in Kasap İlyas. Two people (single men), for instance, were living in a—probably rented—room and another in a coffeehouse. Three people (husband, wife, and son) had their permanent residence in one of the warehouses situated on Helvacı Street. Three of the houses located near the mosque were *vakıf* houses that had been bequeathed to local pious foundations so that they be used (either as a residence or to obtain rental income) by the *imam* or by the *müezzin* of the Kasap İlyas mosque. In one of them, that at 11 Yokuşçeşme Street, lived, together with his wife and mother-in-law, Ahmet Necati efendi, the *imam*. As to Ahmet efendi, the *müezzin*, he lived in the house situated at 52 Samatya Street with his wife and infant daughter.

In 1885, at 8 Cami-i Şerif Street, that is, just behind the Kasap İlyas mosque Osman Efendi (1837–1904), the *muhtar* of Kasap İlyas lived with his family. Born in Istanbul, Osman efendi had been officiating as a local headman for a few years already at the time of the census (see the appendix).[25] His household consisted of five people besides himself: his wife, who was 40, his three children, a boy of 10 and two girls of ages 7 and 4, plus a female servant. Osman efendi and his wife Fatma Şöhret hanım had no other living children. In 1895 Osman was born, their first grandchild. The house in which they lived was theirs. It was officially registered as property of Fatma Şöhret hanım, and the family shared it with no other household. Osman efendi was a haberdasher (*astarcı*) by profession. There was at the time, however, no haberdasher's shop within the Kasap İlyas *mahalle* and Osman efendi's workplace must have been situated in one of the commercial areas of the city, perhaps in the central Grand Bazaar. Osman efendi had a very long tenure as *muhtar* and took his official duties very seriously, as we have had occasion to see.

Our *mahalle* contained two *tekke*s (dervish convents). The first was located at 53 Samatya Street (formerly "Butchers' Road") and the second at 19 Yokuşçeşme Street, on the left-hand side when climbing toward Cerrahpaşa. The first of these dervish lodges was called Gümüş Baba (or Taşçı tekkesi) and the second Bekâr bey (or Kâmil Efendi).[26] They belonged, respectively, to the Kadirî and to the Rufaî sufi orders. The officiating *şeyh*s of these two lodges and their families lived in houses adjacent to their respective *tekke*s. For instance, Ihsan Efendi, the *şeyh* of the Bekâr bey Rufai lodge, was himself a middle-ranking bureaucrat in the Ministry of Finance (*maliye ketebesinden*) and his household consisted of four people: his brother, his sister, a person officially put down as a dervish, and himself. As to İbrahim efendi bin Sadullah, *şeyh* of the Kadirî lodge, he lived in the *tekke* with a familial group consisting of seven people, kin, and servants. The point is that neither of these two *tekke*s were large and religiously or culturally important institutions. Weekly sufi *zikir* ceremonies did take place in both of them (on Saturdays in Bekâr bey and on Tuesdays in Gümüş *baba*) but neither of these *tekke*s can be considered as a principal lodge (*asitane*) or as an important center of attraction, from a religious or a cultural point of view, and none could ever have housed a large number of resident dervishes. They were not very old and venerable institutions either, since they had both been established toward the end of the eighteenth century at the earliest, and more probably at the beginning of the nineteenth century.[27]

The Kasap İlyas *mahalle* contained none of the other large and collective households that existed in many other areas of the capital-city of the Ottoman Empire. There was no *medrese* within the neighborhood, for instance. Kasap İlyas was quite a distance away from the Fatih mosque and from its conglomerate of religious schools. The nearest *medrese* was a rather smallish institution, the Gevherhan Sultan *medrese*, situated in the neighboring Cerrahpaşa District and which, in the middle of the century housed only two teachers and twenty-seven students.[28] There were no *bekârodaları*s (rooms for single men in which migrant bachelors were usually housed) in the neighborhood either. Why would there be one, anyway, in this neighborhood that was not situated anywhere near the commercial heart of the city? According to the 1885 listing of premises (see table 4.7) there were four dwellings qualified as *oda*s within the neighborhood, and only two people were recorded as effectively residing in them. Besides, not being a central *mahalle*, there never had been in Kasap İlyas any of the *han*s or *bedesten*s in which artisans or tradesmen exercised their profession together.

An interesting house in the *mahalle* was the one situated at 11 Yokuşçeşme Street. This house that belonged to the local *vakıf* was officially the residence of Necati efendi, the *imam* of the Kasap İlyas mosque, and of his family. But the same building also functioned as a primary school for girls. This school was known in Istanbul as the Şerif Paşa school for girls (*Şerif Paşa mekteb-i inası*).[29] For all practical purposes this meant that, in this two-story small wooden Kasap İlyas house, Necati efendi more or less regularly welcomed a small number of young female pupils living in the *mahalle*. The locals certainly must not have hesitated in entrusting their young daughters to the hands of the *imam* of the local mosque. To these pupils Necati efendi taught some elementary skills such as reading, writing, deciphering the Holy Coran and, perhaps, the first rudiments of arithmetic. The parents of the pupils were then adding a small contribution to Necati efendi's livelihood. The school's curriculum as well as its teaching methods followed "traditional" norms, and were apparently not affected by the modernizing thrust of the educational reforms of the Tanzimat period. A 1894–1895 official statistical publication clearly records the fact that teaching in this small school was not done according to the new methods (*usûl-i cedid*), but followed the ancient patterns (*usûl-i kadîm*) and mentions that a total of 20 pupils (18 girls and 2 boys) were attending.[30]

"Upper *Mahalle*" and "Lower *Mahalle*": Topographical Harmony

As a settlement the *mahalle* was, so to speak, living in harmony with its general topographical setting. *Samatya Caddesi* (Samatya Avenue, *alias* "Buchers' Road"), running in a more or less east-west direction parallel to the sea and itself at approximately sea level, was in many ways the "high street" of Kasap İlyas (Fig 3.1). Almost all of the shops and all of the public buildings (the mosque, the public bath, the police station, the bakery, one of the two dervish lodges, the main public fountain, and two coffeehouses), as well as the largest *konak*s, were all lined on this street.

Through our "main street" also passed, at that time, one of the newly established horse-drawn tramway lines. This was the Aksaray-Yedikule line, one of the first horse-drawn tramway lines in Istanbul, put in operation in the early 1870s. The electrification of the Istanbul tramway lines was to come only after the turn of the century. Samatya Street had also been newly paved for the occasion and the rails went now between regular pavement-stones, not on the dirt that was trodden by the butchers carrying meat to the Janissaries in previous centuries. The Kasap İlyas "main street" was not wide enough, though, and, before the tramway line could be inaugurated, a number of shops and houses had to be torn down to allow for the simultaneous passage of two streetcars.

The first precise and published measurements of street length and width in and around Kasap İlyas were done by a German land-surveying company just before the First World War. These measurements clearly show that, even after the passage of the tramway line, our newly paved "main street" was neither rectilinear nor uniformly wide. The width of Samatya Caddesi varied between a minimum of 8.4 meters and a maximum of 10.8 meters, sidewalks included, over the portion that passed through the Kasap İlyas *mahalle*. Over some portions there was still, forty years after the tram line was opened, only one set of tramway rails, and two streetcars could not pass abreast. The width of the other important streets of the *mahalle* (e.g., Çavuşzâde or Yokuşçeşme) nowhere exceeded four or four and a half meters, the measurements being always taken from house to house. Over part of their course these streets were even narrower. The bay windows of the houses situated on the two sides were almost touching each other. There were even much thinner passageways in the neighborhood, such as the one leading to the Ispanakçı Viranesi and the whole web of small streets situated between Samatya Caddesi and the sea.[31] One consequence of the operation of the new tramway line that connected the *mahalle* to one of the central districts of the city had, obviously, been a change in the transportation patterns of the local inhabitants of Kasap İlyas. The Davudpaşa wharf totally lost any function it may have had in local urban passenger transportation.

South of Samatya Street, along the old city ramparts, also passed the railway line that connected Istanbul to Vienna, Paris, London, and other European cities through Edirne, Sofia, and Belgrade. That was the line that brought the "Orient Express" to Istanbul. The railway line had been officially opened in 1874. On the same line also operated local urban/suburban trains that went from the Sirkeci train station in the city center to the distant suburb of Küçükçekmece.[32] The nearest two stops were those of Yenikapı and Samatya, both about half a kilometer away along the shore, respectively to the east and to the west of Kasap İlyas. The local inhabitants preferred to use the tramway line, however, which was cheaper and much more convenient for those who worked in the city center.

Sloping gently in a roughly north-south course toward this main commercial street, two other long streets, Çavuşzâde and Yokuşçeşme (with its narrow passageway leading to the cul-de-sac of Ispanakçı Viranesi), delineated the main residential areas of Kasap İlyas. These two streets, as well as those situated south of Samatya Caddesi toward the sea, contained no shops at all. In 1885, more than two thirds of the residents were living either on Samatya Street or in the streets situated to the north of it. Twenty years later, the situation had not changed, as only 24 percent of the residents lived south of the main street in 1907. To the south of the main street was the relatively sparsely populated area that also contained all of the warehouses.

Most of the Kasap İlyas people had to therefore "go down" to Samatya Street for all sorts of everyday activities: to buy a loaf of bread, to do some daily shopping, to pray, to have a hot bath, to get a bucketful of drinking water, to sit idly at a coffeehouse, or to use public transportation to go to another part of the city. There had developed, so it seems, in the *mahalle*, a quite clear functional differentiation between the purely residential areas and the central/shopping area. The residential area consisted of the streets and alleys situated to the north of the central shopping area, and these streets had no shops. On or very near Samatya Street were also located all of the four *konak*s that belonged to the wealthier of the residents. By opposition, less than one fifth of the neighborhood population lived in the three narrow and winding streets (named Helvacı, Horasancı, and Davutpaşa İskelesi) that went from this central area toward the wharf and the sea.

It appears that these three streets south of the main street and that also contained the warehouses for wood, coal, and other bulk goods were, just as the *Ispanakçı Viranesi* further up north, another relatively poor residential section of the *mahalle*. "The neighborhood never contained more than a thousand inhabitants.... The more well-to-do lived on Çavuşzâde street, and the poorest in Yokuşçeşme street and in the Ispanakçı Viranesi.... There were absolutely no immigrants among the inhabitants of Çavuşzâde street." This is a twentieth-century representation of the situation, which prevailed half a century before that, expressed by a native of Çavuşzâde Street.[33] Indeed, not a single native of Arapkir lived on that street in 1907.

The 1885 census documents contain no detailed information on the precise composition of the central shopping area of the neighborhood. The notebooks of Osman Efendi, however, fill up some of the lacunae and give particulars as to some of the shops on Samatya Street.[34] There were two barbershops, a butcher, a locksmith (and tinner at the same time), two groceries, a seller of *boza*, a herbalist (*aktar*), a maker and seller of sweet pudding (*muhallebici*), and another of sweets (*helva*). Of the two bakeries, both located on the main street, one was for bread and the other for sweet pastry. The large public bath, with a *tepidarium/caldarium* couple for men's use and another for women, was one of the oldest and best known of Istanbul.

These shops, together with the nearby vegetable gardens, were quite sufficient to meet the daily needs of the inhabitants. There were, however, no sellers of cloth, shoes, dresses, garments, or related items, nor of any other kind of durable consumer goods within the neighborhood. Kasap İlyas contained no other specialized craftsman or shop, either. People had to buy provisions in nearby markets. The two nearest marketplaces were situated in Aksaray and in Avratpazarı, the first about a kilometer away to the east and the second not too far away, in the neighboring northern district of Cerrahpaşa. There was no primary school for boys within the *mahalle* either. Schoolboys had to climb uphill in order to reach the primary school known as Ahmet Paşa *taşmektebi*, situated in the upper portion of Yokuşçeşme Street, then part of the northern Hûbyâr neighborhood. This school, which operated on a modern mode, was much more important than the small primary school for girls on lower Yokuşçeşme Street. Forty-five male and thirty-one female pupils were enrolled in that primary school in 1894.[35]

The number of shops in the *mahalle* was barely equal to that of the warehouses for wood and coal (see table 4.7). The 1885 census listing of occupations (see table 3.2) shows that the number of artisans and shopkeepers who resided in Kasap İlyas (137) was much larger than the total number of shops (24) that the neighborhood itself contained. Besides, the precise occupations of these artisans and shopkeepers who resided in Kasap İlyas did not correspond at all to the types of shops and trades that existed in the neighborhood. For instance, the owner or manager of what was certainly one of the largest commercial enterprises in the neighborhood, the public bath, does not appear in any of the listings of the inhabitants of Kasap İlyas. Neither do any of those who worked in the same *hamam*. Osman efendi, the *muhtar* of Kasap İlyas, is another case in point. He was a haberdasher (*astarcı*) by profession but there was no haberdasher's shop within the Kasap İlyas *mahalle*. Clearly, he had to spend the day away from his neighborhood. There were bakeries and groceries in Kasap İlyas but no resident professional bakers or grocers. There were twenty-four warehouses (*mağaza*s) in Kasap İlyas in 1885, but their owners or managers are nowhere to be seen in the census listings. By contrast, a cobbler/shoemaker lived in our *mahalle* but his shop was situated elsewhere.

As a matter-of-fact, almost the whole group of artisans and shopkeepers living in Kasap İlyas practiced their profession elsewhere, and the shops and trades in Kasap İlyas were owned or run by people residing in some other neighborhood. Obviously, then, there must have been a considerable number of people, both adults and children, permanently on the move and who commuted, so to speak, daily to and from the *mahalle*. Most of the Kasap İlyas inhabitants probably walked to work and to school, as their habit had been for long centuries, but some of them must have used the new means of public transportation, the tramway.

Wharf and Warehouses: The "Lower *Mahalle*"

Ever since the early sixteenth century (see chapter 1), the presence of a number of shops and warehouses for wood, timber, coal, sand, gravel, straw, and other bulk goods is well documented. These warehouses were functionally dependent on the operation of the Davudpaşa wharf and were, as in the sixteenth century, all situated within the area between Samatya Street and the sea.

The continuity between the sixteenth-century shops for wood and timber (the *dükkân-ı haşşâb*) and the late nineteenth-century warehouses can be followed by the many traces they have left in local documents. In a list of the shops and trades of Istanbul drafted in 1682, for instance, there is a total of forty-nine shops selling wood and coal. Forty-one of these were located in such districts as Cibali and Fener, both of them along the southern shores of the Golden Horn. These were the ports where these bulk goods were traditionally brought; the shores of the Golden Horn contained many wharfs for unloading coal and wood upon their arrival to the city. As to the remaining eight shops and warehouses, they were all situated in our neighborhood.[36]

Less than a century later, in 1772, a shop for wood/timber located in the neighborhood was being donated to establish a local pious foundation.[37] In 1784, the sale of a warehouse for straw neighboring on a storeroom for coal in Kasap İlyas is recorded by the Davudpaşa Court. The description of this piece of real estate makes it clear that both the warehouse for straw itself and the neighboring storeroom for coal were adjacent to the city ramparts (*cidar-ı hısn*)[38] and, therefore, that they were situated between the "Butcher's Road" and the sea.

The fate of one particular Kasap İlyas warehouse can be followed through the local *vakıf* documents for quite a long period of time. When this piece of real estate was first endowed as a local *vakıf* in 1772, it consisted of a "house with a shop for wood and timber under it."[39] According to the deed of trust, the monthly rental income of 25 *akçe*s was to accrue to the *imam* of the Kasap İlyas mosque. This piece of real estate was described in the deed of trust as being surrounded by two other shops for wood and timber. In 1772, then, Kasap İlyas contained at least three of these shops. This house *cum* timber shop was endowed as a *vakıf* in 1772 for the benefit and under the trusteeship of, the Kasap İlyas *imam*, changed hands at least seven times in the fifty years that followed the initial deed of trust. Most of the transmissions of the right of usufruct, all of them approved and signed by the *imam*, who was also the trustee of the *vakıf*, were from a deceased father to his son. After 1780, however, the deeds of transfer of this *vakıf* property do not mention the house that was above the shop at the time of its donation. Half a century later, a record of transfer, dated March 1825, tells us that the donated shop was now used for a different trade. It was not a shop for wood and timber anymore, but a warehouse for straw.[40] As of March 1825, this *vakıf* record redefines the shop's neighbors and indicates that it was now surrounded by another warehouse for straw on one side, and by a shop that sold coal on the other. Just like half a century ago, these shops and warehouses still seem to have been more or less grouped in the same area, between the neighborhood's "main street" and the sea. A few years later, half a share of the ex-timber shop, now a warehouse for straw, was transferred in April 1831 to one Hüseyin Nuri bey, a *kömürcü* (coal-seller) by profession, and the other half to his wife. Hüseyin Nuri bey used this shop for selling coal, not straw. Eight years later, in March 1839, in a last deed of transfer, Hüseyin Nuri bey passed on this shop to Ali bin Ismail, another coal-seller. Neither the wood and timber shop initially donated as a *vakıf*, nor its successor, the warehouse for straw, are mentioned in the 1839 deed of transfer of the shop for coal. This is the last deed of transfer we have, and we lose track of this *vakıf* shop thereafter.

The multiple avatars that this single shop went through, in a period more than three quarters of a century long, have one important thing in common. The successive users of this *vakıf* shop changed its contents and its trade, but not its essential character, namely, that of being a shop/warehouse for the storage and sale of bulk goods (timber and wood at first, then straw, and finally coal), the transportation and distribution of which were dependent on its proximity to the Davudpaşa wharf.

The Davudpaşa wharf and the warehouses cast their shadow on the human landscape of the area, as well. The Davudpaşa area, and the Kasap İlyas *mahalle* that was part of it, acquired a reputation in Istanbul, a reputation that stemmed directly from the presence of the warehouses and their managers and workers. An illustration of this is given by an anonymous early-eighteenth-century tract on the folklore of the various districts and inhabitants of Istanbul. The tract contains a humorous, deprecating, and sometimes even insulting list of the evil deeds supposedly perpetrated by the inhabitants of the various districts of Istanbul. And each of these districts had its own dominant ethnicity, occupational group, specific urban function, or generally perceived overall character or image. Davudpaşa was famous in Istanbul for its wharf and for the warehouses for storing and selling wood that were next to it. Not surprisingly, the inhabitants of our district are qualified in this tract as "... those ruffians from the Davudpaşa wharf who sell wood with counterfeit weights...."[41]

The warehouses left their mark on the street names, too. Although all of them were bearing official names ever since the early 1860s, the people of Kasap İlyas continued to refer to some of the streets in their *mahalle* by the types of warehouses they contained. In 1883, for instance, two different cases brought to the Davudpaşa Court concerned pieces of real estate property situated in the "coal-sellers' street."[42] That misnamed street was certainly one of those situated south of Samatya Caddesi. As late as 1898, another of the streets in the neighborhood was named as the "straw-sellers' street" in an official document.[43]

These warehouses brought not only goods, trade, and activity to the neighborhood but also, from time to time, the odd small disaster. In 1864, a fire ravaged once again the area around the Davudpaşa wharf. Its scope was fairly limited, however, and a total of only twenty-two buildings were destroyed in this local catastrophe. This rather circumscribed (by Istanbul standards) fire was recorded in the annals of Istanbul disasters as "The fire of the coal-sellers in the Davudpaşa Wharf,"[44] thereby signifying that the numerous coal-sellers present in the area and the highly inflammable goods that they stored were not only the victims but perhaps also the cause of this local fire.

These warehouses and their trade did not address themselves solely to the inhabitants of the Kasap İlyas *mahalle*. Given the large number of warehouses (twenty-four) listed in the 1885 census documents (see table 4.7), it is highly unlikely that the small Kasap İlyas *mahalle*, or even the larger Davudpaşa area, could ever have constituted a sufficient outlet for the volume of coal, wood, and so forth that must have been brought in. These warehouses were in fact servicing a much larger area, perhaps the whole portion of the intramural city bordering on the sea of Marmara and situated to the east of the Davudpaşa wharf. Large quantities of these goods could obviously not be brought through the dense, narrow, and hilly maze of streets of the city center. By necessity, they had to be brought by sea and had to be stored in warehouses situated not too far away from their point of entry into the walled city. From there, the retail trade and distribution could normally proceed.

Two of the warehouses in Kasap İlyas were clearly listed in the 1885 census documents as being "warehouses for coal." As to the notebooks of the *muhtar* Osman Efendi, they specify that, at about the same date, two of these warehouses were for timber, three for coal, and another three for straw. Most of the commodities stored and distributed were goods of first necessity, whether for fuel (wood and coal), for transportation (straw), or for construction and repair work (timber, sand, and gravel).

At least some of the porters (*hammal*s) living in Kasap İlyas at the end of the nineteenth century must have been fully or partly employed in the transportation and the retail distribution of these bulk goods stored nearby. Some of these porters might even be sleeping in their workplace. And the presence of this group of poor and destitute porters carrying sand or coal on their backs all day long from boats to warehouses and from warehouses to various houses in and around the *mahalle* was one of the reasons why this part of the Kasap İlyas neighborhood had acquired a plebeian and rather unsavory reputation. "My family lived in Çavuşzade and, when we were children, the lower parts of the neighborhood [meaning the area between the "main street" and the wharf] were strictly out of bounds for us. Some unpleasant things had happened in that area and my father had forbidden us to go down there," declared one of the elderly inhabitants of Kasap İlyas, referring to his childhood period in the 1930s and 1940s.[45] "Only poor people lived over there in small and shabby houses," declared another elderly informant, referring to the same area in about the same period.[46] The area was also qualified as "A sort of large shantytown."[47] Ispanakçı Viranesi was also another such impoverished large area but the traditional shelter of poor Arapkirli migrants never had this sort of unsavory reputation.

It was not the presence of the poor street-porters alone that gave the part of Kasap İlyas nearer to the sea its disreputable character. At all times, there were some even less-esteemed groups of people that haunted the area. A few fishermen, for instance, probably used to live or sleep in the sheds and boathouses down by the wharf, where they also dried and mended their nets. The old city ramparts, which ran along the sea side certainly provided some shelter (and also the occasional building material) to some of the poorest and of the "homeless" of Istanbul. Drunkards and drug addicts also got together, especially in the summer, under the ramparts and by the wharf, far from the ordinary crowd of the *mahalle*. Besides, all along the Marmara shore of the traditional walled city, there were always vagabonds whose main occupation was to stroll by the seaside, on the lookout for the occasional spoils brought by the waves, the southernly wind, or the latest Lodos tempest. The area also had the great advantage of being right next to the large Langa vegetable gardens, which contained a maze of winding tracks and small footpaths, a terrible trap for the newcomer but a practical way of escape for those familiar with the topography of the *bostan*s. No wonder, then, that this outgrowth of the *mahalle* was considered disreputable and unsafe by many of the inhabitants of "upper" Kasap İlyas and declared out of bounds for their young children. As a matter-of-fact, the dubious reputation of the "lower" part of Kasap İlyas persisted well into the 1950s when the wharf was torn down and the warehouses removed once and for all.

This part of the neighborhood, located between Samatya Caddesi and the sea, therefore had, for quite a long time, an overall urban commercial function whose importance exceeded by far, the narrow limits of a single little *mahalle*. It was located on a sort of topographical extension of the neighborhood toward the sea and the warehouses throughout the history of Kasap İlyas, it was directly related to the urban function fulfilled by the wharf. The sorts of goods transported, stored, and distributed did change, but the unloading/storage/retail distribution functions that the wharf and the warehouses of Kasap İlyas together fulfilled, remained intact. In the sixteenth century the goods were wood and timber. Later, coal and straw were added to the list of goods brought and stored there. As for the twentieth-century inhabitants of Kasap İlyas, they remember the Davudpaşa wharf primarily as a place for unloading sand and gravel.

Kasap İlyas was part of the Davudpaşa *semt* of intramural Istanbul. But the definitional role of the homonymous wharf was always perceived as far more important than that of the stately Davudpaşa mosque and its complex, situated up on the hill. Historical documents even present many instances in which the Davudpaşa *semt* is, for reasons of topographical clarity, subdivided in two separate entities: upper Davudpaşa, or Davudpaşa itself (*nefs-i* Davudpaşa) and the Davudpaşa Wharf (Davudpaşa İskelesi). Kasap İlyas was always part of this second section.

The wharf and the warehouses marked not only Kasap İlyas's image, reputation, and social standing, but even its very name, its official denomination. In all official documents Kasap İlyas was defined as "the Kasap İlyas *mahalle* by the Davudpaşa wharf," in the sixteenth as well as in the nineteenth century. This was so in the Davudpaşa Religious Court records, in the local deeds of trust, as well as in the various official lists of Istanbul neighborhoods. The official seal (*mühür*) used by the *muhtar*s of Kasap İlyas for stamping legal documents at the end of the nineteenth century reads; "The *Muhtar* of the Kasap İlyas *mahalle*, near the Davudpaşa wharf."[48]

THE *MUHTAR* AND HIS *MAHALLE*:
RULER, REPRESENTATIVE, AND MIDDLEMAN

Such was the *mahalle* that Osman efendi, the *muhtar*, was expected to rule, control, and represent. He had to have official dealings with a wide variety of people and was expected to know all the residents of his neighborhood. Osman Efendi had a period of tenure of almost a quarter of a century (ca.1880-1904) as *muhtar* of Kasap İlyas. The Istanbul *muhtar*s did not have an official workplace or an office of their own, at the time. The Kasap İlyas residents, therefore, had to pay a personal visit to Osman efendi's home, situated at 8 Cami-i şerif Street, just behind the mosque, each time they needed an official signed document. And a closer look at the three thick notebooks Osman efendi filled with various official and personal annotations provides a different perspective on the intra*mahalle* relationships at the end of the nineteenth century.

Legally, the only types of records the *muhtar*s were officially required to enter in their books or to stamp with their seal of office were those of a demographic type. The Population Registration Regulation (Sicill-i nüfus Nizamnamesi) of 1883 had put all urban and rural *muhtar*s under the obligation of recording demographic events and of reporting them to a centralized population record. This permanent register was to serve for the updating of the results of the 1885 population census.[49] All births, deaths, and marriages that occurred within the *mahalle* and the migrations to and from it were to be reported by the *muhtar*. The system established in 1883 did not meet with success, though, for the regulation offered no real incentive for officially declaring and recording these events, nor did it provide for any significant penalties for abstainers. A second regulation, established in 1902, was more stringent but, still, success was far from being complete.

Looking at Osman efendi's notebooks, however, the number and the variety of entries, which went far beyond what the official regulations imposed, is truly striking. The average number of cases from Kasap İlyas that were brought to the Davudpaşa Court, for instance, did not exceed a yearly average of eight or ten during the nineteenth century. There were even some years with less than five cases. There is, by contrast, not a single year in which less than fifty records had been entered in Osman Efendi's notebooks. Second, the variety of the entries in the *muhtar*'s notebooks was not commensurate with what the law strictly required of him. As a matter-of-fact there are very few birth and death entries in the notebooks (a total of just about sixty, spanning a period of more than ten years). The entries that were related to demographic events (there were more than three hundred of them) mainly consisted of ex post facto justifications given to rural migrants who settled in Istanbul without regular travel documents (see chapter 3). These were, as we have pointed out, more informative of the web of intra*mahalle* relationships and of well-established patterns of migration to Istanbul and of integration to urban life than of purely quantitative population movements.

Help and Control

Among the entries in Osman efendi's notebooks those that were compulsory records were only a small minority. Our *muhtar* was performing a number of functions that went far beyond his strictly official duties. To assist his flock in all of their official dealings Osman efendi was in fact fulfilling the functions of a notary, or those of a witness, of a scribe, a petition-writer, those of a guarantor, and of a middleman. He acted as a scribe for those who could not read or write. He wrote petitions on behalf of those who had to apply to a government office. He apposed his signature as a witness in deeds of sale of real estate situated in the neighborhood and often entered the full deed in his notebooks as if he were a notary. He was often called to witness the conclusion of this or that commercial deal between two residents of the neighborhood. He acted as a guarantor of the identity, moral integrity, and social and marital status of many of the inhabitants of his *mahalle* and this gave them access to some public benefits. Whenever one of them needed to be supported when dealing with government authorities, the first person whose help was required was the *muhtar*. Osman Efendi also had to transmit all official notifications addressed to a resident of his *mahalle*. Besides, he recorded many of the changes in property rights of privately owned land and houses in the neighborhood, as well as the details of the marriage acts performed by the *imam* of the Kasap İlyas mosque.

Helping the inhabitants and controlling the *mahalle* as a whole were functions that had a high degree of overlapping. It will suffice to give but a few examples as illustrations of the types of entries that fill the pages of Osman Efendi's notebooks.

There are, first, what were then called the official declarations of poverty (*fakir ilm-ü haberi*). These were official statements, signed and stamped by the *muhtar*, certifying that such and such a person was poor and was therefore entitled to receive assistance from a public organism (the Red Crescent, a philanthropic foundation, other types of poor relief, etc.). The "poor" could also be exempted from the payment of a fee (e.g., a child's tuition) or of a tax. The statement, stamped by the *muhtar*, contained information on the identity and the address of the person in need. Here is an example of such a statement, entered on November 7, 1887: "Hamam Odaları street, number 18—Vahide Hanım, sister of Mehmet Tevfik Efendi, scribe of the thirty fifth regiment of infantry... is a widow, cannot provide for herself, and is in a pitiful state."[50] Of a similar nature, but more numerous, are those entries that Osman Efendi grouped under the heading of dispatches to the hospital (*hastahaneye sevk*). These were documents given by the *muhtar* to the poor and sick of the *mahalle* and which, it seems, enabled them to receive free or inexpensive medical assistance. For instance an entry in the *muhtar*'s notebooks dated from October 28, 1887 reads: "Samatya caddesi 53—Fidan Kalfa, daughter of Abdullah, born 1250 a.h., ill and to the hospital...."[51] There was a total of about thirty such entries in Osman Efendi's notebooks.

For all practical pupuses, these "dispatch" documents fulfilled the same function as the "official declarations of poverty." The local headman was thereby helping some of the poor of his *mahalle*. With these two types of documents the *muhtar* was creating the legal basis of a specific right. A great service was being rendered to the local poor because it was the *muhtar*'s signed and stamped official declaration that obtained for them the right of access to a free lunch or to medical care. A pauper would not obtain assistance or relief from any official organization without the *muhtar*'s written statement, nor would he be taken care of in a hospital.

In other instances, the origin of a personal right was not the *muhtar* himself, but the law. Nevertheless, the local inhabitant who had that specific legal right, or was legally entitled to a particular benefit could not effectively exercise his right or obtain his benefit without a document signed by the *muhtar*. Osman efendi had to control and guarantee the beneficiary's identity as well as personal and residential status before he or she could benefit from what was, after all, only a full legal right. Two categories of personal benefits were particularly concerned here: the transfers of pay (*sipariş-i maaş*) and the retirement pensions (*tekaüt maaşı*). The transfers of pay were instances in which a civil servant of the Ottoman government (and this was particularly the case for the military) who was posted far away from the capital had ordered his salary to be paid to a member of his family residing in Istanbul. The beneficiaries who resided in Kasap İlyas had to have Osman efendi's written and signed approval. Osman efendi had regrouped the entries concerning the transfers of pay and the retirement pensions under the title of monthly allowances (*mahiyyât*). There are more than forty such entries in his notebooks, all concerning the years from 1883 to 1892.

The *muhtar*'s powers over the inhabitants of his *mahalle* were not, it seems, much smaller than those of the *imam* in former times. A couple of examples will suffice to show how the vested rights and interests of many of the neighborhood residents could be denied a de facto existence without a written statement from the *muhtar*. On July 10, 1890 Saide hanım, living at 2 Sancaktar Street, receives from Osman Efendi a written statement that specifies that "... Saide hanım has the benefit of a transfer of pay *[siparis-i maaş]* from her brother Ismail Zühdü, who is a first lieutenant in the second army, fifteenth regiment, second regular battalion, second squadron...."[52] With that document, Saide hanım could receive her brother's pay. The document, which may seem redundant at first sight, and the parallel entry in the *muhtar*'s notebooks signify simply that, for all practical purposes Osman Efendi had, in the name of the whole *mahalle*, recognized Saide hanım as being precisely Saide hanım. Osman Efendi signs another document on March 9, 1890, and entitles Mehmet Ağa, a former customs house guard living at 5 Samatya Street to receive a monthly retirement pension of 144 *kuruş*. "Samatya street, 5—The former customs house guard Mehmet Ağa has been allotted a retirement pension of one hundred and forty four *kuruş*," reads the entry in the notebooks.[53] Another entry in the notebooks, dated June 22, 1892, for instance, allows a widow to receive the retirement pension that was being paid to her now deceased husband. The document reads: "Hafize Resmiye hanım, the widow of the deceased Halim Efendi, former scribe in the Ministry of Defense, is presently alive and has not contracted a new marriage."[54] The *muhtar* is here controlling and certifying that Hafize Resmiye hanım has apparently no other financial resource than the retirement pension of her deceased husband. These entitlements signify that the *muhtar* had considerable power over those inhabitants of the neighborhood that needed his signature, testimony, and approval.

From a purely formal point of view, what Osman Efendi did was simply to provide a statement confirming a person's identity, kinship situation, and marital status. But without that written statement neither Saide hanım, nor the retired Mehmet ağa, nor the widow of Halim efendi could benefit from what in fact was their full legal rights. The *muhtar* was double checking these entitlements and Osman Efendi, in the name of his whole *mahalle*, was, in a sense, collectively guaranteeing these people's good faith. In a sense, people became full legal entities only through the *muhtar*'s intercession.

Apparently, in the eyes of the Ottoman administrative apparatus, a *muhtar*'s sponsorship had more weight than the official identity papers that began to be delivered by that very same Ottoman administration right after the 1885 population census and registration. These official identity documents (called Ottoman certificates, *tezkere-i Osmani*) had apparently not yet been widely distributed and, a fortiori, were not considered as sufficiently convincing proof of a person's identity. A guarantee/sponsorship by the *muhtar*—the direct eyewitness of an Ottoman subject's daily life and demeanor—was still deemed necessary for official proof of identity and/or of marital and personal status.

The seal authentications (*mühür tasdiki*) were yet another sort of certification of identity that the *muhtar* of Kasap İlyas very often had to deliver. Ottomans used regularly a personal seal in lieu of a handwritten signature. This was totally unrelated to literacy or social status. Personal as well as official documents were stamped with the seal of the writer, the ultimate model being the seal of the Sultan, the imperial *tuğra*. Almost everybody had a personal seal made of metal or of a precious stone. As to the engraving of seals, it was a widespread and honorable occupation—sometimes even an art. The problem, of course, was that these personal seals could be easily reproduced or counterfeited.

And that was precisely when the *muhtar* was asked to intervene. Many residents of the *mahalle* requested from their *muhtar* an authentication of their personal seals, either because they had lost an old seal and had had a new one made or because the transaction that they were about to conclude or the government administration with which they were to deal or to which they had presented a sealed petition had requested a bona fide authentication of their personal seal. Commercial deals between people who did not know each other well enough and that involved a future commitment of one of the parties could, understandably, also be accompanied by an authentication of the seals and identities of the signatories. Osman Efendi's notebooks contain a large number of entries indicating that such a certification had been delivered to a resident of Kasap İlyas. The shortest of these entries simply indicated that such and such a person's seal had been authenticated and really belonged to him or her. More complex authentications delivered by the *muhtar* also specified why the document had been requested. Here is an example, dated from June 10, 1889: ". . . Major İbrahim Şem'i Efendi has lost his old personal seal, and he will use his new one to retrieve his deposits from the Trust bank. . . ."[55] There are also much more detailed entries in the notebooks, entries in which not only the precise transaction in which the authenticated seal is to be used is specified, but also the price of the good sold, and names, occupations, and addresses of the witnesses, and so forth.

In a number of other instances, what the *muhtar* was brought to guarantee was not just the identity or the marital and social status of a person but his very personality, his morals, respectability, and character. Sometimes the *sharia'* courts of Istanbul required such a document in order to accept as valid the testimony of a particular witness. And what government official could know that person and weigh the testimonial value of his word better than his local headman, the *muhtar*, a firsthand eyewitness to that person's primary familial situation and daily social behavior? There were many public administrations that also asked for such a written statement of moral propriety. Hence, Osman efendi not only had to guarantee the identity of the residents of his *mahalle*, but was also often called to evaluate and sponsor their overall "respectability." On August 5, 1887, for instance, a note was delivered to Ali bin Osman who was asked to testify in court. Osman Efendi states that Ali "... is a person of integrity and his testimony is acceptable...."[56] Two years later, on August 16, 1889 another resident of Kasap İlyas, Mehmet Arif Efendi, who had applied to a military school, is given a note from the *muhtar* stating that he is "... a respectable person...."[57] Every time some resident of Kasap İlyas had to move to another Istanbul neighborhood he rightfully asked for a note of introduction addressed to the *muhtar* of his new *mahalle* and stating that, in his previous *mahalle*, he had been well-behaved and "respectable" (Fig. 4.2). Before the *muhtar*, it was the *imam* of the neighborhood mosque who provided the residents of the *mahalle* with similar documents of paternalistic protection and moral patronage.

Osman Efendi also delivered a number of signed and sealed notes (there are eighteen of them in his notebooks) for those who were short-term "guests" in the neighborhood. These notes were very appropriately called notes of overnight stay (*beytutet pusulası*). They concerned almost exclusively students of a boarding school or of a military college who were to spend a night or two a week with a parent, a relative, or a friend living in Kasap İlyas. For the student, these notes had the significance of a temporary legal "residence permit." As to the school or college, it was thus released from its responsibilities for the time the student spent away from the school. Here is an example of such a note, given by Osman Efendi on June 7, 1889: "Hamam Odaları street, 15—Hayri, a first year student in the İmperial medical school, will spend the night at his father's house when he is on permission."[58]

It may indeed seem quite artificial that, on the one hand, so many of those "notes of overnight stay," obviously quite insignificant from the point of view of local control and security, were handed out by the *muhtar* of Kasap İlyas to various schoolboys while, on the other hand, an effective registration and control system for the massive number of rural migrants from Arapkir and elsewhere could never be fully implemented. The Ottoman administration implicitly required that the *muhtar*s, and especially those of the capital, control and be informed of practically *everything* that happened within their *mahalle*. The ideal *muhtar* was supposed to keep all local residents under a sort of moral supervision and check and control even the most minute and insignificant population movement. We understand now that this was not within the realm of possibility. But still, a conscientious *muhtar* would behave *as if* an exhaustive and absolute local control mechanism was within reach. And that is perhaps how the zealous recording activities of Osman efendi should be interpreted. Although they had inherited some of the traditional powers and responsibilities

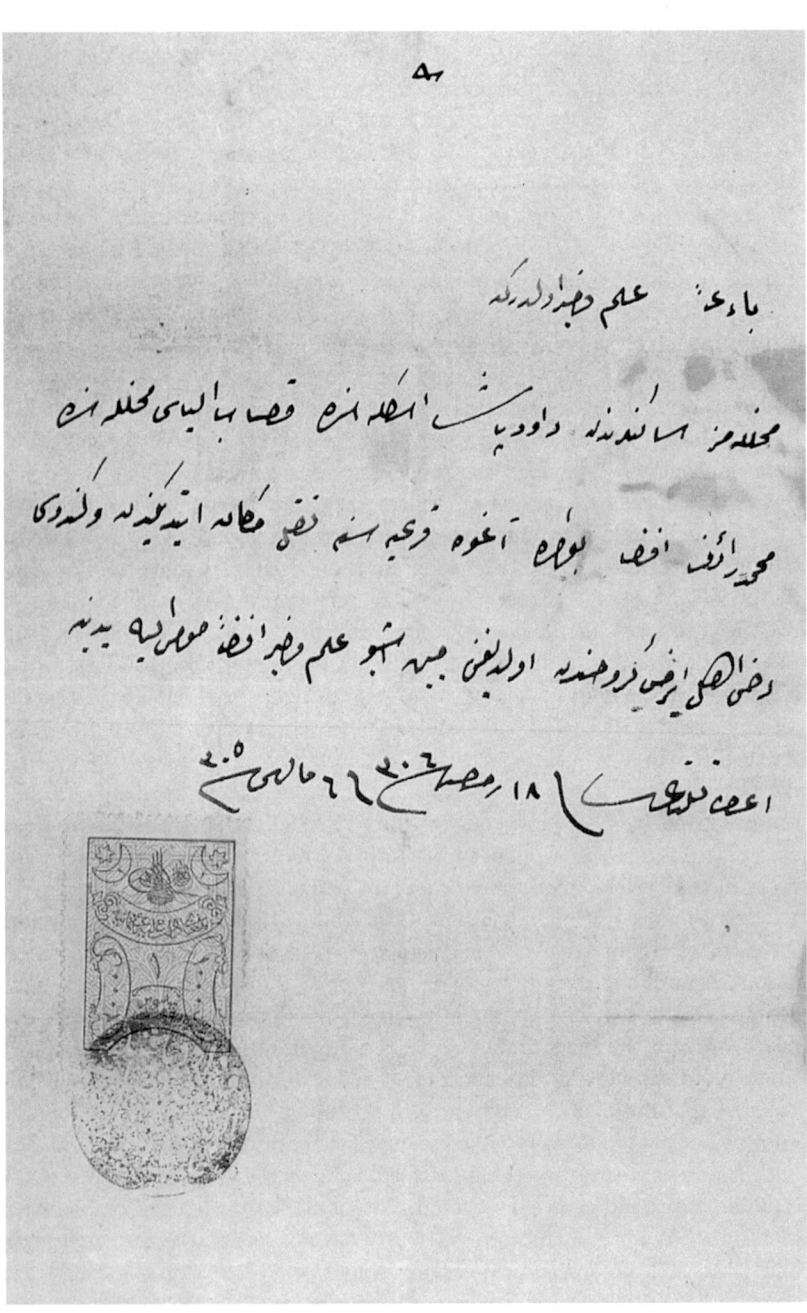

FIGURE 4.2 A Certificate of Good Conduct (*İlmühaber*) Delivered by the *Muhtar* of Kasap İlyas in 1889 (private collection)

of the *imam*s, the *muhtar*s were, after all, the local representatives of the centralizing and modernizing thrust of the post-Tanzimat bureaucratic reforms.

"Somebody to Lean On"

Large numbers of people came to the *muhtar* to get his signature, approval, or his testimonial; to conclude a private business deal in his presence; or simply to seek general information and guidance. His notebooks are, as already indicated, full of entries which, at first sight, seem totally unrelated to his official functions as local headman of Kasap İlyas. The common denominator to all these transactions is, no doubt, the unmitigated confidence and trust that the *muhtar* had inspired in those placed under his administration. For instance, the *muhtar* was fulfilling the functions of a modern public *notary* when he delivered one of the "seal authentication" certificates. This unofficial notarial function of the *muhtar* was in fact being put to a wider variety of uses by residents of the *mahalle*. Many of the inhabitants of Kasap İlyas chose Osman Efendi to witness and record some of their important legal and commercial transactions.

Here are some of the types of transactions that were brought to Osman Efendi's attention and that were recorded in his notebooks: settlements of old debts, partial or total sales of houses situated in the neighborhood, the transfer of the right of use of a *vakıf* property in Kasap İlyas, the renunciation to a legal right of inheritance in favor of another relative, a rental contract, and a spousal statement of agreement for divorce by mutual consent (*hul'* or *muhalaa'*). Most of these transactions were probably later taken to the relevant government office (the land registry, the department of finance, the *shari'a* court, etc.) to complete the full legal process and to be officialized.

In all of these dealings the *muhtar* was acting as an authority in front of which a personal transaction or a commercial deal would receive its legal baptism, so to speak. For instance, there are a total of ten entries in Osman Efendi's notebooks indicating a preliminary agreement concerning the sale of a house in the Kasap İlyas *mahalle*. As an example, on September 14, 1887 a house was sold situated at 27 İskele Street as well as a 50 percent share in the shop right under it. The relevant entry in the *muhtar*'s notebook mentions the names of the buyer and the seller, the price of the house, and adds: "... the cession has been agreed upon with a view to carry out the necessary procedure, ..."[59] meaning thereby that the agreement would later be brought to the land registry to be recorded and the change of ownership to acquire full legality.

Our *muhtar* also took note of a few declarations of divorce by mutual consent. The legal address for such a change in marital status was obviously the *shari'a* court, which would register the parties' intentions in the presence of witnesses and declare the marriage dissolved. Still, a few couples from Kasap İlyas preferred to come first to the *muhtar* and had him record in his notebooks their common intention of obtaining a divorce, although they knew that this registration could have no legal validity whatsoever. We can only speculate on the reasons that pushed them to go to the *muhtar* before going to court. First of all, its practicality might have been appealing to these couples. Indeed, a written note of intention witnessed and signed by the *muhtar* could have eased the process in court either by helping to convince the judge and/or by allowing one of the spouses to be absent during the proceedings. Or, on a purely personal plane, these married couples might have preferred to address themselves first to someone they knew personally who would act like a confident and whom they could trust to protect their privacy.

Osman Efendi's notebooks also contain, however, a number of entries that seem to signal not a provisional protocol pending a final agreement, but a definitive deal or transaction. Some of the entries represented more than just a vague agreement in principle. That is, they did not have to be taken to an administrative office to receive the final stamp of legal existence. They already had full legal validity. Such was the case of many *rental contracts* in Osman efendi's notebooks. Two—perhaps illiterate—people from the *mahalle* got together in the presence of the *muhtar* and signed a deal that they took to be perfectly legal. This deal was to leave no other written trace than the relevant entry in the *muhtar*'s personal notebooks. The rented property was in the *mahalle* and a local testimonial of validity by the local authority seemed sufficient to many people. On August 13, 1889 a warehouse at 42 Iskele Street was rented out, and the transaction in the notebook reads: ". . . Süleyman ağa has rented this warehouse until the beginning of April 1890 to Nikola son of Mihal for the sum of eight hundred *kuruş*. Four hundred *kuruş* have been paid and the rest is to be settled in February. . . ."[60]

In these cases, Osman Efendi was again acting as a public notary, a witness, and a scribe to local private commercial transactions. The notarial function is obviously also present in the many powers of attorney *(vekâletname)* that Osman Efendi witnessed, signed, and issued. These were notes established for the use of two residents of Kasap İlyas, one of which was giving a power of attorney to the other. The notes specified who was giving whom a power of attorney, and for what period of time and specific purpose or transaction it was given. The *muhtar* signed the document and made the corresponding entry in his notebook. These powers of attorney, too, had a validity of their own and did not have to be registered elsewhere. The trust the inhabitants of Kasap İlyas placed in their *muhtar* was sufficient. The notarial function of the *muhtar* was also to be accepted by third parties.

This great confidence was also manifest in the fact that the residents of the Kasap İlyas *mahalle* often used the office of their local headman as a trustee, or as a depository for some of their precious belongings, mostly for the nominative government bonds (*esham*s) they possessed. The *muhtar* kept these bonds at home and gave them back to their owners when an interest coupon was to be cashed personally. There are five such entries in Osman Efendi's notebooks. Here is an example of a certificate of deposit, signed and dated from April 12, 1889: ". . . Helvacı 8—Fatma bint-i Abdullah, wife of Mehmed efendi the haberdasher, has new government bonds bearing a yearly interest of one hundred *kuruş* in four instalments. . . ."[61]

The office of the *muhtar* was also often used as a simple scribe or petition-writer by those—probably illiterate—Kasap İlyas inhabitants who had a request or a petition to address to some government authority. The loss or the modification of some identity papers was the single most frequent subject of these personal petitions. But there were also, for instance, those who wanted to apply for a government job, those who wanted a written testimony of the amount of real estate property they possessed in the neighborhood, those who wanted an authentication of some official document in their possession, and so forth. Whatever the precise administrative problem was, the residents of the Kasap İlyas *mahalle* first sought the help of their *muhtar*. In their dealings with the faraway and formidable-looking Ottoman state apparatus, they knew that they had nearby somebody to lean on.

A "bottom-up" view of the *muhtar*'s local authority and social functions implies that illiteracy,[62] poverty as well as the ignorance of one's legal rights, or of laws and regulations in general, were the main reasons for applying for his assistance. Osman efendi played the role of a sort of mediator between the government and the population at large. He was a paternalistic transmission belt from, for instance, the poor Arapkirli migrants to what was for them the unattainable spheres of the Ottoman government and of the central judicial and administrative apparatus of the Tanzimat period. A close, familiar, and trusted figure in the neighborhood, he was, for many of the locals, the semi-official helper in all public affairs. The *muhtar* of Kasap İlyas provides an example of how the centralizing bureaucratic apparatus of the Tanzimat period made the *muhtar* take over some of the traditional functions of the local *imam*, at the same time the figure of the *muhtar* was made to acquire new areas of authority and intervention.

That Kasap İlyas was neither a central nor a very prosperous neighborhood is significant. This is reflected in the social distribution of the entries in the *muhtar*'s notebooks. We have a sort of *a contrario* indication on the social roles and functions that the *muhtar* was then fulfilling. Kasap İlyas contained, in the second half of the nineteenth century, a few mansions belonging to, and containing, upper-class households. There was, for instance, the household headed by Şevket Paşa, the former cabinet minister and that of Col. Sadettin bey. Both were living in their *konak*s situated on Samatya Street (numbers 62 and 64, respectively). So was Nebil bey, a high-ranking foreign affairs bureaucrat (number 5). As to retired army general Ahmet Faik Paşa, his mansion was on Şimendifer Street (number 19). All of these upper-class household heads appear in the list of property-owners of the *mahalle* drawn by Osman Efendi in 1885.[63] These elite figures are also duly present, with their families, servants, and dependents, in the 1885 census.

Strangely enough, however, none of these elite households, and not a single one of their members, servants, and various dependents included, ever appear by name in the notebooks that Osman Efendi, *muhtar* of Kasap İlyas, kept for almost a quarter of a century. Obviously, they were all living in their *konak*s situated within the neighborhood. But they have left absolutely no trace in the *muhtar*'s notebooks. During the long reign of Osman Efendi as *muhtar* of Kasap İlyas, not even the minutest operation concerning a member of these households was ever entered in his local records. Clearly, these upper-class households constituted quite a different sort of local inhabitant, and their relationship with the *muhtar* must have shown a different profile. They never came to ask for an authentication from Osman Efendi, for instance, nor for any sort of guarantorship. No transaction of theirs ever seem to have needed the legal baptism from the *muhtar* that many residents of Kasap İlyas eagerly sought. Nor did these Paşas and their families ever have to ask for any sort of signed and stamped note or certificate from their local headman. They never deposited their precious belongings or government securities with the *muhtar*. Their becoming full legal entities was never pending on the delivery of a signed certificate by the *muhtar*. It was certainly not for the *muhtar* to certify their moral integrity or propriety. Nor did they ever need him to act as a sort of mediator between them and some higher government authority.

It is difficult to attribute all of this to pure chance, and to dismiss the fact as a simple coincidence. It is the perception that these high-ranking bureaucrats and soldiers had of the *muhtar*'s status, authority, and social function that obviously made all the difference. And Osman Efendi knew his limits. In their multiple dealings with the Ottoman administration, these notables never needed the services of the *muhtar* of the neighborhood in which they happened to reside. Whatever business they had with the law or with some government office, they settled it directly and, quite naturally, did not waste their time with the local headman, who was therefore simply skipped.

The rich and the powerful who happened to live in Kasap İlyas toward the end of the nineteenth century were conspicuously absent from Osman efendi's late nineteenth-century notebooks. A few decades later, another highly respected Kasap İlyas *muhtar* of the '40s, '50s, and '60s knew that the different households in the neighborhood needed different approaches. This is how this *muhtar* (a second-generation Alevî migrant from Arapkir himself) managed to colorfully express the duality: "... there are houses in which I can enter at any time simply by giving a kick at the door. But there are also those houses where, after knocking, I have to turn my back to the door and wait for an answer from inside or for an invitation to come in, and I can not turn back towards the house without having been invited to do so...."[64] There were those numerous households that needed his help and had to submit to whatever authority he happened to hold. And there were those few households that simply did not need him at all. And a good *muhtar* knew the difference.

Epilogue

In 1893, while Osman Efendi was still *muhtar* of Kasap İlyas, an epidemic of cholera struck Istanbul. Whether the epidemic took a particularly heavy toll in Kasap İlyas is not known, but its indirect and long-term effects on our neighborhood as a whole were certainly devastating. The year the epidemic broke, a large *konak* called Takiyüddin Paşa Konağı and situated in Hûbyâr, the northernly neighbor of Kasap İlyas, was bought by the Istanbul municipality and set up as a hospital to treat the victims of the epidemic.[1] This *konak* was situated at the uppermost corner of Yokuşçeşme Street. Its large garden that extended downhill was not too far from the Ispanakçı Viranesi, which was at the northern tip of Kasap İlyas. When the cholera epidemic ended, the *konak* continued to operate as a municipal hospital. Later, a couple of new buildings were added in the garden of the *konak* and the institution continued to function as a general hospital for men. In 1911–1912 the old wooden *konak* was torn down and new construction replaced it.

Until the 1930s the hospital (now called the Cerrahpaşa Hospital, by reference to the district and to the new *mahalle* in which it was situated) remained, topographically speaking, within the bounds of the former Hûbyâr *mahalle*. After the 1928 municipal reform of Istanbul, the limits of the old Hûbyâr *mahalle* were modified, and its name was changed to Cerrahpaşa. In 1933, the Cerrahpaşa Hospital was integrated into the University of Istanbul as a Faculty of Medicine and began to serve as a training hospital for interns and residents for specialization.

In 1936 the president of the Republic Mustafa Kemal Atatürk paid a visit to the institution. During his visit, he is reported to have said: "This hospital should be extended down to the seaside."[2] Between the Cerrahpaşa Hospital and the seaside stood then two traditional Istanbul *mahalle*s: Cerrahpaşa (*alias* Hûbyâr) and Kasap İlyas. Whether the effect of this presidential pronouncement or not, the whole area was marked as a "hospital area" in the urban development plans drawn for Istanbul in the late 1930s. From then on, the inhabitants of Hûbyâr and of the northern section of Kasap İlyas knew that the whole area was to be turned over to the hospital, and that they

FIGURE 5.1 The Cerrahpaşa Hospital Complex and a Late Nineteenth Century House in Kasap İlyas—1994 (author's photograph)

were sooner or later due to be expropriated. "When we decided to build a second floor to our house, we knew very well that the whole area was in fact an expropriation area," declared an elderly inhabitant, referring to the early 1950s.[3] Coming from the wife of a former *muhtar* who had arrived herself to the *mahalle* in 1947, "Atatürk had said long ago that this whole area was to be a hospital"[4] is a statement that shows that the inhabitants of Kasap İlyas were well aware that the fate of their neighborhood was already sealed.

The expropriations and the hospital extension process was quite slow, though, and it took them more than three decades for completion. Closer to the hospital, it was the small Hûbyâr *mahalle* that went first. It had almost completely disappeared by the early 1950s, as new buildings were added to the hospital complex, which extended its limits and came to neighbor the Ispanakçı Viranesi. The centuries-old local community of poor Alevî Arapkirli migrants living in the *Virane* dispersed, never to be formed in this location again. Their dilapidated houses were not worth repair and it was the hospital that was in command of the land, anyway. In the 1960s, one of the many open-air film theaters of Istanbul (*Gülistan sineması*) was operating on the flat piece of land where the *Virane* used to be. The two-centuries-old *Ispanakçı viranesi*, heir to the *konak* of Ispanakçızâde Mustafa Paşa had completely disappeared. The Kasap İlyas *mahalle* had thereby lost one of its historically fundamental social/ethnic identity markers.

Then, in the late '60s and '70s the expropriation procedures were accelerated. As the hospital complex spread toward the sea, scores of houses were vacated and torn down. As a matter-of-fact, whole streets disappeared. Following the western side of Yokuşçeşme Street and tearing down all of its houses with an odd number, the hospital finally reached Samatya Street, leaving nothing of the old *"upper mahalle"* but the Kasap İlyas mosque itself. "This hospital greatly damaged the neighborhood. . . . it took Yokuşçeşme; it took the Ispanakçı Viranesi, the Cami street, Çavuşzade [Street], there was the Çavuşzade fountain here, Hamam odaları [Street], Şeyhülharem [Street] . . . all the land until Esekapısı was taken up by the hospital" was a remark we recorded.[5] "The Cerrahpaşa hospital is the institution that completely destroyed our neighborhood, historical Davudpaşa is gone too."[6] was another bitter comment made by an elderly former inhabitant of Kasap İlyas. After completion of the expropriation process,[7] the following Kasap İlyas streets had completely disappeared: Çavuşzade, Tekke, Cami-i Şerif, Hamam Odaları, Şeyhülharem, Ispanakçı Viranesi, and Ispanakçı Viranesi Street, as well as the whole western side of Yokuşçeşme Street. About one third of the total initial area of the *mahalle* had been swallowed by the hospital. The hospital complex, however, could not completely obey Atatürk's indications of 1936 and had to stop short of reaching the seaside. Obviously, there were obstacles more difficult to overcome between

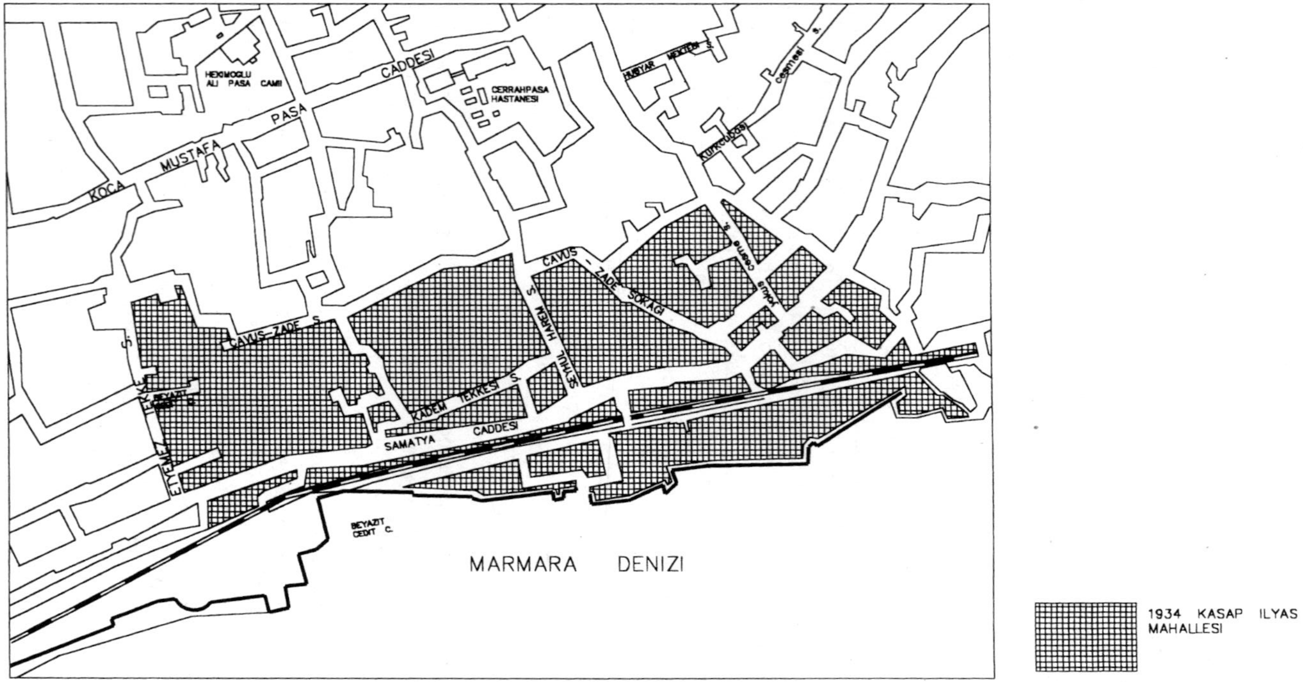

FIGURE 5.2 The Kasap İlyas Neighborhood in 1934

Samatya Street and the sea: the train lines and part of the historical city ramparts. But something just as destructive befell this part of the neighborhood, the *"lower mahalle,"* in the 1950s: the building of a sort of "corniche," a wide four-lane freeway along the whole Marmara coast of Istanbul.

The 1950s saw widespread urban developments in Istanbul. A number of wide and modern boulevards that cut across the urban tissue of the walled city were opened. Among this network of boulevards was the so-called seaside road (*sahil yolu*) that went from the Sirkeci train station in the city center all the way to the airport, about twenty-two kilometers away. This road was designed to be thirty meters across, with wide sidewalks on both sides. It was to run parallel to the railway line and to the ramparts along the Marmara shore. Practically, the opening of such a wide road meant that the whole Marmara coast of the city was to be leveled, that the sea was to be filled in where needed, and that all topographical or man-made obstacles were to be removed.

The Davudpaşa wharf itself, part of the ramparts bordering on the sea, as well as the warehouses near the wharf were among the obstacles to the new seaside road. These basic topographical landmarks, of definitional importance to the neighborhood ever since its foundation in the late fifteenth century, completely disappeared in the middle of the 1950s. After the demise of the Ispanakçı Viranesi, the neighborhood thus lost another of its traditionally important human and social components. With the warehouses, the greater part of the employment opportunities for the street-porters of the neighborhood was taken away. The *bostan*s near the ramparts were expropriated too. In fact, the whole "lower *mahalle*"—with its more modest residents, its reputation, and peculiarities—lost much of its *raison d'être*. The Davudpaşa Wharf was torn down, never to be rebuilt again. Most of the warehouses for wood and coal were expropriated and torn down to make space for the new seaside road and for its promenade. So was the larger part of the old city ramparts that passed through lower Kasap İlyas. As to the occupants of the shoddy wooden houses abutting on these ramparts by the seaside, they were relocated by the municipal authorities in one of the new shantytowns that were spreading then in the northern suburbs of Istanbul.

Not only was the Kasap İlyas *mahalle* totally severed from the sea, but an end was put to the social and economic characteristics that came from its proximity to a wharf and to the centuries-old transportation, wholesale, and retail activities related to it. The "lower *mahalle*" lost its overall urban commercial functions at about the same time the "upper *mahalle*" was truncated of its traditional residents and of many of its streets. Never before, as far as we can surmise, in its entire history that extended over more than four centuries, had the Kasap İlyas *mahalle* experienced such an overwhelming and existential trauma.

It is not only in the creation of a new urban grid of avenues and boulevards,[8] or of a health infrastructure more adapted to modern needs that the

FIGURE 5.3 The Marmara Sea Coast and the Davudpaşa Wharf in the 1940s

modernizing thrust of the republican municipal reforms made itself felt. It is the very definition of the traditional intramural Istanbul *mahalle*s that underwent a radical change in the 1920s. The new rational configuration that was a posteriori superimposed upon the myriads of small neighborhoods signified, in a sense, the beginning of the end for the traditional perceptions of local space in Istanbul.

As already sufficiently underlined (see the Introduction), a *mahalle* was essentially a matter of perception. "The *mahalle* is in the eye of the inhabitant," to paraphrase a better-known aphorism. The neighborhoods of Ottoman Istanbul never had nor needed well-defined borders. Where a *mahalle* ended and another began was a matter for the residents to perceive, to voice, and to enact in their daily lives, not a matter for the legislator or the administrator to determine. Before being anything alse, a neighborhood was a place where people were neighbors. It was the interacting families, the daily contacts of men, women, and children, whether to pray, to shop, to play games, or simply to stroll together, and the relationships that such activities implied that made up the neighborhood gestalt. Local identity was first and foremost dependent on the existence of a web of relationships. The intensity of contacts among the residents created a sense of belonging to the secondary sphere of privacy centered around the home that was the *mahalle*. It is the degree of social integration, not necessarily the precise topographical "address" or the necessary presence of a local mosque that created this.[9] The existence of face-to-face contact and interaction brought a neighborhood community to life and defined it as a *mahalle* having a specific geographic location; not the other way around. Predrawn precise borders were irrelevant. This was so even for those predominantly non-Muslim *mahalle*s with a high degree of ethnic/religious homogeneity. If anything, the "borders" were organic, changeable, and mental.

As to the streets of the eighteenth- and nineteenth-century Istanbul *mahalle*s, they were not just neutral passageways, but loci for play, work, and communication and were constituent parts of local neighborhood consciousness. Face-to-face contact was a reality for houses as well as for people. Both sides of these narrow streets, with the protruding bay windows of the houses lined on opposite sides almost touching each other, obviously belonged to the same *mahalle*. In conformity to this general perception, the Ottoman census returns for Istanbul in 1885 and again in 1907 do not contain a single case where the even-numbered and odd-numbered sides of the same street belong to two different *mahalle*s. An ordinary Istanbul street was never perceived as being a borderline between two neighborhoods, one side of the street belonging to one neighborhood, and the houses facing this side to another.

There were some exceptions to this state of affairs, however. These exceptions were constituted by the very few long and relatively rectilinear arteries of Istanbul. All of them were topographical relics of Byzantine Constantinople, and they had to pass through more than one Ottoman *mahalle*. Samatya Street, *alias* "Butchers' Road," which went through no less than seven *mahalle*s, is one such instance. But even these are doubtful exceptions, since the artery entered the next *mahalle* at a particular crosspoint and, while crossing this *mahalle*, became part of it, with the houses on both sides and all their contents.

The 1927–1928 reform and restructuring of the Istanbul *mahalle*s[10] completely ignored these traditional perceptions of urban local space. The redrawing of the *mahalle* borders by the Istanbul municipality rested on principles totally alien to the century-old conceptions that formed the basic urban culture of local cohabitation in the Ottoman capital. The ideal model was the haussmannian *arrondissements* of Paris, and the cartesian division of each of them into four *quartiers*. The reform reduced the number of intramural Istanbul neighborhoods and fixed it to 114. More importantly, new *mahalle* borders were defined and streets were systematically used as border markers. The frontiers of all of the *mahalle*s were identified with the median line of a street, one side of which was made to belong to a *mahalle*, and the other side to the neighboring one. Kasap İlyas provides some good examples of this type of

FIGURE 5.4 Wooden Houses in the Kasap İlyas Neighborhood—1994 (author's photograph)

border redefinition. Take, for instance, the Ispanakçı Viranesi, that centuries-old traditional landing ground for the poor Arapkirli rural migrants who came to Kasap İlyas. The 1928 redefinition of *mahalle* borders divides the *Virane* in two. The new *mahalle* borderline was put right in the middle of it and the northern part of Ispanakçı Viranesi was attributed to Cerrahpaşa, while the southern part remained within Kasap İlyas. Davudpaşa İskelesi Street (Davudpaşa Wharf Street) which went from Samatya Street to the wharf, and that was lined with many of the local warehouses for wood and coal, is another example. This street was also selected for constituting a limit between Kasap İlyas and the neighboring *mahalle* to its west (*Yalı mahallesi*). Yokuşçeşme Street is yet another instance. The border was drawn right in the middle and the even-numbered houses were attributed to *Kürkçübaşı*. Kasap İlyas was not always on the losing side of the deal, since the western flanks of a couple of streets previously in the easternly *Sancaktar Hayreddin* neighborhood were now, with this sleight of hand, brought into the new domain of Kasap İlyas.

A logical, positivist idea of the urban quarter was thus superimposed upon and, for administrative purposes, substituted to the more fluid and

FIGURE 5.5 The Kasap İlyas Mosque and Part of the Cerrahpaşa Hospital Complex—1994. Kasap İlyas, tomb appears in the lower corner (author's photograph)

flexible conception of the traditional Istanbul *mahalle*. In a sense, with these definite and fixed new borderlines, it was the "bottom-up" view of an Istanbul *mahalle* as a real neighborhood community that went away and was replaced by a more rigid administrative territorial structure. Not that the *mahalle* as a community ceased to exist overnight, of course, but this negation of its existence marked, in a way, the beginning of the end and signified a radical change of local *gestalt*. Henceforth, the traditional *mahalle* and *mahalle* life were set to become a popular subject matter for the expression of regrets and of nostalgia for "a world we have lost." As an elderly inhabitant of Kasap İlyas put it "This was an average neighborhood, which contained both rich and poor. But no one cared about the difference; everybody deserved and got the same respect from everybody else. Now there is none of that anymore, nobody cares, and being neighbors doesn't mean anything anymore...."[11]

Appendix

List of *Imam*s of the Kasap İlyas Mosque

1662–1667	Mustafa Efendi, *imam*.
1737–1747	Ibrahim Efendi, *imam*.
1760–1761	Mustafa Efendi, *imam*.
1782	*Hacı Hâfız* Mahmud Efendi, *imam*.
1784–1799	*Hacı Hâfız* Mehmed Efendi, *imam*, Ibrahim bin Mustafa, *müezzin,* and Hasan Efendi, *hatip* (Friday preacher).
1799–1808	This is an *interregnum* and the Kasap İlyas mosque officially seems to have had no *imam* in this period. The local *vakıf* documents are all signed by a protector (*vasi*), who is temporarily in charge.
1808–1822	Mahmud Efendi, *imam* and Edhem Efendi, *müezzin*.
1822–1846	*Hacı* Aziz Mahmud Efendi, *imam* (Kâmil Efendi *müezzin* ca. 1830).
1854–1855	*Seyyid Hâfız* Mehmed Efendi, *imam*.

The dates only indicate a *terminus ad quem* and a *terminus ad quo*, since they are simply those of the first and of the last legal acts undersigned by the said *imam* in the documents of the local *vakıf*s, of which he was the trustee.[1] These have been here and there supplemented by information drawn from the Davudpaşa Court records in the nineteenth century as, in some court cases the *imam* appeared as a witness or guarantor.[2] The result is obviously patchy, for the much larger portion of the signatures on the local *vakıf* documents give absolutely no clue about the *imam*'s identity, and they read: *el fakir imam-ı cami-i mahalle-yi Kasap İlyas* (the lowly *imam* of the mosque of the Kasap İlyas *mahalle*).

List of Muhtars

1830(?)–1846	Aziz Mahmud Efendi
	(*Muhtar-ı sânî* : 1832-1833 Mustafa ağa
	ca. 1846 Kömürcü Abdullah Ağa)
1865–1883	İsmail bey
	(*Muhtar-ı sânî*: 1865–1870 Süleyman bin Hasan
	1878–1880 Ahmet bin Hacı Ali
	1880–1883 Osman Efendi)
1883–1904	Osman Efendi
	(*Muhtar-ı sânî*: ca. 1899 Mehmed Nuri Efendi)
dates unknown	Muhsin bey
1944–1968	Hüseyin Gidemez ("Karakaş Hüseyin")
1968–1984	Fuat Sağıroğlu ("Laz Fuat")
1984–1994	Nuri Aydınlı
1994–	Hasan Şarkalkan ("Kuşçu Hasan")

The dates given for the nineteenth-century *muhtar*s are all approximate. For the "second *muhtar*s," the dates given indicate only their date of appearance in the documents, either in the Davudpaşa Court records[3] or in the private notebooks having belonged to Osman Efendi.[4]

Notes

NOTES TO THE PREFACE

1. Alan Duben and Cem Behar *Istanbul Households—Marriage, Family and Fertility: 1880–1940*, Cambridge, Cambridge University Press, 1991.

2. Edhem Eldem "Istanbul, from Imperial to Peripheralized Capital," in Eldem, Daniel Goffmann, and Bruce Masters *The Ottoman City between East and West— Aleppo, Izmir and Istanbul*, Cambridge, Cambridge University Press, 1999, pp. 135–207.

NOTES TO INTRODUCTION

1. *Tin Polein*/Istanbul is, etymologically, *the* city. Similarly, Cairo is still today often called *umm'ad-dunia* (mother of the world), and the glorious Isfahan was celebrated in rhyme, as *Isfahan/Nisf-jihan* (Isfahan/half the world).

2. In many Ottoman biographical dictionaries, only those born within the triangular walled inner city of Istanbul were ever granted the posthumous honor of being qualified as urban (*şehrî*). See, for instance, Mehmed Süreyya *Sicill-i Osmani, yahud Tezkire-i Meşâhir-i Osmaniye*, İstanbul, Matbaa-yı Amire, 1890–1899. Even those born in the nearby boroughs of Istanbul were considered slightly "provincial."

3. For a large collection of Ottoman demographic data and various population estimates for Ottoman and early republican Istanbul, see Cem Behar *Osmanlı İmparatorluğunun ve İstanbul'un nüfusu (1500–1927) (The population of the Ottoman Empire and of Istanbul (1500–1927)*, Ankara, Turkey, State Institute of Statistics (Historical Statistics Series, Vol. 2), 1996.

4. See Alan Duben and Behar *İstanbul Households—Marriage, Family and Fertility, 1880–1940*, Cambridge, Cambridge University Press, 1991, p. 30.

5. Suraiya Faroqhi's work on Ankara and Kayseri in the seventeenth century, and André Raymond's books on Arab cities in the sixteenth to the eighteenth centuries are a case in point.

6. A *semt* is, etymologically, a "direction," a "location," or an "address."

7. See Helene Desmet-Grégoire and François Georgeon (eds.) *Cafés d'Orient Revisités*, Paris, CNRS Editions, 1997.

8. For a recent instance, see Edhem Eldem "Istanbul. From Imperial to Peripheralized Capital," in Edhem Eldem, Daniel Goffmann, and Bruce Masters *The Ottoman City Between East and West—Aleppo, Izmir and Istanbul*, Cambridge, Cambridge University Press, 1999, 135–206.

9. For a solid and detailed exposition of the canonical model of the "Islamic city" and of its various offshoots, see "Introduction: Was There an Ottoman City?" in ibid., pp. 1–18. A scathing deconstruction of the idea of the Islamic city is provided by Janet L. Abu-Lughod in "The Islamic City—Historic Myth, Islamic Essence and Contemporary Relevance," *International Journal of Middle Eastern Studies*, 19, 1987, pp. 155–176.

10. S. M. Stern "The Constitution of the Islamic City," in A. H. Hourani and Stern *The Islamic City—A Colloquium*, University of Pennsylvania Press, 1970, pp. 25–50.

11. Gustav E. von Grunebaum "The Structure of the Muslim Town," in *Islam—Essays in the Nature and the Growth of a Cultural Tradition*, Westport, Conn., Greenwood Press, 1961, pp. 141–159.

12. See, for instance, William Marçais "L'Islamisme et la vie urbaine," *Comptes—rendus de l'Académie des Inscriptions et Belles Lettres*," Paris, January 1928, pp. 86–100. Georges Marçais "La Conception des Villes dans l'Islam," *Revue d'Alger*, 2, 1945, pp. 517–533.

13. Ira M. Lapidus *Middle Eastern Cities*, Berkeley, University of California Press, 1969; Lapidus "The Evolution of Muslim Urban Society," *Comparative Studies in Society and History*, 15, 1973, pp. 21–50.

14. Lapidus "Evolution of Muslim Urban Society," p. 48.

15. For Ottoman crafts and guilds, the best review and summary of the literature is in Halil İnalcık and Donald Quataert (eds.) *An Economic and Social History of the Ottoman Empire (1300–1914)*, Cambridge, 1994.

16. The first of these *kadı* injunctions dates from as early as November 1578. See Ahmet Refik Altınay *Onaltıncı Asırda Istanbul Hayatı*, Istanbul, 1935, pp. 144–145.

17. Ömer Lütfi Barkan and Ekrem Hakkı Ayverdi *Istanbul Vakıfları Tahrir Defteri—953 (1546)*, İstanbul, İstanbul Fetih Cemiyeti, 1970.

18. Ibid.

19. Ayverdi *Ondokuzuncu Asırda Istanbul Haritası (A map of Istanbul in the nineteenth century)*, İstanbul, İstanbul Fetih Cemiyeti, 1978.

20. Cem Behar "Fruit Vendors and Civil Servants—A Social and Demographic Portrait of a Neighborhood Community in Intra-mural Istanbul: the Kasap İlyas Mahalle in 1885," *Boğaziçi Journal*, 11/1–2, 1997, pp. 5–32.

21. For a very thorough discussion of the historiography and the basic problematics of *mahalle* formation, definition, and composition in early Ottoman Istanbul, see

Çiğdem Kafesçioğlu *The Ottoman Capital in the Making: The Reconstruction of Constantinople in the Fifteenth Century,* unpublished Ph.D. Thesis, Harvard University, 1996, especially pp. 284 et seq.

22. Barkan and Ayverdi *Istanbul Vakıfları Tahrir Defteri.*

23. Ayvansarayî Hafız Hüseyin *Hadikatü'l-Cevâmi,* Istanbul, Matba'a-yı Amire, 1281(1865).

24. *Esâmi'-i Mahallât,* in *Mebusların Suret-i İntihabına dair Beyannamedir,* Istanbul, Matba'a-yı Amire, 1877; *Mahallât Esamisi,* Istanbul, Arşak Garoyan Matbaası, 1913; *Istanbul ve Bilâd-ı selâsede kâin mahallât ve kurrânın hurûf-u hecâ tertibiyle esâmi. . . .* Istanbul, Matba'a-yı Amire, 1922. Kasap İlyas *mahalle,* however, appears in all of these lists and there is no solid evidence for thinking that its approximate borders have changed to a considerable degree over time.

25. For a thorough listing of the various fires and other natural catastrophies that plagued Ottoman Istanbul, see Mustafa Cezar *Osmanlı Devrinde Istanbul Yapılarında Tahribat Yapan Yangınlar ve Tabii Afetler,* Istanbul, Güzel Sanatlar Akademisi, 1963. New street-grids appeared after many of the nineteenth-century fires. See Zeynep Çelik *The Remaking of Istanbul—A Portrait of an Ottoman City in the Nineteenth Century,* Seattle, University of Washington Press, 1986.

26. A *han* was a "trade center," in most cases a rectangular one- or two-story structure with a central courtyard and a number of shops or warehouses around it.

27. For the details on Servi Mescidi and on the court case involved, see Osman Nuri Ergin *Mecelle-i Umûr-ı Belediye,* Istanbul, 1995, Vol. 7, pp. 3689–3690; for the eventual disappearance of the Servi Mescidi *mahalle,* see also Ekrem Hakkı Ayverdi *Fatih Devri sonlarında İstanbul mahalleleri, Şehrin iskânı ve nüfusu,* Ankara, Vakıflar Umum Müdürlüğü, 1958.

28. A *defterdar* was a bookkeeper as well as a tax assessor for the public treasury.

29. The *avârız* tax was a tax collected in Ottoman urban centers at irregular intervals on special occasions when the treasury was in dire need of funds. The lump-sum tax was apportioned essentially on a geographic basis.

30. Ayvansarayî Hâfız Hüseyin *Hadikat'ül- Cevâmi',* Istanbul, Matbaa-yı Amire, 1281 (1865).

31. Reşat Ekrem Koçu *İstanbul Ansiklopedisi,* Istanbul, 1966, Vol. 8, pp. 4289–4314 (articles on Davud Paşa).

32. See Cem Behar "Kasap İlyas Mahallesi, Istanbul'un bir Mahallesinin sosyal ve demografik portresi: 1546–1885," *Istanbul Araştırmaları,* 4, Winter 1998, p. 27.

33. See Suraiya Faroqhi *Men of Modest Substance—House Owners and House Property in Seventeenth Century Ankara and Kayseri,* Cambridge, Cambridge University Press, 1987.

34. Behar "Fruit Vendors and Civil Servants."

35. Fifteenth- and sixteenth-century examples of a *mahalle* embedded in another *mahalle* do exist. See Ayverdi *Fatih Devri Sonlarında Istanbul Mahalleleri.*

36. See Heath Lowry "The Ottoman Tahrir Defterleri as a Source for Social and Economic History: Pitfalls and Limitations," *Türkische Wirtschafts- und Sozialgeschichte von 1071 bis 1920*, Wiesbaden, Germany, 1995, pp. 183–196. These *defter*s are of good informational value as far as agricultural output and trade, and the relationship of Anatolian towns with their hinterland are concerned. For a good discussion of the problems involved in using exclusively Tapu-tahrir *defter*s see also Amy Singer *Palestinian Peasants and Ottoman Officials: Rural Administration Around Sixteenth Century, Jerusalem*, Cambridge, 1994.

37. For a detailed survey of the history and the methodology of these late Ottoman censuses and on the rich informative content of the original census documents, see Cem Behar "The 1300 (1885) and 1322 (1907) *Tahrirs* as Sources for Ottoman Historical Demography," *Boğaziçi University Research Papers*, Istanbul, 1985; Behar "Sources pour la Démographie historique de l'Empire Ottoman—Les *Tahrirs* (Dénombrements) de 1885 et 1907," *Population*, Paris, 1/2, 1998, pp. 161–178; see also Behar "Qui Compte?—Recensements et Statistiques Démographiques dans l'Empire Ottoman, du XVIe au Xxe siècles," *Histoire et Mesure*, 13-1/2, 1998, pp. 135–146.

38. The personal and household information in the main rosters of these two censuses (the so-called *Esas Defter*s) were used for the first time by Alan Duben and Cem Behar in *İstanbul Households—Marriage, Family and Fertility 1880–1940*, Cambridge, Cambridge University Press, 1991. Previously, historians who had used these census documents had based their conclusions almost exclusively on the district and provincial totals.

39. For a detailed and nuanced survey and evaluation of the very few available Ottoman first-person narrative texts (a small number of seventeenth- and eighteenth-century personal diaries, some personal account books, a couple of dream-logs, some private personal letters, a few autobiographical sketches, etc.), see Cemal Kafadar "Self and Others: The Diary of a Dervish in Seventeenth Century Istanbul and First-Person Narratives in Ottoman Literature," *Studia Islamica*, 69, 1989, pp. 121–150.

Notes to Chapter 1

1. See Ömer Lütfü Barkan and Ekrem Hakkı Ayverdi *İstanbul Vakıfları Tahrir defteri—953(1546) Tarihli*, İstanbul, İstanbul Fetih Cemiyeti, 1970 (see pp. 351–355 for the Kasap İlyas *mahalle*).

2. Of these fourteen *mahalle*s only three have survived to this day: Davud Paşa, Kürkçübaşı, and Kasap İlyas. Another two (Hubyar and Abacızâde) still existed before the municipal reform of the 1920s. The remaining nine had totally disappeared before the nineteenth century.

3. For more details on the various local pious foundations of Kasap İlyas, see Cem Behar "Kasap İlyas Mahallesi: İstanbul'un bir Mahallesinin Sosyal ve Demografik Portresi, 1546–1885" (The Kasap İlyas *mahalle*: a social and demographic portrait of an Istanbul neighborhood, 1546–1885), *İstanbul Araştırmaları*, 4, Winter 1998, pp. 7–110.

4. A double *hamam* has two separate entrances, a double *tepidarium*, and a double *sudatorium* and is open to both men and women. The single *hamam* was used by men and women either on alternate days or at different hours of the day.

5. See Ayverdi *Fatih Devri Sonlarında İstanbul Mahalleleri, Şehrin İskânı ve Nüfusu* (The Istanbul neighborhoods, the settlements, and the population of the city at the end of the era of the conqueror), Ankara, Vakıflar Umum Müdürlüğü, 1958.

6. Robert Mayer *Byzantion, Konstantinoupolis, İstanbul—Eine Genetische Stadtgeographie,* Akademie der Wissenschaften in Wien, Vienna, and Leipzig, 1943. Alexander van Millingen identifies the Byzantine Agios Emilianos gate with the Ottoman Davudpaşa gate. See *Byzantine Constantinople: The Walls of the City and Adjoining Historical Sites,* London, John Murray, 1899.

7. Mayer, *Byzantion, Konstantinoupolis*; Alfons Maria Schneider "Onbeşinci Yüzyılda İstanbul'un Nüfusu" (The population of Istanbul in the fiifteenth century), *Belleten*, 1952, pp. 35–50; Ali Saim Ülgen *Constantinople During the Era of Mohammed the Conqueror, 1453–1481*, Ankara, Publication of the General Direction of Pious Foundations, 1939.

8. For details on the methods of construction and the semiological content of these early Istanbul maps, see Ian R. Manners "Constructing the Image of a City: The Representation of Constantinople in Christopher Buondelmonti's *Liber Insularum Archipelago,*" *Annals of the American Association of Geographers*, 87 (1), 1997, pp. 73–102. For their significance as a document on the topographical distribution of settlements, mosques, churches, and *mahalle*s in early Ottoman Istanbul, see Çiğdem Kafesçioğlu *The Ottoman Capital in the Making: the Reconstruction of Constantinople in the Fifteenth Century,* Unpublished Ph.D. Thesis, Harvard University, 1996.

9. Ekrem Hakkı Ayverdi *Fatih Devri Sonlarında.*

10. Barkan *Süleymaniye Camii ve İmareti İnşaatı (1550–1557)* (The building of the Süleymaniye mosque and imaret [1550–1557]), Ankara, Türk Tarih Kurumu, Vol. 1 (1972) and Vol. 2 (1979).

11. Barkan and Ayverdi *İstanbul Vakıfları Tahrir Defteri* (see pp. 351–355 for the pious foundations of the Kasap İlyas *mahalle*).

12. Two dervish lodges in the neighborhood were founded in the second half of the eighteenth century.

13. On the Islamic Law of Foundations and its implementation in the Ottoman Empire, see Ahmet Akgündüz *İslam Hukukunda ve Osmanlı Tatbikatında Vakıf Müessesesi* (The *vakıf* institution in Islamic law and Ottoman legal practice), Ankara, Türk Tarih Kurumu, 1988.

14. For the—still valid—official *mahalle* boundaries in intramural Istanbul see Osman Nuri Ergin *İstanbul Şehir Rehberi* (Istanbul city guide), 1934.

15. See Maurice M. Cerassi *Osmanlı Kenti—Osmanlı İmparatorluğunda 18. Ve 19. Yüzyıllarda Kent Uygarlığı ve Mimarisi* (The Ottoman city—Urban civilization and architecture in the eighteenth and nineteenth centuries), Istanbul, Yapı Kredi Yayınları, 1999.

16. See Wolfgang Müller-Wiener *Die Hafen von Byzantion, Konstantinupolis, Istanbul,* Darmstadt, Germany, Ernst Wasmuth Verlag, 1994.

17. See Barkan and Ayverdi *Istanbul Vakıfları,* p. 353. As stated in the deed of trust, a warehouse/shop for wood and timber in the vicinity of the Davudpaşa wharf (*dükkân-ı haşşâb der kurb-ü iskele-i Davudpaşa*) was donated by one "Mahmud, the son of Abdullah," in 1511.

18. For the geographic location of the various commercial urban functions in the seventeenth century, see Robert Mantran *İstanbul dans la Seconde Moitié du XVIIème Siècle—Essai d'Histoire Institutionnelle, Economique et Sociale,* Paris, Librairie Adrien Maisonneuve, 1962.

19. The most important of these is certainly Cengiz Orhonlu "Istanbul'da Kayıkçılık ve Kayık İşletmeciliği" (Boatsmen and boat management in Istanbul), in Salih Ozbaran (ed.) *Osmanlı İmparatorluğunda Şehircilik ve Ulaşım Üzerine Araştırmalar* (Research on urbanism and transportation in the Ottoman Empire), Izmir, Turkey, Ege University Publications, 1984.

20. See Ismail Hakkı Uzunçarşılı *Osmanlı Tarihi* (History of the Ottoman Empire), Ankara, Türk Tarih Kurumu, 1988b.

21. Barkan and Ayverdi *Istanbul Vakıfları,* p. 378.

22. See *Vakfiyeler*—I–X.

23. Reşat Ekrem Koçu "Davudpaşa," in *İstanbul Ansiklopedisi,* 1966, Vol. 8, pp. 4289–4314.

24. See Van Millingen *Byzantine Constantinople.*

25. Barkan and Ayverdi *Istanbul Vakıfları,* pp. 353–354.

26. Here is the typical description of a house situated in the Kasap İlyas *mahalle* and donated by a deed of trust dated from 1506: "... a *tahtânî* house in the aforesaid *mahalle* with two entrances (*bâb*s), stables (*ahur*s), an oven or kiln (*furun*), a water well (*bir-i mâ*), a small garden (*bağçe*), and latrines (*kenif*), all surrounded by a wall (*muhavvata*) and bounded by the properties of Hacı İbrahim and that of Ahmet and also by the public thoroughfare (*tarik-i âmm*)." See Barkan and Ayverdi, *Istanbul Vakıfları,* p. 352, *vakıf* numbered 2075.

27. For more details on the house descriptions and the uses to which these houses were put in the *vakıf*s of Istanbul, see Mehmet İpşirli "Arşiv Belgelerine göre İstanbul Vakıf Evleri—Müştemilât, Tamirat, Kira, Satış" (The Istanbul *vakıf* houses according to archival documents—Extensions, repair, rents, and sales), in *Tarih Boyunca Istanbul Semineri-Bildiriler,* İstanbul, İstanbul Üniversitesi Edebiyat Fakültesi, 1989, pp. 183–196.

28. *Taht* and *fevk* being both words of Arabic origin, the first meaning "below, under, lower," and the second "over, above."

29. See, for instance, Tülay Reyhanlı *İngiliz Gezginlerine göre Onaltıncı Yüzyılda Istanbul'da Hayat* (Life in Istanbul in the sixteenth century according to English travelers), Ankara, Ministry of Culture Publications, 1983.

30. Barkan and Ayverdi *Istanbul Vakıfları*, p. XI.

31. Ibid., p. 354.

32. That mode of construction is in fact well-known in many parts of Anatolia. The material used in filling the space between the supporting beams may have varied geographically and with time. Straw, mud, stones, and various types of bricks might have been used. This technique of construction is generally called *hımış*.

33. See Mustafa Cezar *Osmanlı Devrinde İstanbul Yapılarında Tahribat Yapan Yangınlar ve Tabii Afetler* (Fires and other natural disasters in Ottoman times—Destructions caused to buildings in Istanbul), İstanbul, 1963.

34. See Ahmet Refik *Hicrî Onbirinci Asırda Istanbul Hayatı* (Life in Istanbul in the eleventh century after the Hegira), Istanbul, 1930.

35. Gabriel Antoine Olivier *Voyage dans l'Empire Othoman, l'Egypte et la Perse*, Paris, H. Agasse, 1802, Vol. 1.

36. Barkan and Ayverdi *Istanbul Vakıfları*, p. 355. The deed of trust specifies that this particular *bostan* was contiguous to yet another vegetable garden that belonged to a non-Muslim (*bostan-ı zımmî*) and to the city walls (*cidar-ı kal'a ile mahdud*).

37. Vakfiyeler—X.

38. This fountain was listed as being a new fountain in front of the Davudpaşa wharf market (*Çeşme-i nev der nezd-i çarşu-yı iskele-yi Davudpaşa*). See Kâzım Çeçen *Mimar Sinan ve Kırkçeşme Tesisleri* (Sinan the architect and the Kırkçeşme establishment), Istanbul, 1988, p. 168. For the problem of drinking water provision in Istanbul after the Turkish conquest, see Sadi Nazım Nirven *Fatih II. Sultan Mehmed Devri Türk Su Medeniyeti* (Turkish water and civilization in the epoch of Sultan Mehmed II the Conqueror), İstanbul, 1953.

39. See Mayer *Byzantion, Konstantinoupolis, İstanbul*.

40. See Cengiz Orhonlu *Osmanlı İmparatorluğunda* (see pp. 27–66 on road pavement and pavement workers).

41. Uzunçarşılı *Osmanlı Tarihi*, p. 226.

42. A *tekke* was a dervish convent belonging to a sufi order. The *tekkes* might or might not have contained permanent inmates.

43. It must be stressed again at this point that it is utterly impossible to reconstitute with any degree of precision the street plan of the sixteenth-century Kasap İlyas *mahalle*, or that of any neighborhood within the old city of Istanbul, for that matter. It is probable that none of the sixteenth-century Kasap İlyas "streets" kept their initial location or their itinerary in subsequent centuries, with one single exception: Kasap İlyas' "high street."

44. For a thorough discussion of those legal opinions, see Rhoads Murphey "Communal Living in Ottoman Istanbul—Searching for the Foundations of an Urban Tradition," *Journal of Urban History*, 16/2, February 1990, pp. 115–131.

45. See Barkan and Ayverdi, Istanbul Vakıfları, p. 345.

46. *Boza* is a traditional Turkish drink, consumed mostly in winter, and made of mortared and slightly fermented barley

47. See Ayverdi *Fatih Devri Sonlarında.*

48. Evliya Çelebi *Seyahatname*, Istanbul, 1996, Vol. 1; Eremya Çelebi Kömürcüyan *İstanbul Tarihi-XVII. Asırda İstanbul* (The history of Istanbul—Istanbul in the seventeenth century), İstanbul, Eren Yayıncılık, 1988.

49. See Münir Aktepe "Onyedinci Asra ait Istanbul kazası Avârız Defteri" (A seventeenth century Avârız register for the district of Istanbul), *Istanbul Enstitüsü Dergisi*, 3, 1957, pp. 109–139.

50. The term *avârız* is the plural of *ârıza*, meaning "accident" or "occasional, unexpected occurrence."

51. For a compendium of figures and estimates of the population of the Ottoman Empire and its various provinces, see Behar *Osmanlı İmparatorluğu ve Türkiye'nin Nüfusu (1500–1927)* (The population of the Ottoman Empire and of Turkey), Ankara, State Institute of Statistics (Historical Statistics Series, Vol. 2), 1996.

52. Stanford J. Shaw "The Population of İstanbul in the Nineteenth Century," *International Journal of Middle Eastern Studies*, 10, 1979, pp. 265–277.

53. On the 1885 population of Kasap İlyas, see Behar "Fruit Vendors and Civil Servants—A Social and Demographic Portrait of a Neighborhood Community in Intramural İstanbul: the Kasap İlyas *Mahalle* in 1885," *Boğaziçi Journal*, 11/1–2, 1997, pp. 5–32.

54. Derviş Mustafa Efendi *1782 Yılı Yangınları—Harîk Risalesi* (The fires of 1782—The fire epistle), Istanbul, İletişimYayınları, 1994.

55. That is the only manner in which the topographical location of each piece of real estate in Istanbul could have been defined, before the establishment of a cadastral land survey in the middle of the nineteenth century. The name of the neighborhood plus that of a well-known landmark (a mosque, a city gate, a market, etc.) and the names of the owners of the bordering properties were sufficient indicators defining and locating a house or a plot of land in Istanbul.

56. See, for instance, Kömürcüyan *İstanbul Tarihi-XVII. Asırda İstanbul* (The history of Istanbul—Istanbul in the seventeenth century), Istanbul, Eren Yayıncılık, 1988; P. Incicyan *Onsekizinci Asırda İstanbul* (Istanbul in the eighteenth century), İstanbul, İstanbul Fetih Cemiyeti Yayınları, 1976; Sarraf Sarkis Hovhannesyan *Payitaht İstanbul'un Tarihçesi* (A brief history of the imperial capital Istanbul), Istanbul, Tarih Vakfı Yurt Yayınları, 1996.

57. Barkan *Süleymaniye Camii ve İmareti İnşaatı.*

58. *Hatun*, simply meaning "lady," was then an honorific title given to women of some age who commanded general respect.

59. See Mayer *Byzantion, Konstantinoupolis, İstanbul;* also, Celal Esad [Arseven] *Eski İstanbul Abidat ve Mebanisi—Şehrin Tesisinden Osmanlı Fethine Kadar* (Buildings and monuments of old Istanbul—From its foundation to the Ottoman conquest), İstanbul, Muhtar Halit Kütüphanesi, 1922.

60. This name never became an official street name. When the streets of Istanbul received official names in the 1860s, it was baptized Samatya Avenue (*Samatya Caddesi*), referring to one of the districts through which it passes. Unpleasant memories linked to the Janissary Corps, as well as the desire to "modernize" might have played a role in the elimination of this name, although it had roots in the people's daily life, reflected a social and political reality, and had been used for centuries.

61. See, for instance, Osman Nuri Ergin *Mecelle-i Umûr-u Belediye*, Istanbul, Vol. 2, 1995, pp. 794–795.

62. The Kazlıçeşme area remained a tannery center in Istanbul until well into the 1990s.

63. Hovhannesyan *Payitaht Istanbul'un Tarihçesi*, p. 31.

64. For more details on the butchers' daily procession and on the ritual associated with the distribution of meat to the Janissary companies stationed in the Etmeydanı barracks, see Uzunçarşılı *Osmanlı Devlet Teşkilatından Kapıkulu Ocakları—Acemi Ocağı ve Yeniçeri Ocağı*, Ankara, Türk Tarih Kurumu, 1988, pp. 241ff.

65. *Kalfa* (literally, substitute, or helper) was a title given to senior female officials of the harem in the Imperial Palace.

66. Ahmet Efendi *Üçüncü Selim'in sır kâtibi Ahmet Efendi tarafından tutulan Ruzname* (Diary kept by Ahmet Efendi Selim the Third's confident), Ankara, Türk Tarih Kurumu, 1993, p. 201.

67. Idem, p. 217.

68. For a detailed listing of the various fires in Ottoman Istanbul, see Mustafa Cezar *Osmanlı Devrinde Istanbul Yapılarında Tahribat yapan Yangınlar ve Tabii Afetler* (Fires and other natural disasters in Ottoman times—Destructions caused to buildings in Istanbul), Istanbul, 1963. On the network of amateur fire brigades that were set up in Istanbul in the nineteenth century, see Reşat Ekrem Koçu *Yangın var . . . Istanbul Tulumbacıları* (Fire! . . . The Istanbul voluntary fire brigades), Istanbul, Ana Yayınevi, 1981.

69. See Cezar *Osmanlı Devrinde* and Koçu *Yangın Var.*

70. Cezar *Osmanlı Devrinde*, p. 17.

71. Vakfiyeler—I.

72. Derviş Mustafa Efendi *1782 Yılı Yangınları—Harik Risalesi* (The fires of 1782—The fire epistle), Istanbul, IletişimYayınları, 1994, p. 60.

73. See Uzunçarşılı "İstanbul ve Bilâd-ı Selâse Denilen Eyüp, Galata ve Üsküdar Kadılıkları," *Istanbul Enstitüsü Dergisi*, 3 1957, pp. 25–52.

74. The fire of 1782 was a disaster for historiographers, too, for it destroyed a rich archival collection. The Davudpaşa Religious Court was one of the oldest in Istanbul and used to work under the direction of a *naib*, a representative of the *kadı* of Istanbul. The inhabitants of the Kasap İlyas *mahalle* usually went to this religious court for their lawsuits and legal records. The Davudpaşa Court of Justice used to operate in a wooden house abutting on the Davudpaşa mosque itself. The 1782 fire

completely destroyed this house and an archive with about three centuries of court records on the Davudpaşa District were turned to ashes. The first record of the new series is dated 1 Zilhicce 1196 a.h. (November 7, 1782).

75. Archives of the Religious Courts of Istanbul—Davudpaşa Court (*Istanbul Şer'iye Sicilleri Arşivi—Davudpaşa Mahkemesi*) [ISA-DM 8/1 p. 37a; 8/1 p. 73b; 8/1 p. 75a; 8/5 p. 52b; 8/6 p. 82a; etc].

76. Vakfiyeler—IV and VI.

77. Vakfiyeler—VI.

78. A *zira'* or *zira'-yı mimari* (architectural zira'), was equal to about 75 centimeters.

Notes to Chapter 2

1. For an approximate list of the *imam*s of the Kasap İlyas mosque from the middle of the seventeenth to the middle of the nineteenth centuries, see the appendix.

2. See Osman Nuri Ergin *Türkiyede Şehirciliğin Tarihi İnkişafı* (The historical development of urbanism in Turkey), Istanbul, 1936. Also, Musa Çadırcı "Türkiye'de Muhtarlık teşkilâtının kurulması üzerine bir inceleme" (An inquiry into the establishment of the Muhtars' organization in Turkey), *Belleten*, 1970, pp. 409–420; İlber Ortaylı *Tanzimattan Cumhuriyete Yerel Yönetim Geleneği* (The tradition of local administration from the Tanzimat to the republic), Istanbul, Hil Yayın, 1985.

3. See Çadırcı "Türkiye'de Muhtarlık teşkilâtının kurulması üzerine bir inceleme." (An Essay on the establishment of the Muhtar's organization in Turkey), *Belleten*, 1970, pp. 409–420.

4. Çadırcı *Tanzimat Döneminde Anadolu Kentlerinin Sosyal ve Ekonomik Yapıları* (The social and economic structure of Anatolian towns in the Tanzimat period), Ankara, Türk Tarih Kurumu, 1991.

5. See *Vakfiyeler I–X.*

6. For *avârız,* see chapter 1.

7. Vakfiyeler—X, Folio 2.

8. Vakfiyeler—VI. ("... her ne bina ve ihdas ederse vakf-i şerife ait olmak üzere....")

9. Vakfiyeler—VIII. ("... icare-i muaccelesine mahsub....")

10. Vakfiyeler—IV. ("... her ne bina ve ihdas ederse arsası vakıf, binası mülk olmak üzere....)"

11. Ahmet Akgündüz *İslam Hukukunda ve Osmanlı Tatbikatında Vakıf Müessesesi* (The Vakıf institution—Islamic law and Ottoman practice), Ankara, Türk Tarih Kurumu, 1988; Mehmet İpşirli "Arşiv Belgelerine göre Istanbul Vakıf Evleri—Müştemilât, Tamirat, Kira, Satış" (The Istanbul vakıf houses according to archival documents—Extensions, repair, rents and sales), in *Tarih Boyunca İstanbul Semineri—*

Bildiriler, Istanbul, İstanbul Üniversitesi Edebiyat Fakültesi Basimevi, 1989, pp. 183–196.

12. Vakfiyeler—VIII.

13. Vakfiyeler—V.

14. One *kuruş* was equal to 120 *akçe*s.

15. See Akgündüz "*İslam Hukukunda*" and Ipşirli "Arşiv Belgelerine gore."

16. Vakfiyeler—I.

17. See Ipşirli "Arşiv Belgelerine gore."

18. See Şevket Pamuk "Money in the Ottoman Empire, 1326–1914," in Halil İnalcık and Donald Quataert (eds.) *An Economic and Social History of the Ottoman Empire*, Cambridge, Cambridge University Press, 1994, pp. 947–985; Şevket Pamuk, "En büyük tağşiş ve 1844 tarihli Tashih i sikke İşlemi" (The greatest debasement and the coin correction operation of 1844), *Toplumsal Tarih*, 13, January 1995, pp. 12–15; Şevket Pamuk *500 Years of Prices and Wages in Istanbul and Other Cities*, Ankara, State Institute of Statistics, 2000.

19. ("... *bahçe derûnunda bir bâb oda ve köşk ve zulle ve bi'r-i ma ve matbah ve kenif ve havz ve eşcâr-ı müsmire ve cevânib-i erbaasında taş dıvar....*") Vakfiyeler—V.

20. ("... *Beher şehr altmış akçe icareli bahçeye mutasarrıf olan Es-seyyid Aziz Mahmud Efendi mutasarrıf olduğu bahçeyi bin kuruş bedel-i makbuz üzere İsmail Ağa'nın zevcesi Fatma Hatun binti Hasan'a ferağ ve kasr-ı yed edip tevliyetim hasebiyle izin verilip defter-i vakfa kaydolundu...*"), Vakfiyeler—V, ff.4.

21. For more details on the means of circumventing the Islamic prohibition on interest used in the Ottoman Empire, see Murat Çızakça *A History of Philanthropic Foundations: The Islamic World from the Seventh Century to the Present*, İstanbul, Boğaziçi University Press, 2000.

22. "... *beher şehr otuz akçe ile mutasarrıf olduğum bahçeyi hüsn-ü rızam ile nısfını kerimem Hatice Huriye Hatun binti Aziz Mahmud Efendi ve nısf-ı âherini dahi damadım Ahmet bey bin Elhac İbrahim Efendi'ye nısfiyet üzere tasarruflarına izin verilip defter-i vakfa kaydolundu...*" (Vakfiyeler—V, p. 4).

23. See Akgündüz "*İslam Hukukunda.*"

24. "... *talibine arz olunup, ...*" and "... *daha ziyâde bahâ ile talib-i âhari zuhur eylemeyip....*" (Vakfiyeler—I, X).

25. "... *sûk-u sultanide müzayede olunup rağbet-ün nâs bilkülliye münkati' olduktan sonra...,*" or "... *sûk-u sultanide ba'd-el mezâd....*"

26. "... *ebniye ve sukûfa vukuf ve şuûru olan cemm-i gafir ihbar etmeğin....*"

27. Vakfiyeler—IV, p. 2. "... *Beher şehr on akçe icareli mukataa-yı zemin olan bahçeyi hüsn-ü rızamla nısfını kerimem Hatice Huriye Hanıma ve nısf-ı âharını damadım Ahmed bey bin elhac İbrahim efendi'ye ferâğat ve kasr-ı yed etmemle tasarruflarına izin verilip defter-i vakfa kaydolundu....*"

28. 1885 census and population roster for the Kasap İlyas *mahalle*, Fatih District [Atik Defter 14, folio 73].

29. Vakfiyeler—VII, p. 4.

30. This set of really exceptional documents (three thick notebooks, henceforward to be referred to as [D1], [D2], and [D3]) having belonged to the successive *imam*s and the *muhtar*s of Kasap İlyas, are now part of a private collection. They contain property listings and some partial population counts in the *mahalle*, as well as various other entries. There are also markings on the in-migrants and out-migrants to and from the neighborhood. These quite detailed, though certainly not exhaustive, diaries cover the events of the period between 1864 and 1907, with a particular emphasis on the years from 1883 to 1905, when Osman Efendi was *muhtar* of Kasap İlyas.

31. See Çadırcı "Türkiye'de Muhtarlık teşkilâtının kurulması üzerine bir inceleme" p. 411.

32. See Çadırcı "Tanzimat döneminde çıkarılan men'-i mürur ve pasaport nizamnameleri" (The prohibition of passage and passport regulations issued during the Tanzimat period), *Türk Tarih Kurumu—Belgeler*, 15/19, 1993, pp. 169–183.

33. "*Samatya Caddesi 12, Çengi arsası yirmi senedir sahibi zuhur etmediği gibi sahibi malum dahi olmadığından karakolhane ittihaz olunması ihtimaline mebni nizamen lâzım olan muamelesinin icrası için ahâlinin mühürleriyle beraber ilmühaber verilmiştir, 22 Mart 1305*" [D2/35b].

34. For more details on these late Ottoman censuses, the population rosters they contributed to establish, as well as on the modes of registration and their consequences, see Cem Behar "Sources pour la démographie historique de l'Empire Ottoman: les *Tahrir* de 1885 et 1907," *Population* (Paris), 53/1–2, January–April 1998, pp. 161–181.

35. For a thorough review of Ottoman/Islamic marriage law and practices, see Halil Cin *İslâm ve Osmanlı Hukukunda Evlenme* (Marriage in Islamic and Ottoman law), Ankara, Ankara Üniversitesi İlahiyat Fakültesi, 1974; and Mehmet Akif Aydın *Islam-Osmanlı Aile Hukuku* (Islamic/Ottoman family law), Istanbul, Marmara Üniversitesi İlahiyat Fakültesi, 1985.

36. On the marriage procedures in late Ottoman Istanbul, and particularly on the various issues raised by these marriage permissions, the *izinname*s, see Alan Duben and Behar *İstanbul Households: Marriage, Family and Fertility, 1880–1940*, Cambridge, Cambridge University Press, 1991, pp. 107–121.

37. "... *Helvacı 25—Ömer Raşit bin Hüseyin teehhül edeceğinden mani-i şer'isi yoktur....*" [D2/52a].

38. "... *Kerimem Fatma'nın hiç bir kimseye nişanlı olmayıp ve hiç bir gûnâ mani-i şer'isi olmadığı, şayet bir gûnâ mani-i şer'isi zuhur ederse mes'uliyeti bana ait idüğü işbu mahalle şerh ve temhir kılındı. Adliye hademelerinden Ismail Hakkı....*" [D2/ p. 46a].

39. "... *Mezburenin mani-i şer'isi olmadığına dair Rıza bey'in senedi vardır....*" [D3/p. 52a].

40. *"Zevcenin mani-i şer'isi olmadığına Dizdariye mahallesinden ilmühaber ve mezkûr Şeyh Halil Efendi ve kahveci Hasan ve muhallebici Kadri'nin şehadetleriyle sabittir...."* [D3/p. 52].

41. *"Cami-i Şerifin üçyüz dört senesi Martından Şubatına kadar mahiyelerimi tamamen aldığımı mübeyyin işbu mahalle temhir eyledim. 27 Mart 1304. İmza: müezzin Ahmet (mühür)."* [D2/p. 24a].

42. *"Üçyüz yedi senesi maaşımı Hoca efendi yedinden tamamen ahz eyledim. 1 Mart 1307."* [D2/p. 24a].

43. See Ortaylı *Tanzimattan Cumhuriyete yerel yönetim geleneği*.

44. *"... Mahmiye-i İstanbul'da Davudpaşa iskelesi kurbünde Kasap Ilyas mahallesinde vaki ... bir taraftan imam Mustafa Efendi menzili ve bir taraftan Ahmet efendi menzili ve bir taraftan Âtıf Efendi vakfından menzil ve bir taraftan tarik-i 'amm ile mahdûd ... bir bâb arsa...."* Vakfiyeler—IV.

45. *"... Mahmiye-i İstanbul'da Kasap Ilyas mahallesinde ... bir taraftan Ibrahim Ağa menzili ve bir taraftan Halifezâde Mustafa Efendi menzili ve bir taraftan helvacı Ahmet arsası ve taraf-ı rabii tarik-i 'amm ile mahdûd terbi'an iki yüz ondört zira' arsada.... 9 Muharrem 1217* [May 5, 1802],*"* İstanbul Şer'iye Sicilleri Arşivi (The Istanbul Religious Courts' archives)—Davudpaşa Mahkemesi [ISA-DM], 8/40, p. 11a.

46. Vakfiyeler—I–X.

47. İstanbul Şer'iye Sicilleri Arşivi [ISA-DM], 8/1 p. 36b; 8/1 p. 73b; 8/4 p. 31b; 8/5 p. 27a; 8/6 p. 60a; 8/6 p. 71b; etc.

48. [ISA-DM], 8/40, p. 11a, 9 Muharrem 1217 [May 5, 1802].

49. [ISA-DM], 8/1, p. 75a, 17 Jumada I 1197 [April 20, 1783].

50. [ISA-DM], 8/3, p. 55b, 17 Shawwal 1198 [August 30, 1784].

51. [ISA-DM], 8/5, p. 52b, 11 Dhu'l Ka'ada 1199 [September 15, 1785].

52. [ISA-DM], 8/6, p. 82a, 11 Shawwal 1200 [August 2, 1786].

53. Vakfiyeler—IV.

54. [ISA-DM], 8/4 p. 31b; 8/5 p. 52b; 8/5 p. 55a; 8/6 p. 56b; 8/6 p. 60a; 8/6 p. 82b; 8/40 p. 11a; 8/50 p. 56b .

55. [ISA-DM], 8/4 p. 31b; 8/5 p. 52b; 8/5 p. 55a; 8/6 p. 56b; 8/6 p. 60a; 8/6 p. 82b; 8/40 p. 11a; 8/50 p. 56b.

56. *"... Fevkânî üç bâb oda ve bir sofa ve mağsel ve tahtında bir kenif ve abdesthane ve kömürlük ve bi'r-i mâ, avlu ve sokak kapısını müştemil bir bâb menzil...."* [ISA-DM], 8/5 p. 55a.

57. [ISA-DM], 8/1 p. 36b; 8/6 p. 56b; 8/120 p. 3a; etc.

58. Behar "Fruit Vendors and Civil Servants: A Social and Demographic Portrait of a Neighborhood Community in Intramural İstanbul, the Kasap İlyas *mahalle* in 1885," *Boğaziçi Journal*, 11/1–2, 1997, pp. 5–32.

59. Ibid., pp. 8–9.

60. In 1885, 873,575 inhabitants were counted in Istanbul, according to the officially published figures. For longer time series on the population of the capital-city of the Ottoman Empire, see Behar *Osmanlı İmparatorluğunun ve Türkiye'nin Nüfusu: 1500–1927* (The population of the Ottoman Empire and Turkey), Ankara, State Institute of Statistics (Historical Statistics Series, Vol. 2), 1996.

61. In September 2001.

62. Edmondo de Amicis *Constantinople (1874)*, Ankara, Türk Tarih Kurumu, 1993, p. 281.

63. On the vegetable gardens within the walled city of Istanbul, and for maps of these gardens toward the end of the nineteenth century, see Reşat Ekrem Koçu "Bostan," in *İstanbul Ansiklopedisi*, Vol. 6, Istanbul, 1963, pp. 2971–2973.

64. Ekrem Hakkı Ayverdi *Ondokuzuncu Asırda İstanbul Haritası* (An Istanbul map in the nineteenth century), İstanbul, Istanbul Fetih Cemiyeti, 1978.

65. [ISA-DM], 8/140 p. 65a; 8/141 p. 22b; 8/148 p. 87; 8/154 p. 3a; 8/176 p. 30; etc.

66. [ISA-DM], 8/1 p. 36b; 8/6 p. 34b; 8/6 p. 36b.

67. *Boza* is a very popular Turkish soft drink made of fermented millet.

68. Duben and Behar *İstanbul Households*.

69. Vakfiyeler—I–X.

70. Vakfiyeler—I, p. 2–3.

71. Vakfiyeler—VI.

72. Vakfiyeler—X.

73. [ISA-DM] 8/5 p. 4b; 8/5 p. 52b; 8/6 p. 52a; 8/10 p. 54b; 8/70 p. 8b; 8/80 p. 20a; 8/90 p. 7a; etc.

74. [ISA-DM] 8/5 p. 28a; 8/9 p. 13b; 8/50 p. 31a; 8/110 p. 2a; etc.

75. [ISA-DM] 8/50 p. 59a.

76. [ISA-DM] 8/90 p. 7a.

77. On the evolution of the burials and burial grounds within the city of Istanbul, see Nicolas Vatin "L'inhumation intramuros à Istanbul à l'époque ottomane," in Gilles Veinstein (ed.) *Les Ottomans et la Mort*, Leiden, Netherlands, Brill, 1996, pp. 157–175. For the relevant Ottoman government order, see *Vak'anüvis Ahmet Lütfi Efendi Tarihi*, Ankara: Türk Tarih Kurumu, Vol. 11, 1989, p. 30.

78. On the matter of Ottoman tombstones considered as historical sources, see Hans-Peter Lacqueur "Grabsteine als Quelle zur osmanischen Geschichte—Möglichkeiten und Probleme," *Osmanlı Araştırmaları*, 3, Istanbul, 1982, pp. 21–44.

79. "*Kasap İlyas mahallesi sakinlerinden ve Şehremânetinde mahallât odası mukayyidi Ahmet Vehbi Efendi. Ruhuna Fatiha 1276.*"

80. Vakfiyeler—X, p. 2. Neither the religious community to which this person (named as "David, son of Gabriel" in the records) belonged, nor whether he effectively resided in the neighborhood is specified in the relevant *vakıf* documents.

81. [ISA-DM] 8/50 p. 43a; 8/80 p. 20a.

NOTES TO CHAPTER 3

1. Halil İnalcık and Donald Quataert *An Economic and Social History of the Ottoman Empire, 1300–1914*, Cambridge, Cambridge University Press, 1994, pp. 793–795.

2. Ibid., p. 787.

3. Edhem Eldem, Daniel Goffmann, and Bruce Masters *The Ottoman City between East and West—Aleppo, Izmir and Istanbul*, Cambridge, Cambridge Univeristy Press, 1999.

4. For some precise instances see İlber Ortaylı *Osmanlı Toplumunda Aile* (The family in Ottoman society), Istanbul, Pan Yayıncılık, 2000.

5. See Musa Çadırcı "Tanzimat döneminde çıkarılan men-i mürur ve pasaport nizamnameleri" (The passport and certificate of passage regulations issued in the Tanzimat period), *Türk Tarih Kurumu—Belgeler*, 15, 1993, pp. 169–183.

6. Ibid., pp. 170–171.

7. See Cem Behar *Osmanlı İmparatorluğunun ve Türkiye'nin Nüfusu, 1500–1927* (The population of the Ottoman Empire and Turkey), Ankara, Devlet Istatistik Enstitüsü Yayınları, 1996.

8. Alan Duben and Behar *İstanbul Households—Marriage, Family and Fertility in Istanbul, 1880–1940*, Cambridge, Cambridge University Press, 1991, pp. 24–25.

9. See Behar "Fruit Vendors and Civil Servants—A Social and Demographic Portrait of a Neighborhood Community in Intramural İstanbul, the Kasap İlyas *mahalle* in 1885," *Boğaziçi Journal*, Vol. 11/1–2, 1997, pp. 5–32.

10. Duben and Behar, *İstanbul Households*, p. 24.

11. Census rosters for the Kasap İlyas *mahalle* in 1885 and 1907, Fatih Nüfus Müdürlüğü [Atik Defter 14] and [Eski Esas 23].

12. The Ottoman Province (*vilâyet*) of Mamuretülâziz, whose administrative center was the city of Harput, comprised parts of the present-day Turkish provinces of Sivas, Malatya, Elazığ, and Erzincan.

13. Behar "Fruit Vendors and Civil Servants," p. 16.

14. Mehmed Süreyya *Sicill-i Osmani, yahut Tezkire-i meşâhir-i Osmaniye*, Istanbul, Matbaa-yı Amire, Vol. 4, 1893, pp. 446–447.

15. Ayvansarayî Hâfız Hüseyin Efendi *Hadikat'ül Cevami'*, Istanbul, 1864; also in Ömer Lütfü Barkan and Ekrem Hakkı Ayverdi *İstanbul Vakıfları Tahrir defteri-1546*, İstanbul, İstanbul Fetih Cemiyeti 3 1970, p. 351.

16. Abdüsselâm Uluçam "Arapkirdeki mimari anıtların bugünkü durumu" (The present situation of the architectural monuments of Arapkir), *Battal Gazi ve Malatya çevresi Halk Kültürü Sempozyumu Bildirileri*, Malatya, Turkey, İnönü Üniversitesi, 1986, pp. 140–147.

17. Mehmed Süreyya *Sicill-i Osmani, yahut Tezkire-i meşâhir-i Osmaniye*, İstanbul, Matbaa-yı Amire, 1893, Vol. 3/246, Vol. 1/152, Vol. 4/479.

18. *"Ispanakçıbaşı veresesi arsası"* is mentioned as a neighboring property in the relevant court case [ISA-DM, 8/50, p. 56b].

19. ". . . *Vilâyet-i Anadoluda Ağın kazasına tabi Pezenka(?) nâm karye ahâlisinden olup Kasap İlyas mahallesinde sâkin iken bundan akdem vefat eden Kömürcü Hüseyin beşe bin Abdullah. . . .*" [ISA-DM, 8/6, p. 71a].

20. [ISA-DM, 8/20, p. 3b].

21. *". . . vilâyet-i Anadolu'da Arapkir kazasına tâbî Bostancık nâm karye ahâlisinden olup Davudpaşa İskelesinde Kasap İlyas mahallesinde sâkin Kara Ahmed bin Mehmed . . . yine karye-i mezbure ahâlisinden İbrahim Beşe bin Abdurrahman. . . .*" [ISA-DM, 8/20, p. 3b].

22. [ISA-DM, 8/40, p. 44b; 8/90, p. 7a; 8/120, p. 48b; 8/140, p. 53a; 8/148, p. 87a; 8/170, p. 27a].

23. Vital Cuinet *La Turquie d'Asie—Géographie Administrative*, Paris, Ernest Leroux, 1892, Vol. 2, pp. 315–404 (see pp. 357–361 on Arapkir).

24. İbrahim Alaattin Gövsa *Türk Meşhurları Ansiklopedisi* (Encyclopedia of famous Turks), Istanbul, Yedigün Matbaası, 1945–1946; Ahmet Nezih Galitekin "İsmail Saib Sencer," *Müteferrika*, 4, 1994, pp. 137–144.

25. Charles Issawi *The Economic History of Turkey, 1800–1914*, Chicago, University of Chicago Press, 1980, p. 35.

26. Donald Quataert "The Age of Reforms, 1812–1914," in Halil Inalcık and Donald Quataert (eds.) *An Economic and Social History of the Ottoman Empire*, Cambridge, Cambridge University Press, pp. 759–947.

27. See Cuinet *Turquie d'Asie*, p. 345.

28. Ekrem Yalçınkaya *Muhtasar Malatya Tarih ve Coğrafyası* (A short history and geography of Malatya), Istanbul, Cumhuriyet Matbaası, 1940, p. 38. On the decline of the cotton manufactures of Arapkir, see Fikri Yücel *Arapgir Tarihi* (History of Arapkir), Arapkir Matbaası, Arapkir, 1967, pp. 46–48.

29. Vital Cuinet *Turquie d'Asie*, p. 332.

30. [ISA-DM, 8/90, p. 7a].

31. For similar contemporary insertion mechanisms in Istanbul, see Sema Erder *Istanbula bir kent kondu: Ümraniye*, Istanbul, Iletişim Yayınları, 1996; Erder "Where Do You Hail From?—Localism and Networks in Istanbul," in C. Keyder (ed.) *Istanbul between the Local and the Global*, London, Rowman and Littlefield, 2000, pp. 161–173.

32. See, for instance, Quataert *Social Disintegration and Popular Resistance in the Ottoman Empire, 1882–1908*, New York, 1983.

33. Cuinet *Turquie* d'Asie, Vol. 2, pp. 359, 361, 363, 367, 372.

34. So were two *muhtar*s (a father and his son) of the neighboring Kürkçübaşı *mahalle*, which is also part of the Davudpaşa District.

35. Interview conducted on August 12, 1994.

36. Interview conducted on July 29, 1995.

37. Interview conducted on December 2, 1994.

38. [D2/p. 2–8].

39. How this Yeşilin Mehmed Efendi came to build and own such a large number of houses on a plot of land practically abandoned but still apparently legally belonging to the heirs of the Ispanakçızâde family is something that the local records do not reveal. Still, this informal local housing market in the *Virane* functioned unimpeded for long decades, until the Cerrahpaşa Hospital took over the land in the second half of the twentieth century (see the Epilogue).

40. Interview conducted on August 2, 1994.

41. Harold Lubell *The Informal Sector in the 1980s and 1990s*, Paris, Organization for Economic Cooperation and Development (OECD) Development Centre Studies, Paris 1991.

42. Robert Mantran *İstanbul dans la Seconde moitié du XVIIème siècle—Essai d'Histoire Institutionnelle, Economique et Sociale*, Paris, Librairie Adrien Maisonneuve, 1962.

43. See Gabriel Baer "The Administrative, Economic, and Social Functions of Turkish Guilds," *International Journal of Middle Eastern Studies*, 1/1970, 28–50; and Engin Deniz Akarlı "Gedik: Implements, Mastership, Shop Usufruct and Monopoly among Istanbul Artisans, 1750–1850," *Wissenschaftskolleg Jahrbuch*, Berlin, 1986, pp. 225–231.

44. Lubell *Informal Sector in the 1980s and 1990s*, p. 17.

45. Mantran *Istanbul dans la seconde moitié du XVIIème siecle*.

46. "... *gümrük ketebesinden.* ..."

47. "... *telgrafhane ketebesinden.* ..."

48. Quataert "The Age of Reforms, 1812–1914," in Inalcık and Quataert *Economic and Social History of the Ottoman Empire*, particularly pp. 897–898.

49. Suraiya Faroqhi "Crisis and Change, 1590–1699," in ibid., pp. 595–598.

50. The birth, death, and marriage records in the *muhtar*'s notebooks cannot be used as sources of demographic information. The *muhtar*'s registration rate for births and deaths in Kasap İlyas does not seem to have exceeded 10 percent during this period.

51. On late Ottoman demographic registration procedures and their failure see Duben and Behar *İstanbul Households*, pp. 15–20.

52. "Sicill-i Nüfus Nizamnamesi" (Regulation on population registers), 1883, *Düstur- Zeyl II*, pp. 3–8, 15–24.

53. Musa Çadırcı "Tanzimat Döneminde çıkarılan men'-i mürur ve pasaport nizamnameleri."

54. [D2/pp. 106–108]

55. "... *Kasımpaşa'da Sahhaf Muhiddin mahallesinden nakil*. ..."

56. "... *Molla Gürani kurbünde Seyyid Ömer mahallesinde bir numaradan nakil*. ..."

57. "... *Yedi nüfus Kürkçübaşı mahallesi Langa caddesi 156 numaradan nakil*. ..."

58. ... *Cumartesi Pazarı kurbünde Hacı Piri mahallesinin 22 numarasından nakil*. ..."

59. The 251 *mahalle*s of Istanbul are listed in an official document intended for use in the 1877 parliamentary elections. "Esâmi-i Mahallât," in *İşbu 1294 senesi Saferinin 22sinde ve Mart ibtidasında ... mebusların suret-i intihabına dair beyannamedir*, Istanbul, Matbaa-yı Amire, 1293(1876).

60. For surprisingly similar contemporary urban insertion mechanisms in Istanbul, see Erder "Where Do You Hail From?"

61. Literate or not, most people in Istanbul had their personal seals that they used for stamping, in lieu of signing, all official documents. The seal was strictly personal and its authenticity, too, had to be certified by the *muhtar*, if necessary.

62. The *pusula* given by the muhtar to the person who left the neighborhood often contained a brief physical description of the (male) person ("... short, dark hair, brown eyes, fair skin, white beard etc. ...").

63. [D3/pp. 7–23].

64. For more details on the types of coffeehouses in Istanbul in the nineteenth century and their various social and cultural functions, see François Georgeon "Les cafés à Istanbul à la fin de l'Empire Ottoman," in Helene Desmet-Gregoire and François Georgeon *Cafés d'Orient revisités*, Paris, Editions du CNRS, 1997, pp. 39–79. On the social functions of coffeehouses in contemporary Istanbul shantytowns and their role on the local labor market see Erder "Where Do You Hail From?"

65. [Atik Defter 14, various pp.]

66. See S. E. Eisenstadt and L. Roniger *Patrons, Clients and Friends*, Cambridge, Cambridge University Press, 1984.

67. [D2/p. 53b].

68. [D2/p. 54a].

69. "... *altı sene evvel memleketinden gelmiş bilâ kayd İzmire* ..." [D2/p. 55b].

70. "... *üç sene akdem gelip tezkere-i mecidisi zayi*. ..." [D2/p. 57a].

Notes to Chapter 4

1. [Atik Defter 14].

2. See Alan Duben and Cem Behar *İstanbul Households: Marriage, Family and Fertility, 1880–1940*, Cambridge, Cambridge University Press, 1991, pp. 189–193.

Notes to Chapter 4   203

3. Stanford J. Shaw "The Population of Istanbul in the 19th Century," *International Journal of Middle-Eastern Studies*, 10, 1979, pp. 265–277.

4. "Esami-i mahallât, . . ." 1877. In this listing Kasap İlyas is cited as *Mahalle-i Kasap İlyas kurb-ü iskele-i Davutpaşa* (the Kasap İlyas *mahalle* near the Davutpaşa wharf).

5. To calculate median and mean ages, the ages stated in the census in lunar years (Hegirian calendar) had to be converted to solar years (Gregorian calendar).

6. Duben and Behar *İstanbul Households*, pp. 49–50.

7. We have assumed that the person ranked first in the ordering of the household members in the census documents was the head of that household.

8. State Institute of Statistics *1990 Population Census, Social and Economic Characteristics*, Ankara, 1993.

9. Duben and Behar *İstanbul Households*, pp. 48ff.

10. Ibid., p. 59.

11. Ibid., p. 59.

12. Behar "Polygyny in Istanbul (1885–1926)," *Middle Eastern Studies*, London, 27/3, 1991, pp. 477–486.

13. Duben and Behar *İstanbul Households*, p. 126.

14. Shaw "Population of Istanbul in the 19th Century," pp. 265–277.

15. For the details of the classification, see Peter Laslett "Family and Household as Work Group and Kin Group: Areas of Traditional Europe Compared," in Richard Wall, Jean Robin, and Peter Laslett (eds.) *Family Forms in Historic Europe*, Cambridge, Cambridge University Press, 1983, pp. 513–563. On household types in the whole of Istanbul during the 1885 census, see Duben and Behar *İstanbul Households*, pp. 48–69.

16. On slavery and slave trade in the Ottoman Empire in the second half of the nineteenth century see Ehud R. Toledano *The Ottoman Slave Trade and Its Suppression*, Princeton, Princeton University Press, 1982; and Hakan Erdem *Slavery and its Demise in the Ottoman Empire, 1800–1909*, London, Macmillan, 1996. This last work provides a large number of insights into the social status of slaves and slavery in the late Ottoman Empire.

17. For more details on these communities of black female manumitted slaves in Istanbul see Erdem *Slavery and Its Demise in the Ottoman Empire*.

18. Ibid.

19. Toledano *Ottoman Slave Trade and Its Suppression*.

20. [D3/pp. 1–23].

21. ". . . *tabaka-yı ulyâda üç bab oda ve bir kiler ve bir abdesthane ve kenif ve bir sofa ve vüstada üç bab oda ve bir abdesthane ve kenif ve bir sofa ve süflâda bir matbah ve bir kenif ve bir kömürlük ve selâmlık tâbir olunan mahalde ulyâda bir bab oda ve abdesthane ve vüstada bir bab oda ve abdesthane ve bir kenif ve bir ahır ve bir-i ma ve bir miktar*

bahçe ve sokak kapılarını müştemil bir bab mülk konak...." [ISA-DM], 8/110, p. 2a, 1 Jumada II 1261, [June 7, 1845].

22. "*...fevkânî iki bab oda ve sofa ve tahtânî iki bab oda ve hamam ve berber ma' dükkân....*" [ISA-DM], 8/120, p. 3a, 6 Shaban 1270 [May 4, 1854].

23. 1907 Census Roster for the Kasap İlyas *mahalle* [Eski Esas 23].

24. [D3/pp. 1–26].

25. The last entry by his own hand in the *muhtar*'s notebooks is dated from November 1903 [D3/p. 126]. Subsequent entries are by another hand. In 1907 Osman Efendi had already passed away, and the new census entries mention his daughter as "daughter of the late Osman Efendi." We have accepted 1904 as the probable year of his death.

26. For more details on the history of these two dervish lodges, see the two entries by Baha Tanman "Bekâr bey tekkesi," and "Taşçı tekkesi," in *Dünden Bugüne İstanbul Ansiklopedisi* (Encyclopedia of Istanbul yesterday and today), Istanbul, Tarih Vakfı Yayınları, 1995, Vols. 2 and 7.

27. See Klaus Kreiser "Medresen und Derwischkonvente in İstanbul: Quantitative Aspekte," *Economie et Sociétés dans l'Empire Ottoman*, Paris, Editions du Centre National de la Recherche Scientifique, 1983, pp. 109–127.

28. See Mübahat S. Kütükoğlu "1869'da faal İstanbul Medreseleri" (The Istanbul *medrese*s active in 1869), *İstanbul Üniversitesi Edebiyat Fakültesi Tarih Enstitüsü Dergisi*, 7–8, 1977, pp. 277–393.

29. See Sedat Kumbaracılar "İlk kız Okullarımız nasıl kuruldu?" (How were our first schools for girls founded?), *Hayat Tarih Mecmuası*, 4, May 1969, pp. 77–83.

30. See Mehmet Ö. Alkan *Tanzimattan Cumhuriyete Modernleşme Sürecinde Eğitim İstatistikleri, 1839–1924* (Educational statistics in the modernization process from the Tanzimat to the republic, 1839–1924), Ankara, State Institute of Statistics (Historical Statistics Series, Vol. 6), 2000, p. 55.

31. Maps drawn in 1913–1914 by the *Deutsches Syndikat für Stadtebauliche Arbeiten in der Türkei—Konstantinopel*, Istanbul, Istanbul Municipality Atatürk Library, Maps Section [912-563 IST, L/5, 1913–1914].

32. See Zeynep Çelik *The Remaking of Istanbul—Portrait of an Ottoman City in the Nineteenth Century*, Seattle, University of Washington Press, 1986.

33. Interview conducted on July 29, 1995.

34. [D3/pp. 1—26].

35. See Alkan *Tanzimattan Cumhuriyete Modernleşme Sürecinde Eğitim İstatistikleri*, p. 56.

36. See Ziya Kazıcı "1093(1682) Yılında çeşitlerine göre İstanbul'da dükkânlar" (Different types of shops in Istanbul in 1093–1682), *Tarih Boyunca İstanbul Semineri—Bildiriler*, İstanbul, İstanbul Üniversitesi Edebiyat Fakültesi, 1979, pp. 239–279.

37. Vakfiyeler—X.

Notes to Chapter 4 205

38. The warehouse for straw is described as follows: "*... bir taraftan beygir hanı, bir taraftan Hacı Ahmed'in kömür mahzeni, cidar-ı hısn ve tarik-i 'amm ile mahdûd bir bâb samanhane....*" [İSA-DM 8/5, p. 27a].

39. "*... bir bâb menzil ve tahtında bir bâb keresteci dükkânı, ...*" Vakfiyeler—X.

40. "*... fi'l-asl keresteci dükkânı elyevm ifrazdan bâki kalan saman mağazası, ...*" Vakfiyeler—X.

41. "*... Davudpaşa İskelesinde eksik çeki taşıyla odun satan gidiler, ...*" Hayati Develi (ed.) *XVIII. Yüzyıl Istanbul Hayatına dair Risale-i Garibe* (A strange tract on life in Istanbul in the eighteenth century), Istanbul, Kitabevi, 1998, p. 23.

42. [ISA-DM 8/141], pp. 23a and 128a. There is another instance of a street being identified by reference to its inhabitants in the late nineteenth century. In a court case dating from 1879 a street in the *mahalle* was referred to as the street of the Arabs (*arablar sokağı*), probably because a number of the manumitted female black slaves were living in it.

43. [ISA-DM 8/154], p. 3a.

44. "*... Davudpaşa İskelesinde Kömürcüler yangın, ...*" Osman Nuri Ergin *Mecelle-i Umûr-u Belediye*, Vol. 3, Istanbul, 1995, p. 1228.

45. Interview conducted on July 29, 1995.

46. Interview conducted on December 2, 1994.

47. Interview conducted on September 11, 1994.

48. "*Davud Paşa İskelesi kurbünde Kasap İlyas mahallesi muhtarı.*"

49. Two regulations were issued on the matter, in 1883 and in 1902. For more details on the late Ottoman population registration schemes and the information contained therein see Behar "The 1300 (a.h.) and 1322 (a.h.) *Tahrir*s as Sources for Ottoman Historical demography," Istanbul, *Boğaziçi University Research Papers*, 1985; Behar "Sources pour la Démographie Historique de l'Empire Ottoman: les Tahrir de 1885 et 1907," *Population* (Paris), 53/1–2, 1998, pp. 161–181.

50. "*... Hamam Odaları—18—Piyade Nizamiye otuz beşinci alayın dördüncü taburunun kâtibi Mehmet Tevfik efendinin hemşiresi Vahide hanım dul olup ve maişeti olmayıp şayan-ı rahmet bulunduğu....*" [D3/p. 7].

51. "*... Samatya Caddesi 53—... Fidan kalfa bint-i Abdullah, mevlidi 1250, nâmizaç olup hastahaneye....*" [D3/p. 21].

52. "*... Saide hanımın biraderi İsmail Zühdü efendi'den ki ikinci ordu, onbeşinci alay ikinci nizamiye taburu ikinci bölük mülâzım-ı evvelidir, sipariş-i maaşı vardır....*" [D2/p. 78b].

53. "*... Samatya Caddesi 5—Gümrük kolcusu Mehmet ağa'ya tekaüt maaşı yüz kırk dört kuruş olarak tahsis olunmuştur....*" [D2/p. 15b].

54. "*... Bab-ı seraskeri ketebesinden müteveffa Halim efendi zevcesi Hafize Resmiye hanım elyevm berhayat ve ere varmamıştır....*" [D3/p. 86].

55. "... *Kolağası İbrahim Şem'i efendinin eski mühr-ü zatisi zayi olup elyevm ittihaz etmiş idüğü mührü mühr-ü zatisi olup emniyet sandığında olan emanetini ahz edeceğini. . . .*" [D2/p. 25b].

56. "... *âdil ve makbûlü'ş-şehadet idüğü. . . .*" [D2/p. 4a].

57. "... *ehl-i ırz gürûhundan idüğü. . . .*" [D2/p. 46a].

58. "*Mekteb -i idadi-yi tıbbiye-i şâhâne birinci senesi şâkirdanından Hayri, müddet-i mezuniyetinde pederinin yanında beytutet edeceği. . . .*" [D2/p. 20b].

59. "... *kat'iyen ferağ ile muamele –i lâzımesinin icrası zımnında. . . .*" [D2/p. 5b].

60. "... *İskele 42—Süleyman ağa işbu mağazayı Nisan 1306 iptidasına kadar Nikola veled-i Mihale sekiz yüz kuruşa icar edip dört yüzü peşinen bakiyesi Şubat iptidasında alınacaktır. . . .*" [D2/p. 49a].

61. "... *Helvacı 8—Astarcı Mehmed efendi zevcesi Fatma bint-i Abdullah'ın dört taksit senevî yüz kuruş faizli esham-i cedidesi olduğu. . . .*" [D2/p. 52a].

62. The literacy rate for adult males was around 25 percent in late nineteenth- and early twentieth-century Istanbul. We have reached this estimate by using declared occupations as a proxy for literacy. No literacy rate can be calculated for females, though, very few having any declared occupation in the Ottoman censuses. The literacy rate for adult males in the Kasap İlyas *mahalle* was probably slightly lower than that for Istanbul as a whole.

63. [D3/pp. 1–23].

64. Interview conducted on July 29, 1995.

Notes to Epilogue

1. See Osman Nuri [Ergin] *Müessesât-ı Hayriyye-yi Sıhhiye Müdiriyeti*, Istanbul, 1911; Nil Sarı and M. Bedizel Zülfikâr "Tarihle içiçe bir eğitim kurumu: Cerrahpaşa Tıp Fakültesi," *Tıp Tarihi Araştırmaları (History of medicine studies)*, 4, Istanbul, 1992, pp. 41–61.

2. Sarı and Zülfikâr, p. 44.

3. Interview conducted on December 2, 1994.

4. Interview conducted on August 12, 1994.

5. Interview conducted on August 12, 1994.

6. Interview conducted on July 29, 1995.

7. The hospital was sued a number of times by some of the former residents of Kasap İlyas for insufficient compensation of the expropriated houses and lands, but to no great avail. See Erdem Yücel "Davudpaşa Iskelesi ve Kamulaştırma," *Türk Dünyası Araştırmaları*, 1/1, August 1979, pp. 130–139.

8. Terminating with the "old" urban landscape of Istanbul and replacing it with a "modern" (i.e., Parisian or Viennese) look was an idea that was often toyed with in the Tanzimat period. Many urban projects with that view in mind (long, straight avenues, large and monumental piazzas, arching bridges, towers, a right-angled grid of streets, etc.) saw the day in the nineteenth century. See Zeynep Çelik *The Remaking of Istanbul*, Los Angeles, University of California Press, 1992. The basic social building blocks of the urban tissue, the *mahalle*s, however, were not part of this new urban ideal and were left to their own devices.

9. This seems to have been so in the inceptive fifteenth century as well, when the Ottoman *mahalle*s of Istanbul were just taking shape. See Çiğdem Kafesçioğlu *The Ottoman Capital in the Making: The Reconstruction of Constantinople in the Fifteenth Century*, unpublished Ph.D. Thesis, Harvard University, 1996.

10. See "Yeni mahalle, mıntıka ve daire taksimatı," *Şehremaneti Mecmuası*, Istanbul, 1928, pp. 43–51.

11. Interview conducted on August 12, 1994. Kasap İlyas is now one of the smallest *mahalle*s of intramural Istanbul, and is located within the Fatih District (*ilçe*). It contains a total of nine streets and, according to the *muhtar*, fifteen hundred inhabitants.

Notes to Appendix

1. See *Vakfiyeler* (I–X).

2. Istanbul Şer'iye Sicilleri Arşivi—Davudpaşa Mahkemesi (Istanbul Religious Courts' Archives—Davudpaşa Court), ISA-DM 8/4, p. 31b; 8/20, p. 15a; 8/50, p. 6a, etc.

3. Istanbul Şer'iye Sicilleri Arşivi—Davudpaşa Mahkemesi (Istanbul Religious Courts' Archives—Davudpaşa Court), ISA-DM 8/9, pp. 43a, 49a; ISA-DM 8/140, pp. 47a, 55a; ISA-DM 8/154, p. 33b.

4. [D1], various entries.

Bibliography

ARCHIVAL SOURCES

Vakfiyeler (I–X)

Copies of Deeds of Trust, and of sales or transfers of the Right of Disposal of *vakıf* property under the trusteeship of the *imam* of Kasap İlyas (*Kasap İlyas mahallesi imamlarına ait vakfiye ve temessük senedi suretleri, ferağ ve intikal kayıtları*), manuscript, 19 folios (17 × 49 cm), 10 deeds of trust covering the period 1662–1855, and various operations attached thereto.

Notebooks of the *Muhtar* of the Kasap İlyas *Mahalle*

Covering the 1864–1910 period and containing marriage, birth, death, and migration records, as well as various other entries on topics of local interest.

[D1] Leatherbound notebook with marbled paper, 40 pages (42 × 17 cm).
[D2] Unbound notebook, 178 pages (20 × 27 cm).
[D3] Clothbound notebook, 136 pages (24 × 33 cm).

1885 Census Roster and Population Register (Tahrir Defteri ve Sicill-i Nüfus) for the Kasap İlyas *Mahalle*

Bound black roster, 49 × 37cm., 300 pages (Kasap İlyas pp. 1–153).
İstanbul, Fatih Kaymakamlığı, İlçe Nüfus Müdürlüğü [Atik Defter 14].

1907 Census Roster and Population Register (Tahrir Defteri ve Sicill-i Nüfus) for the Kasap İlyas *Mahalle*

Bound dark blue roster, 49 × 32.5 cm, 92 pages.
İstanbul, Fatih Kaymakamlığı, İlçe Nüfus Müdürlüğü [Eski Esas 23].

BIBLIOGRAPHY

Archives of the Istanbul Religious Courts

İstanbul Müftülüğü Şer'iye Sicilleri Arşivi, Davud Paşa Mahkemesi [İSA-DM].

Register Numbers: 8/1, 8/2, 8/3, 8/4, 8/5, 8/6, 8/7, 8/8, 8/9, 8/10, 8/20, 8/30, 8/40, 8/50, 8/60, 8/70, 8/80, 8/90, 8/100, 8/110, 8/120, 8/129, 8/130, 8/140, 8/141, 8/145, 8/148, 8/154, 8/157, 8/166, 8/170, 8/176, 8/179, 8/183, 8/189, 8/192.

Maps of the Neighborhood

Map of 1875 (scale: 1/2000) published by Ekrem Hakkı Ayverdi, *Ondokuzuncu Asırda İstanbul Haritası*, Istanbul, Istanbul Fetih Cemiyeti, 1978 (Part D3).

Map of 1913–19/14 (scale: 1/500), *Deutsches Syndikat für Stadtebauliche Arbeiten in der Türkei—Konstantinopel*, Istanbul, Municipal Atatürk Library, Maps section, [912-563, IST, L/5, 1913/14].

Map of 1934 (scale: 1/10000), *Istanbul Şehri Rehberi*, Istanbul, 1934 (Map number 11).

Interviews

A series of ten interviews, conducted in 1994 and 1995, with present and former elderly inhabitants of Kasap İlyas.

Printed Sources

Abu-Lughod, Janet L. (1987) "The Islamic City-Historic Myth, Islamic Essence, and Contemporary Relevance," *International Journal of Middle Eastern Studies*, 19, 155–176.

Efendi, Ahmet. (1993) *Üçüncü Selim'in Sırkâtibi Ahmet Efendi Tarafından Tutulan Ruzname*, Ankara, Türk Tarih Kurumu.

Akarlı, Engin Deniz. (1986) "Gedik: Implements, Mastership, Shop Usufruct and Monopoly among Istanbul Artisans, 1750–1850," *Wissenschaftskolleg Jahrbuch*, 225–231.

Alkan, Mehmet Ö. (2000) *Tanzimattan Cumhuriyete Modernleşme sürecinde Eğitim İstatistikleri, 1839–1924*, Devlet İstatistik Enstitüsü Yayınları (State Institute of Statistics, Historical Statistics Series, Vol. 6).

Akgündüz, Ahmet. (1998) *İslam Hukukunda ve Osmanlı Tatbikatında Vakıf Müessesesi*, Ankara, Türk Tarih Kurumu.

Bibliography

Aktepe, Münir. (1957) "Onyedinci Asra ait İstanbul Kazâsı Avarız Defteri," *İstanbul Enstitüsü Dergisi*, 3, 109–139.

Esad, Celal. [Arseven] (1912) *Eski İstanbul Abidat ve Mebanisi-Şehrin Tesisinden Osmanlı Fethine Kadar*, İstanbul, Muhtar Halit Kütüphanesi, 1328.

(Ayvansarayi) Hafız Hüseyin (1864) *Hadikat'ül-Cevami*,' İstanbul.

Aydın, Mehmet Akif. (1985) *İslâm-Osmanlı Aile Hukuku*, Istanbul, Marmara Üniversitesi Ilahiyat Fakültesi.

Ayverdi, Ekrem Hakkı. (1953) *Fatih Devri Mimarisi*, İstanbul, Fetih Cemiyeti Neşriyatı.

———. (1958) *Fatih Devri Sonlarında İstanbul Mahalleleri, Şehrin İskanı ve Nüfusu*, Ankara, Vakıflar Umum Müdürlüğü Neşriyatı.

———. (1978) *Ondokuzuncu Asırda İstanbul Haritası*, İstanbul, İstanbul Fetih Cemiyeti.

Baer, Gabriel. (1970) "The Administrative, Social and Economic Functions of Turkish Guilds," *International Journal of Middle Eastern Studies*, 1, 28–50.

Barkan, Ömer Lutfü. (1972–1979) *Süleymaniye Camii ve İmareti İnşaatı (1550–1557)*, Ankara, Türk Tarih Kurumu, Vol. 1 (1972) and Vol. 2 (1979).

Barkan, Ömer Lütfü and Ekrem Hakkı Ayverdi. (1970) *Istanbul Vakıfları Tahrir Defteri-953 (1546) Tarihli*, İstanbul, İstanbul Fetih Cemiyeti.

Bayındır, Abdülaziz. (1986) *İslâm Muhakeme Hukuku (Osmanlı Devri Uygulaması)*, İstanbul, İslami İlimler Araştırma Vakfı.

Behar, Cem. (1985) "The 1300 (a.h.) and 1322 (a.h) Tahrirs as Sources for Ottoman Historical Demography," *Boğaziçi University Research Papers* (85-03), Istanbul.

———. (1991) "Polygyny in İstanbul (1885–1926)," *Middle Eastern Studies* (London), 27/3: 477–486.

———. (1996) *Osmanlı İmparatorluğu'nun ve Türkiye'nin Nüfusu (1500–1927)*, Ankara, Devlet İstatistik Enstitüsü Yayınları (State Institute of Statistics, Historical Statistics Series, Vol. 2).

———. (1997) "Fruit Vendors and Civil Servants—A Social and Demographic Portrait of a Neigborhood Community in Intra Mural İstanbul: The Kasap İlyas *Mahalle* in 1885," *Boğaziçi Journal*, 11/1–2, 5–32.

———. (1998) "Kasap İlyas mahallesi: Istanbul'un bir mahallesinin sosyal ve demografik portresi: 1546–1885," *Istanbul Araştırmaları*, 4, 7–111.

———. (1998) "Sources pour la Démographie Historique de l'Empire Ottoman: les *Tahrir* de 1885 et 1907," *Population*, 53/1–2, 161–181.

———. (1998) "Qui Compte? 'Recensements' et statistiqued démographiques dans l'Empire Ottoman, du XVIe au XXe siècle," *Histoire et Mesure*, 13/1/2, 135–146.

Behrens-Abouseif, Doris (1994) *Egypt's Adjustment to Ottoman Rule. Institutions, Waqf and Architecture in Cairo (16th–19th Century)*, Leiden, Netherlands, Brill.

Cerassi, Maurice M. (1999) *Osmanlı Kenti*, İstanbul, Yapı Kredi Yayınları.

Cezar, Mustafa (1963) *Osmanlı Devrinde İstanbul Yapılarında Tahribat Yapan Yangınlar ve Tabii Afetler*, İstanbul, Güzel Sanatlar Akademisi Yayını.

Cin, Halil (1974) *İslâm ve Osmanlı Hukukunda Evlenme*, Ankara, Ankara Üniversitesi İlâhiyat Fakültesi.

Cuinet, Vital (1892) *La Turquie d'Asie-Géographie Administrative*, Paris, Ernest Leroux.

Çadırcı, Musa (1970) "Türkiye'de Muhtarlık Teşkilatının Kurulması Üzerine bir İnceleme," *Belleten* (Türk Tarih Kurumu), 409–420.

———. (1991) *Tanzimat Döneminde Anadolu Kentlerinin Sosyal ve Ekonomik Yapıları*, Ankara, Türk Tarih Kurumu Yayınları.

———. (1993) "Tanzimat Döneminde çıkarılan men'-i mürur ve pasaport nizamnameleri," *Türk Tarih Kurumu-Belgeler*, 15/19, 169–183.

Çeçen, Kâzım (1988) *Mimar Sinan ve Kırkçeşme Tesisleri*, İstanbul, İstanbul Büyükşehir Belediyesi.

Çelik, Zeynep (1986) *The Remaking of İstanbul—A Portrait of an Ottoman City in the Nineteenth Century*, Seattle, University of Washington Press.

Çizakça, Murat (2000) *A History of Philanthropic Foundations. The Islamic World from the Seventh Century to the Present*, İstanbul, Boğaziçi University Press, 2000.

De Amicis, Edmondo (1993) *İstanbul (1874)*, Ankara, Türk Tarih Kurumu.

Derviş Mustafa (1994) *1782 Yılı Yangınları (Harik Risalesi-1196)*, İstanbul, İletişim Yayınları.

Doumani, Beshara (1995) *Merchants and Peasants in Jabal Nablus, 1700–1900*, Los Angeles, University of California Press.

Duben, Alan and Cem Behar (1991) *İstanbul Households, Marriage, Family and Fertility, 1880–1940*, Cambridge, Cambridge University Press. (Turkish translation: *İstanbul Haneleri-Evlilik, Aile ve Doğurganlık 1880–1940*, İstanbul, İletişim Yayınları, 1996).

Eisenstadt, S. E. and L. Roniger (1984) *Patrons, Clients and Friends*, Cambridge, Cambridge University Press.

Eldem, Edhem, Daniel Goffmann, and Bruce Masters (1999) *The Ottoman City between East and West—Aleppo, Izmir and Istanbul*, Cambridge, Cambridge University Press.

Erdem, Hakan (1996) *Slavery and its Demise in the Ottoman Empire, 1800–1909*, London, Macmillan.

Erder, Sema (1996) *Istanbul'a bir kent kondu: Ümraniye*, Istanbul, İletişim yayınları.

———. (1999) "Where Do You Hail From?—Localism and Networks in Istanbul," in C. Keyder (ed.) *Istanbul, Between the Local and the Global*, London, Rowman & Littlefield, 161–173.

Ergin, Osman Nuri (1911) *Müessesat-ı Hayriyye-yi Sıhhiye Müdiryeti*, Istanbul.

———. (1934) *İstanbul Şehri Rehberi*, İstanbul.

———. (1936) *Türkiye'de Şehirciliğin Tarihi İnkişafı*, İstanbul.

———. (1995) *Mecelle-i Umur-u Belediye*, İstanbul, Büyükşehir Belediyesi Yayınları.

Esami-i Mahallat (1876) in *İşbu 1294 Seferinin 22sinde... mebusların suret-i intihabına dair beyannamedir*, İstanbul, Matbaa-yı Amire.

Evliya Çelebi (1996) *Seyahatname, Vol. I* (Transciption from TKS B.304 made by Orhan Şaik Gökyay), İstanbul, Yapı Kredi Bankası Yayınları.

Faroqhi, Suraiya (1984) *Towns and Townsmen of Ottoman Anatolia, 1520–1650*, Cambridge, Cambridge University Press.

———. (1987) *Men of Modest Substance—House Owners and House Property in seventeenth century Ankara and Kayseri*, Cambridge, Cambridge University Press.

Gövsa, Ibrahim Alaeddin (1946) *Türk Meşhurları Ansiklopedisi*, Istanbul, Yedigün Neşriyat.

von Grunebaum, Gustav (1961) "The Structure of the Muslim Town," *Islam: Essays in the Nature and Growth of a Cultural Tradition*, London.

Hanna, Nelly (1998) *Making big money in 1600, The life and times of Ismail Abu Taymiyya, Egyptian merchant*, Syracuse, Syracuse University Press.

Hourani, Albert and S. M. Stern (1970) *The Islamic City—A Colloquium*, Philadelphia, The University of Pennsylvania Press.

Hovhannesyan, Sarkis Sarraf (1996) *Payitaht İstanbul'un Tarihçesi*, İstanbul, Tarih Vakfı Yurt Yayınları.

İnalcık, Halil and Donald Quataert (eds.) (1994) *An Economic and Social History of the Ottoman Empire (1300–1914)*, Cambridge, Cambridge University Press.

İncicyan, P. (1976) *Onsekizinci Asırda İstanbul*, İstanbul, İstanbul Fetih Cemiyeti Yayınları.

İpşirli, Mehmet (1989) "Arşiv Belgelerine göre İstanbul Vakıf Evleri (Müştemilât, Tamir, Kira, Satış)," in *Tarih Boyunca İstanbul Semineri-Bildiriler*, İstanbul, İstanbul Üniversitesi Edebiyat Fakültesi Basımevi, 183–196.

"İstanbul ve bilâd-ı selâsede kâin mahallât ve kurranın huruf-u hecâ tertibiyle esami ve mensub oldukları maliye şu'ubatı ve mülhak bulundukları liva ve kazâ esamisini mübeyyin rehberdir," Istanbul, Matbaa-yı âmire, 1922.

Kafesçioğlu, Çiğdem (1996) *The Ottoman Capital in the Making: The Reconstruction of Constantinople in the Fifteenth Century*, Unpublished Ph.D. Thesis, Harvard University.

Karpat, Kemal (1978) "Ottoman Population Records and the Census of 1881/82–1893," *International Journal of Middle Eastern Studies*, 9, 237–174.

Kazıcı, Ziya (1989) "1093 (1682) yılında çeşitlerine göre İstanbul'daki dükkanlar," in *Tarih Boyunca İstanbul Semineri-Bildiriler*, İstanbul, İstanbul Üniversitesi Edebiyat Fakültesi Basımevi, 239–279.

Kent Tarihçiliği (Sempozyum-Atölye), İstanbul, Toplu Konut İdaresi/Tarih Vakfı, 1994.

Koçu, Reşat Ekrem (1966) *İstanbul Ansiklopedisi* (articles on "Davud Paşa"), Vol. 8, 4289–4314.

———. (1981) *Yangın Var... İstanbul Tulumbacıları*, İstanbul, Ana Yayınevi.

Kömürcüyan, Eremya Çelebi (1988) *İstanbul Tarihi-XVII. Asırda İstanbul*, İstanbul, Eren Yayıncılık.

Kreiser, Klaus (1983) "Medresen und Derwischkonvente in İstanbul: quantitative Aspekte," in *Economie et Sociétés dans l'Empire Ottoman*, Paris, CNRS, 109–127.

Kumbaracılar, Sedat (1969) "İlk Kız Okullarımız Nasıl Kuruldu?" Hayat Tarih Mecmuası, 4, 77–83.

Kütükoğlu, Mübahat S. (1977) "1869'da Faal İstanbul Medreseleri," *İstanbul Üniversitesi Edebiyat Fakültesi Tarih Enstitüsü Dergisi*, 7–8, 277–393.

Lapidus, Ira M. (1969) *Middle Eastern Cities*, Berkeley, University of California Press.

———. (1973) "The Evolution of Muslim Urban Society," *Comparative Studies in Society and History*, 15, 21–50.

Lubell, Harold (1991) *The Informal Sector in the 1980s and the 1990s*, Paris, OECD (Center for Development Studies).

Mahallat Esamisi. Şehremaneti Hududu Dahilinde Bulunan Mahallat ve Kurrânın Huruf-u Heca tertibi üzere mürettep esamisiyle semt-i meşhurlarını ve devair-i belediyenin, . . . İstanbul, Arşak Garoyan Matbaası, 1329 (1913).

Manners, Ian R. (1997) "Constructing the Image of a City: The Representation of Constantinople in Christopher Buondelmonti's Liber Insularum Archipelago," *Annals of the Association of American Geographers*, 87/1, 1997, 73–102.

Mantran, Robert (1962) *İstanbul dans la Seconde Moitié du XVIIéme Siécle—essai d'Histoire Institutionnelle, Economique et Sociale*, Paris, Librairie Adrien Maisonneuve (Türkish translation: *Onyedinci Yüzyılın İkinci Yarısında İstanbul*, Ankara, Türk Tarih Kurumu, 1990).

Mayer, Robert (1943) *Byzantion, Konstantinupolis, İstanbul-Eine Genetische Stadtgeographie*, Akademie der Wissenschaften in Wien, Viyana ve Leipzig.

Meriç, Rıfkı Melûl (1957) "Birkaç mühim arşiv vesikası," *Istanbul Enstitüsü Dergisi*, 3, 33–42.

Millingen, Alexander van *Byzantine Constantinople, The Walls of the City and Adjoining Historical Sites*, London, John Murray at Albemarle Street, 1899.

Müller-Wiener, Wolfgang (1977) *Bildlexikon zur Topographie Istanbuls*, Tübingen, Germany, Ernst Wasmuth Verlag.

———. (1994) *Die Hafen von Byzantion, Konstantinupolis, Istanbul*, Tübingen, Germany, Ernst Wasmuth Verlag.

Murphey, Rhoads (1990) "Communal Living in Ottoman Istanbul—Searching for the Foundations of an Urban Tradition," *Journal of Urban History*, 16/2, 1990, 115–131.

Nirven, Sadi Nazım (1953) *Fatih II. Sultan Mehmed Devri Türk Su Medeniyeti*, İstanbul.

Olivier, Gabriel Antoine (1802) *Voyage dans l'Empire Othoman, l'Egypte et la Perse*, Paris.

Orhonlu, Cengiz (1984) *Osmanlı İmparatorluğunda Şehircilik ve Ulaşım Üzerine Araştırmalar* S. Özbaran (ed.) İzmir, Turkey, Ege Üniversitesi Edebiyat Fakültesi Yayınları.

Ortaylı, İlber (1985) *Tanzimattan Cumhuriyete Yerel Yönetim Geleneği*, İstanbul, Hil Yayın.

———. (2000) *Osmanlı Toplumunda Aile*, Istanbul, Pan Yayıncılık.

Öz, Tahsin (1987) *İstanbul Camileri*, Ankara, Türk Tarih Kurumu Basımevi.

Pakalın, Mehmet Zeki (1983) *Osmanlı Tarih Deyimleri ve Terimleri Sözlüğü*, İstanbul, Milli Eğitim Basımevi.

Pamuk, Şevket (1994) "Money in the Ottoman Empire, 1326–1914," in Halil İnalcık and Donald Quataert (eds.) *An Economic and Social History of the Ottoman Empire*, Cambridge, Cambridge University Press, 947–985.

———. (1995) "En Büyük Tağşiş ve 1844 Tarihli Tashih-i Sikke İşlemi," *Toplumsal Tarih*, 13, 1995, 12–17.

Pamuk, Şevket (2000) *500 Years of Prices and Wages in Istanbul and Other Cities*, Ankara, State Institute of Statistics.

Quataert, Donald (1983) *Social Disintegration and Popular Resistance in the Ottoman Empire (1882–1908)*, New York.

Raymond, André (1984) *The Great Arab Cities in the 16th–18th Centuries*, New York, New York University Press.

———. (1985) *Grandes Villes Arabes à l'Epoque Ottomane*, Paris, Editions Sindbad.

Reyhanlı, Tülay (1983) *İngiliz Gezginlerine göre XVI. Yüzyılda İstanbul'da Hayat (1582–1599)*, Ankara, Kültür ve Turizm Bakanlığı Yayınları.

Risale-i Garibe-İstanbul'a dair (1998), Hayati Develi (ed.) Istanbul, Istanbul Kitabevi.

Sarı, Nil and M. Bedizel Zülfikar (1992) "Tarihle İçiçe bir Eğitim Kurumu: Cerrahpaşa Tıp Fakültesi," *Tıp Tarihi Araştırmaları* (History of Medicine Studies) 4, 41–60.

Schneider, Alfons Maria (1952) "Onbeşinci Yüzyılda İstanbul'un Nüfusu," *Belleten* (Türk Tarih Kurumu), 1952, 35–50 (offprint from *Nachricten des Akademie der Wissenchaften*, Göttingen, Germany, 1949).

Shaw, Stanford J. (1978) "The Ottoman Census System and Population," *International Journal of Middle Eastern Studies*, 9, 325–338.

———. (1979) "The Population of İstanbul in the 19th Century," *International Journal of Middle Eastern Studies*, 10, 265–277.

State Institute of Statistics (1993) *1990 Census of Population (Social and Economic Characteristics)*, Ankara.

Süreyya, Mehmed (1893) *Sicill-i Osmani, yahut Tezkire-i Meşâhir-i Osmaniye*, İstanbul, Matbaa-yı Amire.

Toledano, Ehud R. (1982) *The Ottoman Slave Trade and Its Suppression*, Princeton: Princeton University Press.

Turnham, David, Bernard Salome, and Antoine Schwarz (1990) *The Informal Sector Revisited*, Paris, OECD, Development Centre Publications.

Uluçam, Abdüsselam (1986) "Arapgir'deki Mimari Anıtların Bugünkü Durumu," *I. Battal Gazi ve Malatya Çevresi Halk Kültürü Sempozyumu*, Malatya, Turkey, İnönü Üniversitesi, 140–147.

Uzunçarşılı, İsmail Hakkı (1957) "İstanbul ve Bilad-ı Selâse Denilen Eyüp, Galata ve Üsküdar Kadılıkları," *İstanbul Enstitüsü Dergisi*, 3, 25–52.

———. (1988) *Osmanlı Devlet Teşkilatından Kapıkulu Ocakları-I (Acemi Ocağı ve Yeniçeri Ocağı)*, Ankara, Türk Tarih Kurumu.

———. (1988) *Osmanlı Tarihi*, Ankara, Türk Tarih Kurumu.

Ülgen, Ali Saim (1939) *Constantinople During the Era of Mohammed the Conqueror, 1453–1481*, Ankara, General Direction of Pious Foundations (Evkaf).

Ünver, Süheyl (1976) *İstanbul'un Mutlu Askerleri ve Şehit Olanlar*, Ankara, Türk Tarih Kurumu.

Vak'anüvis Ahmet Lütfi Efendi Tarihi (1989) Vol. 11, Ankara, Türk Tarih Kurumu.

Vatin, Nicolas (1996) "L'inhumation Intra-muros à Istanbul à l'Epoque Ottomane," in Gilles Veinstein (ed.) *Les Ottomans et la Mort*, Leiden, Netherlands, Brill, 157–175.

Wall, Richard, Jean Robin, and Peter Laslett (eds.) (1983) *Family Forms in Historic Europe*, Cambridge, Cambridge University Press.

Yalçınkaya, Ekrem (1940) *Muhtasar Malatya Tarih ve Coğrafyası*, Istanbul, Cumhuriyet Matbaası.

Yerasimos, Stéphane (1992) "A propos des Réformes Urbaines des Tanzimat," in Paul Dumont and François Georgeon (eds.) *Villes Ottomanes a la Fin de l'Empire*, Paris, L'Harmattan, 17–33.

Yurt Ansiklopedisi ("Malatya") (1983), İstanbul, Yurt Yayınları, Vols. 7–8.

Yücel, Erdem (1973) "Davud Paşa Semti," *Türkiye Turing ve Otomobil Kulubü Belleteni*, 316, 16–20.

———. (1979) "Davud Paşa İskelesi ve Kamulaştırma," *Türk Dünyası Araştırmaları*, 1/1, 130–139.

Yücel, Fikri (1967) *Arapkir Tarihi*, Arapkir.

Index

Abacızâde *mahalle* 31, 36; *tekke* 100
Abdullah, Cevdet 104
Abdülhamid II 97
Abu-Lughod, J. 186n 9, 210
age 135; median age 135, 203n 5; age composition 135, 140
ağa 53
Ağın 97, 103
Akarlı, E. D. 201n 43, 210
Akgündüz, A. 189n 13, 194n 11, 195n 15, 210
Aksaray 5, 54, 55, 58, 60, 152, 154
Aktepe, M. 192n 49, 211
Aleppo 9, 19
Alexandretta 105
alevi 109, 110, 116, 134, 171, 175
Alkan, M. Ö. 204n 30, 204n 35, 210
Altınay, A. R. 186n 16
Anatolia 18, 19, 20, 33, 95, 96, 98, 110, 124, 141
Ankara 16, 19
arap (*see* blacks)
arap düğünü 144
Arapkir 13, 20, 95, 97, 98, 100–105, 106–110, 116, 126, 127, 128, 134, 140, 171
arapkirli 98, 100–103, 105–108, 110, 111, 117, 118, 120, 124, 125, 127–129, 134, 137, 140–143, 145, 150, 154, 169, 180
Arap Taceddin *mahalle* 32
Arcadius column 33
Archives of the Religious Courts (*see* *şer'iye sicilleri*)

Arguvan 97, 116, 128
Armenians 12, 38, 52, 55, 61, 89
Arseven, C. E. 192n 59, 211
artisans and shopkeepers 154, 155
'asabiyya 8, 23
Atatürk, M. K. 173, 175, 176
autarky 10
avârız 15, 22, 50, 66–68, 187n 29, 192n 50
Aydın, M. A. 196n 35, 211
Ayvansarayî Hâfız Hüseyin 100, 187n 23, 187n 30, 199n 15, 211
Ayverdi, E. H. 30, 50, 186n 17, 186n 19, 187n 22, 187n 27, 188n 1, 189n 5, 189n 9, 190n 17, 190n 25, 190n 26, 191n 30, 191n 36, 191n 45, 198n 64, 199n 15, 211
Aziz Mahmut efendi 69, 70, 71, 72, 73, 74, 75, 76, 77, 107, 195n 20, 195n 22

bâb 41
Baer, G. 201n 43, 211
Bagdad 100
Balkan wars 3, 123
Barkan, Ö. L. 30, 52, 186n 17, 188n 1, 189n 10, 189n 11, 190n 17, 190n 25, 190n 26, 191n 30, 191n 36, 191n 45, 192n 57, 199n 15, 211
Bayezid 50
Bayezid-i cedid *mahalle* 16, 36, 38, 39
Bayındır, A. 211
beggars (*see* *se'ele*)
Behar, C. 185n 1, 185n 2, 186n 20, 187n 32, 187n 34, 188n 36, 188n 38,

Behar, C. *(continued)*
  192n 51, 192n 53, 196n 34, 196n 35, 197n 58, 198n 60, 198n 68, 199n 7, 199n 8, 199n 10, 199n 13, 201n 51, 202n 2, 203n 6, 203n 9, 203n 12, 205n 49, 211
Behrens-Abouseif, D. 211
Beirut 105
Bekâr bey *tekke* 150, 151
bekârodaları 96, 151
Bekir Paşa *mahalle* 15, 16, 17
bektaşi 57
Belgrade 153
beytülmâl kâtibi 91
bilâd-ı selâse 1
blacks 143, 144
blind alleys (*see* dead-end streets)
bostan 12, 39, 40, 43, 44, 60, 69, 85, 87, 110, 114, 115, 116, 117, 149
Bostancık 103, 104, 106, 129
boza 50, 88, 154, 192n 46, 198n 67
Bursa 19
Butchers' Road 53, 54, 55, 57, 58, 60, 61, 76, 88, 150, 152, 156, 179
Byzantium 33, 54, 88, 179

cadastral land survey 5, 83, 192n 55
Cairo 1, 9, 185n 1
Castle of the Seven Towers 33, 54, 58
Caucasus 145
cemetary 92, 93
censuses 12, 14, 20, 21, 96; census of 1885 12, 15, 16, 20, 21, 22, 51, 80, 86, 87, 97, 98, 106, 108, 134, 135, 146, 154, 157, 160, 163, 179, 196n 28, 209; census of 1907 12, 15, 16, 20, 21, 22, 97, 124, 134, 136, 145, 146, 179, 204n 33, 209
Cerasi, M. 189n 15, 211
Cerrahpaşa *semt* 11, 33, 89, 154, 173, 180; Cerrahpaşa hospital 173, 174, 175, 201n 39
Cezar M. 187n 25, 191n 33, 193n 68, 193n 69, 193n 70, 211
Cezerî Kasım Paşa *mahalle* 14

Cibali 37, 155
Cin, H. 196n 35, 211
city walls (*see* ramparts)
civil servants 113, 114, 118
coal sellers' street 88
coffeehouses 126, 127, 128, 134, 149, 150
Coran 34, 35, 152
Coranic school 57, 68, 152
covered bazaar (*see çarşû-yı kebir*)
Cuinet, V. 104, 105, 106, 110, 200n 23, 200n 27, 200n 29, 201n 33, 211
cul-de-sac (*see* dead end streets)
currency 71, 72 ; currency debasement 72

Çadırcı, M. 194n 2, 194n 3, 194n 4, 196n 31, 196n 32, 199n 5, 202n 53, 211
Çarşamba 5
çarşû-yı kebir 4, 12, 50, 76, 150
Çatalca 59
Çavuşzâde mosque 16, 88
Çavuşzâde street 17, 58, 88, 90, 129, 152, 153, 158, 175
Çeçen, K. 191n 28, 211
Çelik, Z. 187n 25, 204n 32, 207n 8, 211
çerkes 145
Çetintaş, S. 104, 105
Çizakça, M. 195n 21, 211
Çorlu 59

Damascus 100
Davud paşa (grand vizier) 11, 23
Davudpaşa court 222, 39, 61, 84, 85, 92, 103, 104, 107, 108, 149, 156, 157, 159, 160, 193n 74
Davudpaşa double bath 32, 45, 48, 154
Davudpaşa gardens 12, 36, 44, 51, 87
Davudpaşa gate 5, 11, 15, 32, 39, 61
Davudpaşa *semt* 5, 11, 22, 31, 32, 45, 47, 50, 59, 89, 157, 159
Davudpaşa wharf 5, 6, 11, 13, 32, 36, 37, 38, 39, 51, 59, 83, 88, 104, 114,

126, 129, 155, 157, 158, 159, 160, 177, 180, 191n 38, 203n 4
Davudpaşa wharf street 88, 126, 128, 129, 154, 167, 180
dead-end streets 16, 24, 44, 48, 49, 84
de Amicis, E. 87, 198n 62, 211
deed of trust (*see vakfiye*)
defter 18, 188n 36
defterdar 15, 187n 28
Dersaadet 1
dervish convent/lodge 12, 34, 48, 100, 150, 151, 189n 12, 191n 42
Derviş Mustafa 192n 54, 193n 72, 211
Desmet-Grégoire H. 186n 6, 202n 64
district (*see semt*)
Divanyolu 57
divorce 167, 168
Divriği 97, 126, 128
Diyarbakır 100
Doumani, B. 211
Duben, A. 185n 1, 185n 4, 188n 38, 196n 36, 196n 68, 199n 10, 201n 51, 202n 2, 203n 6, 203n 9, 211

earthquakes 42, 131
Edirne 153
Edirnekapı 5
Eğin 110
Eisenstadt, S. E. 202n 66, 212
Eldem, E. 185n 2, 186n 8, 199n 1, 212
endogamy 108, 110, 112, 138, 139
endowments 31, 34, 89, 90, 156
Erdem, H. 145, 203n 16, 203n 17, 211
Erder S., 200n 31, 202n 60, 212
Ergani 101
Ergenç, Ö. 19
Ergin, O. N. 104, 105, 187n 27, 189n 14, 193n 61, 194n 2, 205n 44, 206n 1, 212
Erzurum 100
esham 169
Etmeydanı 55
Etyemez 11, 16, 29, 51, 59, 60
Eyüp 1

family structures (*see* household composition)
Faroqhi, S. 16, 185n 5, 187n 33, 201n 49, 213
Fatih 5, 11, 21, 58, 89, 138, 151, 207n 11
Fener 5, 155
ferâiz 35
ferman 54, 66
fetva 49
fires 14, 42, 51, 58, 87, 88, 100; fire of 1660 58, 59, 60; fire of 1782 58, 60, 61, 62, 63, 101, 103, 193n 74; fire of 1864 157
First World War 3, 4, 51, 89, 105, 152
forced settlements (*see sürgün*)
Forum bovis 46, 54, 55
fruits and vegetables 43, 44; fruit and vegetable vendors 106, 112, 114, 115, 117, 118, 119, 120

Galata 1, 18
Galitekin, A. N. 200n 24
gardens 42, 43, 69, 85, 86
gecekondu 120
gedik 115, 118 119, 210
Georgeon, F. 186n 7, 202n 64
Gerber, H. 19
Goffmann, D. 19, 185n 2, 186n 8, 199n 1, 211
Golden Horn 12, 36, 37, 46, 58, 59, 114, 155
Gövsa, İ. A. 200n 14, 213
Grand Bazaar (*see çarşû-yı kebir*)
Greek Orthodox 12, 38, 52, 60, 61, 93, 146
greengrocers 115, 118, 119
guarantor (*see kefil*)
guilds 9, 113, 115, 118, 119; guild wardens 118, 119, 127, 128
Gümüş Baba *tekke* 150
Günaltay, Ş. 104

Hagios Emilianos 33
Halvetî order 34

hamal 5, 91, 114, 118, 128, 158
hamam 6, 12, 32, 33, 36, 37, 45, 49, 51, 62, 90, 149, 155, 189n 4
Hamam odaları street 58, 144, 165, 175
han 14, 41, 151
hane 21, 40, 86, 149, 150
Hanna, N. 213
hara 9, 10
Hasdek 106
Haysellers' street 88
hazire 92
Hourani, A. H. 8, 186n 10, 213
house 40, 41, 112, 146, 147, 150; house building materials 41, 42, 58, 60, 88; number of houses in Kasap İlyas 51, 69, 70, 86, 87, 98, 135, 146, 147; house prices 72; house quality 40, 41, 42, 85, 86, 158; house rents 68, 69, 71, 72, 112; size of houses 40, 41, 49, 85, 86, 149
households 21, 101, 108, 117, 136, 137, 146, 147, 151; household composition 136, 137, 139, 140–143; household head 109, 112, 136, 137; household size 136, 147
Hovhannisyan, S. 55, 192n 56, 193n 63, 213
Hûbyar *mahalle* 31, 36, 173, 175, 188n 2

Ispanakçızâde family 100, 102, 103
Ispanakçızâde Mustafa paşa 100–103, 105, 127, 175
Ispanakçı Viranesi 17, 97, 98, 104, 110, 111, 112, 113, 116, 120, 128, 133, 149, 153, 154, 158, 173, 175, 177, 180

icare-i kadime 72
icare-i muaccele 71, 75
icare-i müeccele 71, 75
icare-i vahide 71
icareteyn 71
ihtiyar heyeti 67
ilmühaber 121, 161, 162, 166

imam 6, 14, 15, 19–21, 24, 25, 31, 35, 50, 53, 60, 62, 65–70, 73, 74, 75, 76, 78, 80, 131, 132, 133, 150, 151, 156, 162; duties of *imam*s 78, 79, 80, 82; dynasties of *imam*s 66; revenues of *imam*s 70, 71, 72, 76; *imam*s of Kasap İlyas 53, 60, 67–69, 71, 74, 75, 76, 80, 83, 132, 133, 134, 150, 151, 156, 183, 194n 1
İnalcık H. 186n 15, 195n 18, 199n 1, 213
İncicyan P. 192n 46, 213
inflation 72
informal sector 114–117, 119
interviews 23, 109, 110, 210
İpşirli M. 190n 27, 194n 11, 195n 15, 213
"Islamic city" 7, 8, 9, 10
Islamic Law 74, 80, 82
Issawi C. 200n 25
izinname 80
İzmir 19
izn-i şürekâ 49

janissaries 55, 56, 57, 91, 95, 117, 193n 60, 193n 64
janissary barracks 55, 56

kadı 6, 9, 22, 42, 54, 66, 81, 82
Kadirî 150, 151
Kafadar, C. 188n 39
Kafesçioğlu, Ç. 187n 21, 189n 8, 207n 9, 213
kapıcıbaşı 100
kapıkulu 102
Karagümrük 5
Karaman 5
Karpat, K. 213
Kasap yolu (*see* Butchers' Road)
Kasımpaşa 122
kâtip 113
Kayseri 16, 19
Kazıcı, Z. 204n 36, 214
Kazlıçeşme 54, 55, 193n 62
Keban 97, 101, 105, 110

kefil 123, 124, 125, 126, 127, 161
keresteci 92
kethüda (*see* guild warden)
Kızılbaş 110
kinship 108, 111, 116, 128, 141, 142
Koçu, R. E. 187n 31, 190n 23, 193n 68, 193n 69, 198n 63, 213
kolbaşı 144
konak 13, 86, 87, 100, 102, 103, 106, 111, 113, 127, 133, 136, 147, 149, 154, 170, 173
Konya 100
Koska 89
Koraltan, R. 104
köle (*see* slave)
kömürcü 91, 92, 118, 156
Kömürcüyan E. 50, 192n 48, 192n 56, 213
Kreiser, K. 204n 27, 213
Kumbaracılar, S. 204n 29, 214
Kumkapı 50, 59
küfeci 5, 114, 116, 117, 138
külliye 32
Kürkçübaşı *mahalle* 16, 31, 36, 50, 57, 122, 180, 188n 2
Kütükoğlu, M. 204n 28, 214

Lacqueur, H. P. 198n 78
Langa 11, 12, 33, 34, 47, 38, 52, 59, 87, 122
Langa gardens 12, 13, 43, 44, 54, 59, 60, 115, 159
Lapidus, I. 8, 186n 13, 186n 14, 214
Laslett, P. 203n 15
Lebanon 105
legal residence 120
local administration 65, 66, 80, 165, 167, 180, 181; local archives 19, 20, 25; local authority 72, 77, 78, 81, 128, 162, 163, 165; local chronicles 25; local history 19; local headman (*see muhtar*); local identity 11, 12, 21, 27, 31, 110, 178, 179, 180, 181
London 1, 3, 153
Lowry, H. 188n 36

maden emini 100
mahalle 1, 3, 4, 7, 9–12, 13, 14, 19–23, 25 etc.; *mahalle* areas 36; *mahalle* borders 4, 9, 13, 14, 16, 35, 178–181, 189n 14; *mahalle* formation 13, 15, 45, 178, 179; *mahalle* numbers in Istanbul 13, 14, 135, 179, 202n 59; *mahalle* reform of 1928 178, 179, 180, 181, 207n 10
mahiyyat 162
mahlûl 75
Mahmud Paşa *mahalle* 14, 15
Malatya 104, 105, 110, 199n 12
Mâmuretülaziz 97, 104, 199n 12
manav (*see* greengrocers)
Manisa 38
Manners, I. 189n 8, 214
mansion (*see konak*)
Mantran, R. 117, 190n 18, 201n 42, 201n 45, 214
maps 2, 12, 33, 88, 99, 176, 189n 8, 204n 31, 210
Marcus, A. 19
Marçais, G. 8, 186n 12
Marçais, W. 8, 186n 12
Marmara sea 11, 13, 32, 36, 37, 38, 39, 46, 50, 52, 59, 89, 157, 177
marriage age 138, 139; marriage contracts 19, 20, 80, 81; marriage records 80, 81
Masters, B. 185n 2, 186n 7, 199n 1, 211
Mayer, R. 189n 6, 189n 7, 191n 39, 192n 59, 214
medrese 32, 41, 51
Mehmed II (the Conqueror) 1, 27
Mehmed Süreyya 199n 15, 200n 17, 215
men-i mürur 79
Meriç R. M. 214
mescit 6, 14, 15, 16
Mêsê 57
meşrûtâ 68
Middle Eastern cities 8, 19
Migration 95, 98, 103, 107, 108, 109, 116, 139, 140, 143; mass migration

Migration *(continued)*
  95, 107, 123; chain migration 95, 96, 98, 107, 108, 109, 116, 139, 140, 143; migration records and regulations 120, 121, 122, 123, 124, 128, 161
muallimhane 35
muhavvata 44, 190n 26
muhtar 6, 16, 19, 20, 23, 24, 25, 66, 78–81, 109, 110, 120, 121, 122, 123, 124, 125, 128, 129, 131, 133, 134, 146, 160, 161, 162, 163, 164, 165, 167–171, 209; *muhtar*s of Kasap Ilyas 78, 79, 80, 124, 184: duties of the *muhtar* 79, 80, 82, 83, 128, 160, 165, 168, 169; *muhtar* records 160, 161, 162, 164, 165
Murad IV 15
Murphey, R. 191n 44, 214
Mutmur 106
müezzin 15, 31, 32, 35, 52, 67, 77, 81, 82, 132, 136, 144; *müezzin*s of Kasap İlyas 53, 81, 82, 92, 132, 136, 144, 150, 183
Müeller-Wiener, W. 190n 16, 214
mürûr tezkeresi 79, 96, 121, 122, 123, 124, 125, 127, 128

naib 22, 82
nâzır 69
Nazperver Kalfa 57, 58
neighborhood (*see mahalle*)
Neş'et kadın 144, 145
"new *mahalle*" 15, 16, 32
Nirven, S. N. 191n38, 215
Nişanca 59
non-guild labor 9, 113, 116, 117, 118, 119
non-Muslims 52, 93, 134, 146, 191n 36
notary 82, 161
nüfus tezkeresi (*see* population certificate)

occupations 113, 117, 154, 155
Odun İskelesi 37

Olivier, G. A. 42, 191n 35, 215
Orhonlu, C. 190n 19, 191n 40, 215
orientalism 7
Ortaylı, İ. 194n 2, 197n 43, 199n 1, 215
Osman efendi (*muhtar* of Kasap İlyas) 79, 87, 120, 122, 128, 131, 132, 133, 134, 145, 150, 154, 155, 160, 161, 162, 163, 164, 165, 167, 168, 169, 170, 173, 196n 30, 204n 25
Ottoman cities 4, 8, 10, 25, 83, 95
outhouses 41, 44, 46

Öz, T. 215

Pakalın, M. Z. 215
Palace 12, 18, 102
Pamuk, Ş. 195n 18, 215
Paris 1, 3, 153, 207n 8
paşa 5, 53, 100, 101, 102, 103, 106, 133, 143, 170
patronage 101, 102
Pera 18
pious foundations 12, 13, 14, 30, 31, 35, 39, 40, 41, 53, 62, 66, 67, 68, 81, 90, 91, 132, 156; trustees of pious foundations 65, 71, 73, 74, 75, 76, 81
Police department 79
Polygyny 137, 138
population certificate 21; population density 12, 14, 16, 18, 31, 33, 40, 46, 49, 50, 51, 70, 86, 87; population growth 18, 52, 86, 139; population mobility 17, 18, 62, 120, 124, 143; population registers 21; population of Istanbul 1, 3, 51, 87, 135, 198n 60; population of *mahalle*s 4, 14, 18, 49, 50, 51, 52, 86, 87, 124, 134, 135
privacy 48
public fountains 12, 57, 88, 149
public bath (*see hamam*)

quarter (see mahalle)
Quataert, D. 186n 15, 195n 18, 199n 1, 200n 26, 200n 32, 201n 48, 215
Quételet, A. 21

railway line 153
ramparts 13, 32, 39, 42, 59, 156, 158, 177
Raymond, A. 19, 215
refugees 123, 124, 139
registration 25, 160, 165, 201n 50
rençber 117
residential patterns 4, 6, 8, 9, 89, 90, 91, 146
Reyhanlı, T. 190n 29, 215
Rufâi 150, 151
Rumelia 127, 141, 143
Russian war 97, 123, 139, 140, 143
ruznamçeci 91

Saldak 106, 128
samancı 91,
Samatya 11, 12, 33, 34, 38, 52, 87, 114, 126, 129, 133, 136, 150, 152, 153, 157, 174, 175, 179, 180, 193n 60
Sancaktar Hayreddin mahalle 17, 30, 36, 50, 180
Sarı, N. 206n 1, 215
scribe (see kâtip)
Schneider, A. M. 215
security 66, 78, 96, 106
se'ele 5, 13, 89, 114, 143, 146
seğirdim çavuşu 55, 56
Selim III 57, 58
semt 1, 3, 4, 5, 6, 12, 13, 31
Sencer, İ. S. 104, 105
Servi mescidi mahalle 14, 15, 187n 27
Shaw, S. J. 192n 52, 203n 3, 203n 14, 215
Silivri 59,
Sinan 16, 52
slaughterhouses 54, 55
slaves 90, 102, 143, 144, 145, 203n 16; slave trade 90, 144, 203n 16; manumitted slaves 13, 90, 143, 144, 145

solidarity 23, 67, 116, 127, 128, 134
Stern, S. M. 186n 10, 213
streets 44, 45, 46, 47, 48, 84, 85, 86, 87, 111, 129, 146, 152, 153, 179, 191n 43; street names 5, 36, 47, 53, 54, 57, 58, 88; street plan 45, 47, 63, 84, 85, 86, 88, 191 n43; "high street" 46, 53, 54, 88, 152, 191n 43
sub-mahalles 17
Sultanahmed 5
sultanic mosques 65
Sulumanastır 33
Süleyman "the magnificent" 1
Süleymaniye 34, 52
sürgün 1, 13, 33
synagogue 4
Syria 105

Şah ü Gedâ mosque 16
Şehremini 5
şer'iye sicilleri 3, 20, 22, 194n 75, 197n 47, 207n 2, 207n 3, 210
şeyh 150, 151
şeyhülharem 113, 133
şeyhülislâm 49

tahrir-i nüfus (see censuses)
Takiyüddin Paşa konağı 173
Tanman, B. 204n 26
Tanzimat 14, 16, 18, 65, 78, 79, 102, 127, 152, 167, 169, 207n 8
tapu tahrir registers 18, 22
tarîk-i 'amm 46
tarîk-i hass (see dead-end streets)
tatar 91
Taxes 6, 9, 18, 20, 21, 22, 50, 67, 78, 79, 80
tekke (see dervish convent)
Tenants 112, 147, 148
Toledano, E. 203n 16, 203n 19, 216
tezkere-i osmânî 163
Tramway 38, 54, 152, 155
Travel documents (see mürur tezkeresi)
Tuğra 4
tulumbacı 4

'*ulema* 90, 103
Uluçam, A. 200n 16, 216
'*umma* 7
Unkapanı 5
Uzunçarşılı 190n 20, 191n 41, 193n 64, 193n 73, 216

Ülgen, A. S. 189n 7, 216
Ünver, S. 216
Üsküdar 1

vakfiye 11, 30, 31, 36, 40, 84, 85, 86, 209
vakıf (*see* pious foundations)
van Millingen 189n 6, 190n 24, 213
Vatin, N. 198n 77, 216
Vefa 89
vegetable garden (*see bostan*)
Veinstein, G. 198n 77, 216
Vienna 153, 207n 8
virane 100, 103, 111, 112, 113, 120, 175, 180, 201n 39
Vital events 25, 80, 121, 160, 161
Vlanga (*see* Langa)
Von Grunebaum, G. 8, 186n 11, 213

Wall, R. 203n 15, 216
warehouses 12, 37, 38, 39, 146, 150, 154, 155, 156, 157, 158, 159, 177, 180, 205n 38
water-wells 31, 35, 41, 43
Weber, M. 7, 8

Xerolophos 11, 33

Yalçınkaya, E. 200n 28, 216
Yalı *mahalle* 180
Yedikule 54, 152
Yerasimos, S. 216
Yokuşçeşme fountain 88
Yokuşçeşme street 88, 129, 150, 151, 152, 153, 154, 173, 175, 180
Yusuf Kâmil Paşa 104
Yücel, E. 206n 7, 216
Yücel, F. 200n 28, 216
zenci (*see* blacks)
zira' 62, 73, 84, 85, 194n 78
Zeyrek 89
Zülfikâr, B. 206n 1, 215
zürri vakıf 35

Volumes in SUNY Series in the Social and Economic History of the Middle East

Thabit A. J. Abdullah, *Merchants, Mamluks, and Murder: The Political Economy of Eighteenth Century Basra.*

Ali Abdullatif Ahmida, *The Making of Modern Libya: State Formation, Colonization, and Resistance, 1830–1932.*

Rifa'at 'Ali Abou-El-Haj, *Formation of the Modern State: The Ottoman Empire, Sixteenth to Eighteenth Centuries.*

Cem Behar, *A Neighborhood in Ottoman Istanbul: Fruit Vendors and Civil Servants in the Kasap İlyas Mahalle.*

Palmira Brummett, *Ottoman Seapower and Levantine Diplomacy in the Age of Discovery.*

Palmira Brummett, *Image and Imperialism in the Ottoman Revolutionary Press, 1908–1911.*

Ayse Buğra, *State and Business in Modern Turkey: A Comparative Study.*

Guilian Denoeux, *Urban Unrest in the Middle East: A Comparative Study of Informal Networks in Egypt, Iran and Lebanon.*

Hala Fattah, *The Politics of Regional Trade in Iraq, Arabia, and the Gulf, 1745–1900.*

Samira Haj, *The Making of Iraq, 1900–1963: Capital, Power, and Ideology.*

Çağlar Keyder and Faruk Tabak, eds., *Landholding and Commercial Agriculture in the Middle East.*

Issa Khalaf, *Politics in Palestine: Arab Factionalism and Social Disintegration, 1939–1948.*

M. Fuad Köprülü, *The Origins of the Ottoman Empire*, translated and edited by Gary Leiser.

Zachary Lockman, ed., *Workers and Working Classes in the Middle East: Struggles, Histories, Historiographies.*

Heath W. Lowry, *The Nature of the Early Ottoman State.*

Donald Quataert, ed., *Manufacturing in the Ottoman Empire and Turkey, 1500–1950.*

Donald Quataert, ed., *Consumption Studies and the History of the Ottoman Empire, 1550–1922, An Introduction.*

Sarah Shields, *Mosul Before Iraq: Like Bees Making Five-Sided Cells.*